Future directions in literacy: international conversations conference 2007

Edited by Alyson Simpson

SYDNEY UNIVERSITY PRESS

Future Directions in Literacy: International Conversations Conference 3–6 September, 2007, Sydney, Australia (The University of Sydney, Division of Professional Learning), edited by Alyson Simpson. Sydney, Sydney University Press, 2007, 310p. (Research papers, selected conference materials: keynotes, feature speakers).

Contact address:
Division of Professional Learning
Faculty of Education and Social Work (A35)
The University of Sydney
Sydney, NSW 2006, Australia
Phone: 93512634   FAX: 93515027
www.proflearn.edsw.usyd.edu.au

Published by
SYDNEY UNIVERSITY PRESS
University of Sydney Library
www.sup.usyd.edu.au

© Copyright individual authors, 2007
© Sydney University Press 2007
Reproduction and Communication for other purposes
Except as permitted under the Act, no part of this edition may be reproduced, stored in a retrieval system, or communicated in any form or by any means without prior written permission. All requests for reproduction or communication should be made to Sydney University Press at the address below:

Sydney University Press
Fisher Library F03
University of Sydney
NSW 2006 AUSTRALIA
Email: info@sup.usyd.edu.au

ISBN   978-1-920898-77-9

Contents

About this book 1
About the conference 2
Acknowledgements 3

1   Reading places: creative and critical literacies for now and the
    future 5
    Barbara Comber – Feature Speaker

2   Stories from an Indigenous perspective in the reading resources
    mix, and the role they play in literacy success for Indigenous
    Australian students 29
    Margaret Cossey – Feature Speaker

3   How much can we learn from literacy assessment tasks? ® 40
    Ann Daly

4   University–school partnerships: literacy and students with
    additional learning needs® 58
    David Evans, Criss Moore, Iva Strnadova

5   The entry knowledge of Australian pre-service teachers in the area
    of phonological awareness and phonics® 73
    Barbara Fisher, Merle Bruce, Cedric Greive

6   Building literacy education: pasts, futures, and "the sum of
    effort" 96
    Peter Freebody – Keynote Speaker

7   Conversations across borders: interactions between literacy
    research, policy and practice® 115
    Pauline Harris

8   Catching the reading bug: looking at how to immerse children in
    the literary experience using visual and textual literacy® 136
    Jacqueline Hicks

9   Literacy meets technology in the primary school: symbiosis of literacy and technology®.. 151
    Karen McLean

10 Looking for clarity amongst the challenges faced by teachers as they consider the role of ICT in classroom literacy learning experiences®.. 170
    Jessica Mantei, Lisa Kervin

11 Applying multiple literacies in Australian and Canadian contexts®.. 190
    Diana Masny, David Cole

12 icurricula, ipedagogies and outmoded ideologies: literacy teaching and learning in the digital era.. 212
    Jackie Marsh – Keynote Speaker

13 Eyes in the back of our heads: reading futures for literacy teaching 234
    Jo-Anne Reid – Keynote Speaker

14 The significance of text in the teaching of reading in the early years®... 256
    Kathleen Rushton

15 Debating and public speaking as oral literacy: promoting democratic education.. 269
    Benjamin Spies-Butcher – Feature Speaker

16 Research based criteria for the design and selection of literacy and thinking tools®.. 280
    David Whitehead

® indicates refereed paper

About this book

The National Conference on Future Directions in Literacy was held at the University of Sydney, Australia from 3rd to the 6th September 2007.

The papers in this book comprise the proceedings of the Future Directions in Literacy Conference: International Conversations. The proceedings include selected full research papers. All papers are original, peer-reviewed and based on the research originally disseminated at the meeting. Papers presented at this conference reflect the state of the art of global research and development in the area of literacy. The themes addressed were chosen to reflect key issues that face academics and teachers in their drive to improve the literacy outcomes for all groups.

The link between research and practice has never been more significant as global awareness about literacy pushes us to question the success of programs in schools. National reports on literacy were challenged during the conference. Grounded evidence was given of literacy programs that work to make a difference for groups with diverse needs. The collection of ideas in the conference represents a broad concept of literacy that includes the ability to communicate in multimodal, digital texts and values creativity alongside testing for skills. Classroom based research from the sum of these perspectives presents significant reason for change to practice and policy. To make a difference to future generations of students, we need to take the research out of the classroom and make it the centre of informed debate. This publication is a step towards achieving that goal.

The selection of scholarly papers for presentation and publication was based on the outcomes of a rigorous peer review process. Papers reflect the authors' opinions and their inclusion in this publication does not necessarily constitute endorsement by the editor. The proceedings also include other selected conference materials: keynotes and feature speakers, which are not full scientific papers.

The papers which are marked with the symbol ® next to the author's name are refereed papers. The full papers were blind reviewed by two referees who were independent of the author.

About the conference

Proceedings of the National Conference on Future Directions in Literacy: International conversations
3rd to the 6th September 2007, Sydney, Australia

Organised by
Division of Professional Learning, The University of Sydney

Hosted by
Division of Professional Learning, The University of Sydney

Conference Chair
Dr Alyson Simpson, The University of Sydney, Australia

International scientific committee and board of reviewers
Professor Trevor Cairney, Australia
Professor Frances Christie, Australia
Dr David Cole, Australia
Professor Marie Emmitt, Australia
Associate Professor David Evans, Australia
Associate Professor Pauline Gibbons, Australia
Dr Annah Healy, Australia
Rhonda Hoare, Australia
Dr Eileen Honan, Australia
Dr John Hughes, Australia
Jessica Mantei, Australia
Dr Lorraine McDonald, Australia
Professor Stuart McNaughton, New Zealand
Professor Diana Masny, Canada
Marion Meiers, Australia
Guy Merchant, England
Dr Kate Pahl, England
Dr Alyson Simpson (Chair), Australia
Associate Professor Maureen Walsh, Australia
Dr David Whitehead, New Zealand
Professor Geoff Williams, Canada

Local program committee
Alyson Simpson   Ann Cheryl Armstrong
Margaret Day

Local organizing committee
Alyson Simpson   Margaret Day
Nina Goodwin   James Bourke

Editorial and website production group
Alyson Simpson   Margaret Day
Nina Goodwin   James Bourke
Nick Fei Li

Acknowledgements

This conference would not have been possible without the sponsorship of the Australian Government, the Primary English Teaching Association, the Australian Literacy Educators' Association and QANTAS.

Special thanks are extended to Margaret Day, Nina Goodwin and Jim Bourke for their assistance with the conference.

Citations of individual works in this book should have the following format:

Example

Hicks, J (2007). Catching the reading bug: looking at how to immerse children in the literary experience using visual and textual literacy. In A.Simpson (ed.) *Future Directions in Literacy: International Conversations conference 2007*. (pp134–148). Sydney: Sydney University Press.

1
Reading places: creative and critical literacies for now and the future

Barbara Comber
School of Education
Hawke Research Institute for Sustainable Societies
University of South Australia

Introduction

This paper explores the productive literacy learning possibilities inherent in young people reading and writing about the environment. It draws on two projects where young people have had opportunities to develop new knowledge about their local places and to become involved in communication about the care of, and the improvement of, those places. *Urban renewal from the inside out* involved primary school children working with architects to redesign and remake an area of the school grounds into the Grove Gardens. *River literacies* involved teachers and young people from schools around the Murray-Darling Basin studying and representing their local environment in various media. Developing future directions in literacy education, the theme of this collection of papers, is contingent upon us on learning from our pasts, getting beyond professional bandwagons (which have characterised literacy education) and exploring the affordance of various media.

If we are to educate for the present and the future, today's young people need access to the rich cultural resources of their varied histories, the best in the contemporary cultural landscape, and dispositions towards inventing and appropriating new ways with words and images. The kinds of communicative resources young people need to develop for the future should include traditional literacies and new emergent forms of literate practices. It is not about either/or. Indeed as Dyson (1989, 1993) showed many years ago now, if and when the curriculum is permeable, children are able to skilfully appropriate and work with the resources of school, peer and home worlds in order to make meaning and represent their thinking. The table below (Table 1.1) displays just a few of the literate practices in which young people and their teachers were engaged during the projects which I go on to describe. The point I wish to make here is quite simply that teachers work cumulatively with a range of genres and repertoires of practices which suit the particular purposes of the learning for which they are aiming. With reference to bringing place-based pedagogies and critical literacy together I will discuss several instances of how and why it makes sense for teachers to work across a continuum of literate practices developed in different eras.

Traditional school literacies	Emergent school literacies
literature	radio broadcasts and talk-back
diaries	web-pages
surveys	computer aided design
formal speeches	community announcements
cards and letters	film production
alphabet books	spatial literacies
anthologies	installations
debates	

Table 1.1: Traditional and emergent school literacies

A number of writers have indicated important differences between *in-school* and *out-of-school literacies* (Hull & Schultz, 2001; Pahl & Rowsell, 2005), the pervasive tendency for policy to demand limited forms of literate practices (Luke & Luke, 2001; Marsh, 2007), the need for teachers to allow young people to articulate their out-of-school literate practices and pedagogies with those of the school (Moje, 2000), and increasingly, scholars write of *new literacies* (Lankshear & Knobel, 2006, 2007; Marsh, 2007). Contrasting in- and out-of-school literate practices has been useful in highlighting what is missing from a typical authorised school literacy curriculum. Pahl and Rowsell (2005, p6) ask "Why does identity breathe life into literacy?" Indeed the rationale for articulating out-of-school literate practices more closely with those of schooling recognises that literate practices involve identity work and that for some young people the literacies of schooling may be alienating or undesirable. Whilst Hull and Schultz (2001, p577) contrast what goes on in school with young people's out-of-school literate practices, they also point out that "contexts are not sealed tight or boarded off ... one should expect to find ... movement from one context to another". The school as an institutional context does not necessarily determine that classroom literacy practices will be inauthentic or purposeless or indeed *new* or *old*. I do not wish to contest the notion of new literacies, per se; indeed there is considerable evidence of the material differences between emergent digital literacies and traditional print literacies (see Merchant, 2007 for a useful review).

School literacies cannot be taken for granted. As our longitudinal case studies indicate there is considerable variation from classroom to classroom, school to school and even between children in the same classroom (Comber, Badger, Barnett, Nixon & Pitt, 2002). Young people's portfolios of products and performances will vary hugely by the end of a school year, not to mention the end of a school career. Our studies suggest that young people are acquiring very different repertoires of practices and they also show that what teachers do matters greatly. School literacy practices are not the same everywhere. Indeed we can ask what might happen if in-school literacies were more social, goal-directed, participatory, consequential, communicative and aesthetically satisfying. In the context of this paper, what might happen if young people's literate endeavours were at least in part designed to connect with, represent and even work towards enhancing local environments? The content of students' reading and writing is very important in terms of motivation to tackle the challenges of literate work. The content of school literacy tasks needs to respect young people's intelligence and recognise their potential for understanding and acting in the world as citizens here and now as well as into the future. Place-based pedagogies offer new possibilities for rethinking curriculum and pedagogy in productive ways in these times.

> Place-based pedagogies are needed so that the education of citizens might have some direct bearing on the well-being of the social and ecological places people actually inhabit (Gruenewald, 2003 p3).

We now face major new challenges for a sustainable future – an ailing global environment, escalating wealth/poverty divides, and increasing threats to peace. We need to educate young people to live in a world of our making with all of its complexities and potential. I go on now to illustrate how different teachers are grappling with these challenges and at the same time creating engaging, inclusive classroom cultures and producing high quality student artefacts incorporating both traditional school literacies, though critically inflected, and emergent school literacies. In the projects I discuss below, teachers brought together their knowledge and practices about critical literacy, creative arts, place-based pedagogies, environmental science and multi-media communication in order to design meaningful and motivating curriculum for middle and upper primary children.

Urban renewal: A context and landscape for learning

Whilst educators and educational researchers may understand differences between children in terms of class, race, gender and poverty and occasionally in terms of locality (e.g. Gregory & Williams, 2000; Hicks, 2002) – urban, rural, remote and so on – rarely is the spatial nature of literate practice, nor the relationships between textuality and space made central in research (see Jones, 2006; Leander & Sheehy, 2004). Place and indeed spatial elements of literate practices are often seen as static, contextual backdrops to other identity markers. We have come to be more conscious of place and space as constitutive, and central, as our work is consistently located in high poverty areas, which brings us back to particular places – neighbourhoods, suburbs and regions, and to groups of people who are subject to poverty. One such project was conducted in the western suburbs of Adelaide in an area undergoing urban regeneration. This community is one of the poorest in Australia with an extremely diverse population, including many refugee and immigrant families, who have moved to Australia seeking a better life.

> Westwood, the largest urban renewal project in Australia, is a $600 million joint development between the South Australian Housing Trust, Adelaide-based real estate developer Urban Pacific Limited, and the local government City of Port

Adelaide Enfield that covers an area of six square kilometres and encompasses five suburbs. (Westwood, 2007, see www.westwoodsa.com.au, accessed 6 December 2007)

We had already developed a co-researcher relationship with Marg Wells, a primary teacher and her school principal, Frank Cairns when they were at Ferryden Park Primary School, one of the first inner western suburb precincts to be 'renewed'. Marg Wells has taught for over 25 years. She has a strong personal and professional commitment to western suburbs, having grown up in the area and living nearby in her adult life. Over an extended period she has assisted young children to develop an analysis of the neighbourhood and other social spaces. We have documented that work elsewhere (Comber, Thomson & Wells, 2001; Comber & Nixon, 2005; Janks & Comber, 2006), here I briefly draw attention to positive identity work done through literacy practices focussing on place, before turning explicitly to the *Urban renewal* project.

Significantly Wells' pedagogical repertoire included traditional print-based literacies and classroom pedagogies such as studying and making of a class alphabet book and a picture book, wider community literacies such as conducting and analysing surveys, as well as more contemporary emerging literate practices such as the use of digital photography of the neighbourhood and *Kid Pix*. The point to note here is that the design of the literacy curriculum and the associated tasks were contingent upon what the teacher was attempting to accomplish – in this instance, understanding and agency with respect to urban renewal. In other words, Wells wanted the children to understand what urban renewal meant and how they might take active roles in contributing to new public and school places, not simply be the passive observers of the development of an improved suburb for other people's children. In terms of the classroom literacy practices, new literacies were not included for the sake of trendiness, nor traditional literacies as a retreat to the supposed safety of a bygone era. Rather the pedagogical program was based on what might be productive for these young people learning to represent themselves and their places (real and imagined) in a variety of media for different audiences. Importantly, in this curriculum the young people were variously positioned as researchers, analysts, designers and producers of texts, each time taking an agentive position with respect to textual practices.

A is for Arndale: Alphabet book revisited

If we consider briefly just one task based on children's literature we can see the powerful way in which Wells positions her students with respect to place and identity. A consistent feature of her pedagogy is her innovation on the basis of existing published texts in order to produce class-made shared books – a traditional strategy in early childhood literacy classrooms. However, her approach is inflected with her knowledge of critical literacy and place-based pedagogies. In the one case she took a post-colonial approach to the alphabet book genre (Russell, 2000) and in another, she developed a class-made picture book drawing from the work of an architect, Indigenous studies, and author Jeannie Baker (2002), around the concept of *belonging places*. As a result two child-produced class texts were created, entitled *A is for Arndale* and *Windows* which allow children to represent complex and changing relationships between people and places.

Wells began by having her Grade Three/Four class closely study Elaine Russell's *A is for Aunty* (2000). This alphabet book works as a counter-narrative, in that it tells a different history of Australia and life in the bush from the perspective of a female Aboriginal artist and writer. Without being didactic, Russell cleverly conveys insights about the Stolen Generation into her alphabet book for children. In direct contrast with many alphabet books which were produced in the colonial fashion portraying Aboriginal people in tokenistic and stereotypical poses, Russell narrates and illustrates compelling stories of her childhood places and practices. In reading contrastive versions of alphabet books children can begin to see the ways in which texts enshrine certain times, places and ways of life; to understand the kinds of narrative they tell about the past; and note the different representations of cultural groups they portray.

When Wells' class started to create their own version of an alphabet book, *A is for Arndale*, (Arndale being the local shopping mall) based on Russell's book, to send to children in Atteridgeville, a township settlement in Pretoria South Africa, they had to make decisions as writers and artists about how to represent their lives and places. It is in taking up the position of producers (having first analysed a range of texts in the selected genre) that children's understandings of textual resources become evident. The letters of the alphabet allowed for a range of stories to be told about place and the young people's experience of that place. The relationships between critical and creative literacies, between deconstructive and productive literacy practices and the affordances of place-based literacies for meaning-making require further study and are beyond the scope of this paper. Nevertheless, it is important to note here that particular textual practices may have distinctive pedagogical affordances.

Figure 1.1. Q is for Quiet

With the help of their teacher concerning overall aesthetics of the design, the young people in this Grade Three/Four classroom produced a very high standard of art and writing. The artworks for each letter of the alphabet, inspired by Elaine Russell, were the products of many hours of thought, sketching and careful crafting. The written text entries were revised many times to achieve a high degree of clarity and reader-friendliness for their South African peers. In this instance the re-appropriation of the alphabet book allows children to portray their perceptions about place within the landscape of urban renewal. Their entries and illustrations their awareness of their changing places, from the trauma of busy traffic to the order of the neat picket fences surrounding the new houses (see Figs. 1.1 and 1.2).

Figure 1.2. W is for Westwood

Hence in planning literacy curriculum, it is not just a question of whether certain genres are, or are not, suitable for schoolwork, or how they might be modified to engage young people, it is important to think about the pedagogical affordances of introducing children to a range of particular textual practices in order to accomplish particular social and pedagogical goals.

Grove Gardens: Redesigning and remaking places

Having documented Wells' early innovative curriculum about urban renewal, we developed a project entitled *Urban renewal from the inside-out:*

Students and community involvement in re-designing and reconstructing school spaces in a poor neighbourhood[1] (which was funded by the Myer Foundation 2004–2005[2]). The project was designed to have primary school children become place-makers and designers, as well as text-makers. The specific brief was to redesign and develop the empty space between the primary school and the preschool. The educational brief was to explore and develop a repertoire of spatial literacies, aiming to:

- explore the constructedness of space
- explore the social nature of space
- imagine and represent new spaces and their place in relation to them
- explore potential relationships between spatial, imaginary and material worlds
- expand their repertoires of literacy practices

The basic idea of the project was to work with architecture students and academics, journalism students and academics, and student teachers and educational researchers to redesign and remake a part of the school grounds, and to closely document that process of change in a variety of media and genres. Together the architect and the collaborating teachers Marg Wells and Ruth Trimboli introduced children to the languages and

---

[1] The project was conducted by Barbara Comber, Helen Nixon & Louise Ashmore from the Centre for Studies in Literacy, Policy and Learning Cultures, Stephen Loo, Louis Laybourne School of Architecture and Design and Jackie Cook, School of Information, Communication and New Media, University of South Australia with teachers Marg Wells and Ruth Trimboli and young people from Ridley Grove R-7 School, Woodville Gardens, South Australia. See the Myer Foundation website at www.myerfoundation.org.au/main.asp. It describes its mission in the following way: "The Myer Foundation works to build a fair, just, creative and caring society by supporting initiatives that promote positive change in Australia, and in relation to its regional setting." The views expressed in this paper are those of the authors only and do not necessarily represent those of the Myer Foundation.

[2] River Literacies is the plain language title for 'Literacy and the environment: A situated study of multi-mediated literacy, sustainability, local knowledges and educational change', an Australian Research Council (ARC) Linkage project (No. LP0455537) between academic researchers at the University of South Australia and Charles Sturt University, and The Primary English Teaching Association, as the Industry Partner. Chief Investigators are Barbara Comber, Phil Cormack, Bill Green, Helen Nixon and Jo-Anne Reid.

practices of spatial literacies including map-making, architecture and specifically to notions of belonging spaces. Stephen Loo, the architect leading the design aspects of the project, presented a PowerPoint showing unusual buildings and asked questions like:

- What kinds of buildings are these?
- What might happen in them?
- Who might use them? How?

Wells' and Trimboli's classes (Grades Three/Four and Five/Six) visited the architecture studio and worked with architecture students to learn ways of representing spatial relations in different media, from drawing to model-making. They also visited new public garden areas which had been developed as part of the wider urban renewal project. Below is one child's response to his visit to the nearby Vietnamese garden.

- What design elements did you notice?
  I noticed shelter, water features, seating, grass, platforms.
- What did you like about it?
  I liked the shelter best because it is a design of a hat that people wear in Vietnam.
- Did you feel a sense of belonging here?
  Yes I did because I felt like I've been to Vietnam.

In this short framed reflection we can see the way Wells builds upon the language introduced by the architects, namely design elements, even as she seeks personal response.

Back at the school, Trimboli's students were involved in range of research activities – such as a PMI (positive, minus, interesting) analysis of their school grounds – not often the kind of task assigned to school children. The children conducted their research, analysed their findings, displayed the results and presented at a school assembly. Involving these young people in research about their school grounds and the surrounding suburb led to the design and exploration of a range of research and spatial literacies that were *new* to the teachers and their students and which afforded different insights on place and space.

Wells' class was invited to think about current dwellings and possible dwellings.

- Do you like living in the house you are in?
- What do you like about your house?
- What is your favourite place in the house?
- What do you like to do there?
- Where do you go when you want to be on your own?
- Would you like to live in this house? Or a new house?

In making the impending urban change the object of classroom study, Wells recognises that children are competent citizens, with complex opinions, hopes and fears, who benefit from discussion. However Wells also encourages a playfulness with respect to re-imagining dwellings. They were invited to choose an interesting building from Stephen Loo's PowerPoint or from the architecture magazines with which we had flooded the classroom and to imagine life from the perspective of a selected window.

Windows: Becoming place-conscious

Based on *Window* by Jeannie Baker, Wells developed a class picture book, entitled *Windows*. In pairs students selected and photocopied a picture of a window (from a magazine or newspaper), taken from the outside looking in. The selection of windows across the class ranged from port-holes to windows in castles, skyscrapers, lighthouses and aeroplanes. Students were asked to imagine themselves inside that window looking out and to write about their imagined space, what they might be doing there and what they could see out of the window. Students also drew the inside of the window and then what they imagined they could see outside the window.

Taking just one example produced by two boys, I note that the writing about the inside space displays a strong sense of ownership (my bed, my bag, my room, my cat), belonging (warmth, sitting by the fire, talking to my dad), social history (toys that I had for my birthday, my photos, awards; dad and his memories) (see Appendix 1 for the written text). It represented how the inside space was configured, their feeling of belonging in it, and how it operated as a social space. Visually they have made the bedroom window a frame. The yellow and red curtaining is reminiscent of a coat of arms. A poster immediately above the window depicts a red dragon arranged in a maze-like shape. Through the window in the expanded view we can see a blond-haired woman waiting at a bus stop at a busy intersection (see Figs. 1.3 and 1.4).

The writing about the outside space displays a strong sense of their ability to imagine possible socio-spatial scenarios (a fancy car, a bus carrying children, mum waiting for the bus); their awareness of the material nature of neighbourhood places (old rubbish bin, new pathway, new traffic light); their capacities for inventing of possible futures and imaginary worlds (potential new neighbours, favourite tree complete with squirrels). Working pairs with the props of the photocopied windows, children were able to draw on their knowledge developed over time to construct complex narratives of people, place and time. These tasks allowed children to imagine figured social worlds (Holland, Lachicotte, Skinner & Cain, 1998) inhabited by themselves and others using a range of semiotic resources – word, image and layout – to represent what it was like to inhabit spaces behind, and outside of, a particular window.

Figure 1.3 Window Frame and View

Figure 1.4 View through the window

As children wrote and drew about their experiences of their belonging spaces, they called on both material and virtual realities, and like the architecture students they had visited and worked with, they began to present their ideas for the re-imagined Grove Gardens in various media and forms. The teachers put together their collected designs into a laminated book which was circulated around the school and wider community for feedback. A two page text from one pair of Grade Three/Four boys indicates the ways in which students drew on different resources to make a case for their design (see Figs. 1.5 and 1.6).

> **What I would like to see in the area?**
> A big maze with some switches
> **Why?**
> So kids who are waiting can play in it while they are waiting for their mum and dad to pick them up and kids can get tricked because they won't know which is the beginning and which is the end
> **What would it look like? Describe:**
> The walls around the maze are made of cement and painted in gold. It will be 10 metres high and it will have traps inside it. You have to find a key to get out and you have to take a friend with you.
> *Adrian and Tan*

Figure 1.5 Adrian and Tan's text from Consultation book

Figure 1.6 Adrian and Tan's image from Consultation book

The boys' verbal text and their design both indicate the ways they are taking up various insights from the architects in terms of concepts, language and spatial literacies in their repertoires, including walls, height, materials, and surfaces. In addition they indicate their awareness of the social nature of space as they populate the garden and its features with children of different ages and waiting parents. Moreover they take up the invitation from Stephen Loo and their teachers to be imaginative as they draw on their experiences with game-playing to imagine the space as a maze with switches.

Thus far, I have tried to show that urban renewal can provide a rich landscape for young people to study their places, and further, that as they investigate and represent their places that this in turn provides meaningful material for literacy curriculum. In addition, I have argued that teachers can and should draw on a range of literate practices in order to engage with the affordances of place-based pedagogies. In this case young people worked across media and genres to explore and portray their understandings of place and space. These necessarily included old (model-making) and new technologies (CAD) and traditional (alphabet books, picture books) and new emergent school literacies (digital photographs, PowerPoint and so on). Young people need inclusive repertoires of literate practices in order to be powerful and productive citizens. I turn now to the second project, *River literacies*, to illustrate how the environment more broadly conceived can become the object of literacy in primary classrooms.

River literacies: environmental communication in primary schools

In considering the *River literacies* project I wish to reiterate some of the arguments made for place-based pedagogy through the example the urban school above, but at the same time to show that a wider understanding of place involves an appreciation of the complex relationships between people and places, between humans and non-human inhabitants, between land and water. These relationships are ecological, political, cultural, social and geographic and significantly these are captured largely through semiotic resources which in various ways inform policy and practice at local sites. In the past few years Australians have had to learn the hard way what inattention to environment might mean – lack of water, increasing carbon emissions, extinction of many species of flora and fauna, destruction of coral reefs and so on. The impact of climate change is now beginning to hit and it is impacting differently on communities located in different bio-regions and economies. We are now beginning to realise that the long dry period we are experiencing is not simply a drought. As Tim Flannery recently argued:

> I believe Australians need to stop worrying about 'the drought' – which is transient – and start talking about the new climate. (Tim Flannery, *Wetter north only temporary*. *AAP* http://newsninemsn.com.au/article.aspx?id=273233&print=true, accessed 16/06/07)

Some 15 years ago now the Murray-Darling Basin Commission must have had an inkling of where we were headed when it engaged the Primary English Teaching Association to develop a program called *Special Forever*, where young people attending schools located in the Murray-Darling Basin bio-region were invited to represent their special places in art and writing. As it describes itself, *Special Forever* aims to:

- involve students in becoming critically aware of their environments locally, and across the Murray-Darling Basin;
- assist teachers in developing programs that enable students to communicate their understanding of environmental issues effectively; and
- produce and publish a range of student texts focusing on local environmental issues for a range of audiences. (www.peta.edu.au/PETA_projects/Special_Forever/page__1253.aspx, accessed 6/12/2007)

I will not go into the history of *Special Forever* here (but see Comber, Nixon & Reid, 2007; Green, Cormack & Nixon 2007).

My aim is to provide brief vignettes which show how primary school teachers are working creatively and critically to educate young people about the environment and some of the complex issues they grapple with. I consider two sites from our field trips around the Murray-Darling Basin. I sketch these practices somewhat broadly as details of the practices are outlined in a collection of chapters by the teacher-researchers themselves (see Comber et al., 2007).

Fighting for survival

When we visited Kingston-on-Murray we realised just how small the school is and how close it is to the Murray River itself (literally a stone's throw) and the nearby wine producing and eco-tourism centre Banrock Station. The school has been actively involved in the wetlands and bilby habitat rejuvenation programs. The school needs to recruit more students in order to keep its doors open. Its involvement with environmental education may offer one possibility for its survival. In the meantime it is getting a reputation for the way it engages young people in learning about, caring for and communicating about the river. Students produce fliers for city peers who might only visit Banrock for a day; they broadcast on ABC local radio weekly reporting their data on salinity and turbidity in that part of the river; they produce posters voicing their objections to poor treatment of the riverbanks by visiting weekend boaties; they produce photo-stories on local endangered animals; they work at Banrock Station by helping to produce bat-boxes and detecting the tracks of feral animals. These young people are literally learning to read the landscape. As well they get explicit instruction from their teachers about science, from their grandparents about the history of the place, and an appreciation of local crafts from Indigenous elders and artists.

The literacy and communication curriculum here is very much designed around the affordances and complexities of the place. Yet there is no attempt to protect the young people from complex and contested issues – the politics of water rights, the risks and contributions of the tourist industry for the environment and the economy, the fencing off of protected areas of the river – are considered appropriate for these young people to research and discuss. They learn that it is the tourists who are keeping the local deli open with their healthy weekend trading. They learn that whilst they can study the environment at Banrock itself, they cannot access its websites about its sponsorship of research into endangered animals internationally due to its status as a wine producer and exporter. The politics and representation of places is open to discussion.

Searching for balance

Tongala is famous for Nestlé's condensed milk and the Golden Cow. Recently the dairy factory operation has been down-sized significantly. A snack bar complete with special milkshakes and souvenirs remains, as well as a small educational centre. It's one way a rural town keeps itself going in the face of changing conditions. The impact of climate change and the costs of water have already resulted in many services in the town being reduced as the farming community and employment in related industry begin to shrink. Many dairy farmers have already sold up; others are selling their water. Some struggle on. Meanwhile Pam Davis, a Special Forever Coordinator and teacher, long committed to environmental education, tries to help her middle school Grade Five/Six Class to understand what's going on and how to act ethically. She explains her priorities.

> I think one of the main things in our community is for them to see the issue of balance; that because we live in a farming community, in particular, that they have to see that we have to look after the environment and the people, and I think … that's perhaps a really huge issue. Water of course is a major issue in our community, and again the balance or the sharing of water … during this unit it's been the balance between humans and the natural world.

Davis wanted young people not only to gather information, but to become advocates for the environment. In an extended project where they researched local endangered animals children became articulate about what they had learned:

> That we need to save these animals because like when you think about it, there is 12 in our area, and that's only Tongala in Victoria … There's 12 main animals in Tongala, and that's only Tongala, it's tiny, so imagine how many there are in Australia, it's quite sad.

Each student decided on a particular endangered animal for which they wanted to become an advocate. Then Davis and class carried out extensive research using newspapers (local, state and national), websites, children's literature, informational books and encyclopaedia, local experts, field trips, research at home. Davis built a folio of information to avoid students printing out copious amounts of paper. The overall objective was to be able to persuade their peers and members of the local community what needed to be done to save their animal. Her aim was:

> to get the children to be advocates for the animals, so more ... to go beyond just knowledge [long pause] so we went beyond engagement to, yeah, just what do I need to do to get them to have that real understanding and that real desire to make a difference, and real desire to care...

Davis made time for students to rehearse and get feedback. Their presentations were videotaped so that they could review them and try again. Over the course of the study the students engaged in complex forms of reading, research and communication using a variety of media and genres which Davis judged would help them to develop an understanding of *balance* at the same time as it would assist them in becoming persuasive *advocates* whose research might inform others. This meant working with the best models of textual practices that could be accessed about specific content and taking particular points of view into account. Once again a combination of creative and critical, new and traditional literacies was brought together in order to assemble the desired dispositions, knowledge and communication repertoires needed for the task at hand. Inspired by her students' commitment and capacities to work on such a project Davis went on to successfully bid for the development of an environmental centre in her school.

Conclusion

> It is a perennial part of the role of education and educational science to make the world-as-it-has-come-to-be interpretable, understandable, and thus prepare rising generations to address their inheritance of challenges to our present and their future. (Kemmis, 2006, p465)

Across these urban and rural school sites I have show the ways in which teachers are designing new literacy curriculum around an ethics of caring for places. As Kemmis argues above, education does has a critical role in helping young people make meaning of the world, not simply to train them in pre-given basics. As I have discussed place-based curriculum offers some tangible and highly motivating reasons for reading, writing, designing, public speaking and communicating more broadly. We need to engage young people in these projects for their immediate and future health and well-being, yet this cannot be taken for granted.

> Not only may there be less nature to access, but children's access of what remains may be increasingly sporadic … Just as they need good nutrition and adequate sleep, children may very well need contact with nature. (Taylor & Kuo, 2006. p124, p136)

In analysing and synthesising what these teachers do we have found the following commonalities in their literacy education practices. Teachers committed to place-based literacy pedagogies:

- start with research about subjects that matter to students and their community
- build conceptual and knowledge resources over an extended period of time
- work in the 'field' and document those experiences
- introduce students to a range of genres, media and communication technologies
- ensure time for the production and dissemination of high quality student-produced texts for real or imagined audiences (Comber, Reid & Nixon, 2007).

In undertaking this work they draw on all their and their students' critical and creative resources for tackling complex problems and imagining better futures. More expansive interpretations of literacy in contemporary policy would allow teachers more room to design and enact the kinds of innovative pedagogy that are now needed.

References

Baker J (2002). *Window*. London: Walker Books.

Comber B, Nixon H, Ashmore L, Loo S, Cook J (2006). Urban Renewal from the Inside Out: Spatial and Critical Literacies in a Low Socioeconomic School Community. *Mind, Culture and Activity*, 13(3): 228–246.

Comber B, Nixon H (2005). Children re-read and re-write their neighbourhoods: critical literacies and identity work. In J Evans (Ed), *Literacy moves on: Using popular culture, new technologies and critical literacy in the primary classroom* (pp127–148). Portsmouth, NH: Heinemann.

Comber B, Nixon H, Reid J (Eds) (2007). *Literacies in place: Teaching environmental communication*. Newtown: Primary English Teaching Association.

Comber B, Thomson P, with Wells M, (2001). Critical literacy finds a 'place': Writing and social action in a neighborhood school, *Elementary School Journal*, 101(4): 451–464

Comber B, Badger L, Barnett J, Nixon H, Pitt J (2002). Literacy after the early years: A longitudinal study, *Australian Journal of Language and Literacy*, 25(2): 9–23

Davis P (2005). Environmental Communication. *PEN* 147. Sydney: Primary English Teaching Association.

Davis P (2007). From knowledge to action: A pedagogy of hope. In B Comber, H Nixon & J Reid (Eds) *Literacies in place: Teaching environmental communication* (pp96–110). Newtown: Primary English Teaching Association.

Dyson A (1989). *Multiple Worlds of Child Writers: Friends Learning to Write*. New York: Teachers College Press.

Dyson A (1993). *Social Worlds of Children Learning to Write in an Urban Primary School*. New York: Teachers College Press.

Green B, Cormack P, Nixon H (2007). Introduction: Literacy, place, environment. *Australian Journal of Language and Literacy*, 30(2): 77–81.

Gregory E, Williams A (2000). *City Literacies: Learning to read across generations and cultures*. London & New York: Routledge.

Gruenewald D (2003). The best of both worlds: A critical pedagogy of place. *Educational Researcher*, 32(4): 3–12.

Hicks D (2002). Reading lives: *Working-class children and literacy learning*. New York: Teachers College Press.

Holland D, Lachiotte W, Skinner D, Cain C (1998). *Identity and agency in cultural and social worlds*. Cambridge, Massachusetts: Harvard University Press.

Hull G, Schultz K (2001). Literacy and learning out of school: A review of theory and research. *Review of Educational Research*, 71(4): 575–611.

Janks H, Comber B (2006). Critical literacy across continents. In K Pahl & J Rowsell (Eds). *Travel notes from the New Literacy Studies: Instances of Practice* (pp95–117). Clevedon: Multilingual Matters.

Jones S (2006). *Girls, social class & literacy: What teachers can do to make a difference*. Portsmouth, NH: Heinemann.

Kemmis S (2006). Participatory action research and the public sphere. *Educational Action Research*, 14(4): 459–476.

Lankshear C, Knobel M (2007). Researching New Literacies: Web 2.0 practices and insider perspectives, *E-Learning*, 4(3): 224–240. http://dx.doi.org/10.2304/elea.2007.4.3.224

Lankshear C, Knobel M (2006). *New literacies: Everyday Practices and classroom learning*, 2nd Edn. Maidenhead: Open University Press.

Leander K, Sheehy M (2004). *Spatializing literacy research*. New York: Peter Lang.

Luke A, Luke C (2001). Adolescence lost/childhood regained: On early intervention and the emergence of the techno-subject. *Journal of Early Childhood Literacy*, 1(1): 91–120.

Marsh J (2007). New literacies and old pedagogies: recontextualizing rules and practices. *International Journal of Inclusive Education*, 11(3): 267–281.

Merchant G (2007). Writing the future in the digital age. *Literacy* 41(3): 118–128.

Moje E (2000). "To be part of the story": The literacy practices of "gangsta" adolescents. *Teachers College Record*, 102(3): 651–690.

Nixon H (2007). Expanding the semiotic repertoire: Environmental communications in the primary school. *Australian Journal of Language and Literacy*, 30(2): 102–117.

Pahl K, Rowsell J (2005). *Literacy and education: Understanding the New Literacy Studies in the Classroom*. London: Paul Chapman Publishing

Reid J (2007). Literacy and environmental communications: Towards a 'pedagogy of responsibility'. *Australian Journal of Language and Literacy*, 30(2): 118–133.

Russell E (2000). *A is for Aunty*. Sydney: Australian Broadcasting Corporation.

Taylor A F, Kuo F E (2006). Is contact with nature important for healthy child development? State of evidence. In C Spencer & M Blades (Eds) *Children and their environments* (pp124–140). Cambridge: Cambridge University Press.

Appendix 1

My Window

In my room I can see the clothes that my mum bought me, my bag and a closet that I put my clothes in. There is a TV by the fireplace and my cat is sitting by the fire. My bed is done so I don't have to do it. I can see my poster hanging up on the wall. I am sitting by the fire talking to my dad. He's telling me about the time when he was young. I can see toys that I had for my birthday and I can also see my drawers. On top of my drawers there is a telephone, my photos, awards and a radio.

Outside my room I can see a fancy car. I can see a bus carrying children. I think they're going to swimming because they have got their bathers. Outside I can see my mum waiting for the bus. I hope she doesn't have to wait long out there. I can see a rubbish bin that's very old. I think the workers are going to break that down and build a new one because that bin has been there since we moved in. I can see they have built a new pathway because the other one was very hard to walk on and it was old. They also put up a new traffic light. This one is very clean but the old one was old and broken. I can see the Optus building. My dad bought his mobile phone from there. My friend is moving to a different house. I hope out new neighbours are very friendly. I see our new neighbours coming to their new house. I hope they have some kids so I can play with them. I can see my favourite autumn tree. I always go and play on that tree with my friends. I can see some squirrels in that tree. I hope they're not cold over there. Oh, it's five o'clock. It is time for me to go to maths school. I will see you after maths school.

2
Stories from an Indigenous perspective in the reading resources mix, and the role they play in literacy success for Indigenous Australian students

Margaret Cossey

Margaret Cossey is a non Indigenous Australian. She has been a special needs literacy teacher in both government and Catholic schools. For the last fifteen years she has been involved in the development of the processes and protocols and the resulting stories, lesson notes, AV materials and the publishing company that has become Indij Readers Ltd.

I would like to acknowledge the traditional Custodians of the land we are on today, the Gadigal people of the Eora Nation, and their Elders past and present. I thank them for taking care of this land for thousands of years.

The circumstances in all aspects of life, that prevail for most Aboriginal and Torres Strait Islander people in Australia today, do not need more explanation.

In this presentation, I will discuss shared experiences with Indigenous people in Indigenous communities in Australia over the last 15 years, the understandings we came to together, the all-important role we believe functional literacy plays in addressing disadvantage and disempowerment, and how this can be achieved. I will outline what Indij Readers has done and is doing in Indigenous communities, in this regard.

Most people here today would know that most children, and I think it's about 65 per cent, learn to read effectively, no matter what process, system or teaching is in place. We also know that about 30 per cent of all students in schools across Australia experience varying degrees of difficulty in acquiring appropriate literacy skills. Often these are minor and quickly addressed, others require more careful attention. Difficulties occur for myriad reasons, including illness at critical times, regular absenteeism, poor or unhelpful teaching, lack of motivation or engagement in the formal learning process, lack of understanding of the special needs of some students by teachers and family issues.

Indigenous students, particularly boys, are highly over-represented in this problematic cohort and the educational inequality stemming from this literacy delay in the early years of schooling can impact on every part of life thereafter.

We also know that students who can read age and grade appropriate material usually have better school attendance, blossom in other academic areas, have higher self esteem, are less likely to have interactions with the police, are less likely to miss school with minor ailments and are a cohesive element in home and community. It is therefore in our best interests to ensure that all children achieve functional literacy sooner rather than later.

This issue as it relates to Indigenous kids, has been the main focus of my attention for the last 15 years.

What I'm going to speak to you about today is the reasoning behind the approach I have taken to address this issue through the company Indij Readers. I have to preface this by saying I'm not a world authority on anything. I taught children to read and write for about 20 years. I chose to teach those who had difficulty with literacy, and especially those with behaviour issues, so there were a few Indigenous kids over the years.

My teaching experience has been in government schools, Catholic schools K–10 and some experience with kids in and out of detention.

I am a Reading Recovery teacher, a Spalding teacher, in fact nearly every literacy intervention program that has been devised in the last couple of decades, I've done it, got it and got the T-shirt.

Every literacy system has good ideas but quite frankly, I believe the most important factor in the whole process, is that you enjoy being with your students, that they know you actually like being with them, especially if they are regularly in trouble in the system, and that as far as their literacy learning is concerned, you stay firmly tuned into what they say, what they do and don't do, observe their literacy behaviours to see what they know, where they're at and what they need to progress to the next stage. This does presuppose that you have a reasonably solid understanding of the process of acquisition of literacy skills.

And it's safe to say, it's a universal understanding, that good literacy skills are fundamental to success for anyone living at this time — as Dr Paul Brock says, a human right, the inalienable right of every child.

I'm convinced that story is what can link the emerging literacy learner, whatever age, to functional literacy skills.

In my experience, students with special needs as well as those in and out of detention need you to establish some rapport, some warmth with them. That can sometimes take a while, but during that time, if story and meaning are at the centre of the teaching process, the learning has a good chance of starting. Story also has to have relevance to them, has to be within their reach or their experience.

That's not to say that phonics, grammatical features, conventions of print, spelling etc aren't important, but they're the housekeeping. We all have to get across all those skills to be effective readers and writers but they are not the centrepiece. I have never yet met anyone who learnt to read and write just to be hot at phonics.

Many of the understandings that underpin the way I've approached storymaking with our Indigenous authors have been developed out of the experience of being a Reading Recovery teacher. If they teach you nothing else about literacy, good Reading Recovery tutors certainly teach you to be forensic in your observations of the literacy behaviours of your students.

What I also learnt was that, if the new story selected for that day's lesson was about a topic or concept familiar to the student, then the book orientation was a breeze, the running record on the book the next day was often up over the 95 per cent accuracy rate and the child and I were both happy little vegemites.

If the reverse was the case, the lesson that day was stressful for both the student and myself. Over time I realised that everything seemed to hinge around story selection.

Most kids do well in the Reading Recovery environment, they usually progress well and move back into the middle of the literacy range in their class inside the 20 weeks of tutoring. But for some, it doesn't always go so well and I started to think that one of the factors could be that for those students there weren't enough published stories within their life and cultural experience. And this was certainly the case with the Indigenous students I taught in the Reading Recovery program.

I'd like to tell you I had an epiphany and it all fell into place. Not so. It took a while and other people have gradually become involved and eventually the circumstances arose in the early '90s to actually explore the idea of facilitating first time authors in Indigenous communities to make contemporary stories. That's how this project started and at the first communities, Lake Cargelligo and Murrin Bridge, we talked together, about the idea of making contemporary stories from an Indigenous perspective. The question we talked around was, "do we think this is a good idea and if so, will we have a go at it together?" That was 1993. It wasn't just a cold call. I live in Cootamundra in south west NSW and was teaching at Sacred Heart Central School there. St Francis Xavier School at Lake Cargelligo is also in our diocese, so going out to that school and talking this idea over with the AEAs was straight forward. We'd all attended diocesan conferences together so we were slightly known to each other and we had things in common. For me, from the beginning of this project, that's always been fundamentally important, to have some links, some connections, so that Indigenous people can have confidence that it's safe to engage in the work and with me, and that it will be a good thing to be involved in.

I'd been told by a lecturer of mine at CSU that the world already had enough stories for Aboriginal kids by middle-aged, middle-class white women, so I had to be very clear that was not what I would be doing.

What I knew I could do, was be the facilitator for others to make stories. From my experience teaching children – both little ones and older kids – I had an idea of the sorts of stories that worked and engaged them. I was fairly confident I could support first time authors to make such stories.

In those early days I was also very aware of the perception in many Aboriginal communities that most white fullas turn up long enough to get their PhD and then piss off, never to be seen again. Black fullas call them seagulls, they fly in, grab the food and fly out.

I recently read a quote by a black activist who said, "'if you've come to help us, bugger off, but if part of your liberation is working with us, then join us."

I think it comes down to friendship and common interest and that takes time. The common interest is that we all want all kids to learn to read and write well, do as well at school as they can, get the training to get the job they will enjoy doing, and have a happy and productive life.

The central factor to help make that happen, the protocol that took place and still takes place today, is that we all spend time getting to know each other. There's no rushing. The old Aunties call it, 'being on Koori time, sista', and together we decide if it's a good idea to work up some stories in that community at that time. It's much easier now because we've got stories from other communities to show. The Elders and community decide if they would like to be a part of Indij Readers. We haven't had a knock back yet.

By visiting communities one at a time for a long time, asking people what they thought of the idea of making stories in this way, and getting to know Indigenous parents, children, Elders, hearing stories, making friends, and I guess, living life together, making memories together, stories emerged that eventually became our first series of books. The model was collaborative, both Indigenous and non Indigenous participants. Ownership of the process and the final product was inclusive and we all wanted the same things, contemporary Indigenous stories represented in the mix of reading resources available, and everyone reading and having school success.

Two stories came out of that initial experience, those two AEAs at St Francis Xavier were our first authors, Aunty Joy Kelly's story of the Min Min and Aunty Sharon Thorpe's story of the Emu Egg.

Between us, that is, the aunties and I, we worked out other things like, the stories would be written the way they were told, natural language, which included Aboriginal English. We would support teachers with lesson notes, cultural notes and activity sheets for each book. We knew that was very important, so that non Indigenous teachers could take on our materials with confidence. The Aboriginal English and the activity sheets weren't so popular at first, in some quarters with education hierarchies. Nevertheless we persevered and for the most part we have very supportive and helpful relationships with most education department offices. The good part about it all is that, all the people who work for all the education service providers in Australia really do have the same hope, that all the kids will learn to read and write well.

It wasn't long before everyone involved, knew that the model developed to do this work was solid, very labour intensive, but solid. After that, all that was needed was total commitment to see it all through to publication, no matter what. The details of incorporating a company, raising substantial funds, building a business model that was sustainable, working extensive hours for years, arguing with people who held entrenched positions and trying to convince them to think outside the square, ad nauseam, well all I can say is, you don't have to be mad, but it certainly helps.

So Indij Readers has been set up as a not-for-commercial-profit publishing company. We approach corporations, philanthropic organisations and government departments, both federal and state in all states, for funding support. We have been fortunate to have developed long-term strategic partnerships with some very supportive corporations including Clayton Utz, Rio Tinto Aboriginal Foundation and Westpac. We have DGR and ITEC status and all our profits support ongoing development, literacy initiatives and capacity-building initiatives in Indigenous communities. We pay each author and illustrator a fee in lieu of royalty. They always own the copyright of their story or art, and they sign a contract with us which allows us to print and publish their stories.

There are two of us managing the development and business operations of Indij Readers and we have a majority Indigenous Board.

What sustains everyone involved in Indij Readers is that when we go to a new community, everyone loves the stories, and there's pride in them, that they are the contemporary experience from an Indigenous perspective.

Indij Readers has been developed on that premise, story and meaning are at the centre. Our aim is to develop the kind of texts that are effective in engaging literacy learners, both Indigenous and non Indigenous, especially those little fullas and big fullas who don't always find it plain sailing. Our texts are written with a clear purpose: that the books will be read by students learning to read. The wider audience is envisaged as Indigenous and non Indigenous readers and those who want to find out more about Indigenous Australia or just enjoy a good story. All texts share a common purpose: to describe life as it is or has been lived by Indigenous Australians. Importantly, all texts are authentic in that the way they are written supports the purpose of the text: to entertain, inform or recount and not as part of a levelled reading scheme. We know stories should often make us smile and sometimes make us laugh out loud. It's also okay if they make us think a bit. One of the things that especially the Aunties and I hope Indigenous kids think about, is that their stories belong and take their rightful place in the mix of resources that they and all their peers use, when they are learning to read and write. Their stories and their art are a part of the literature that everyone experiences. There can be many other agendas for texts as well, and you will notice with our stories, there is certainly no shortage of agendas.

Because they are classroom reading resources we have accompanying teachers' guides. We use an explicit teaching model and we encourage teachers to use the guides with discernment, as they see fit, for their own particular students.

How effective have we been so far? Well we don't know. What we do know is anecdotal. Teachers phoning in and saying they and their students are enjoying the stories and lessons, wanting to know when there will be more. Since we incorporated the company and started selling our materials we've penetrated about 12 per cent of the target market, that is literacy classrooms in Australian schools. We're not sure how good that is in business terms but we're still in business so that's a good sign.

In late 2004 we decided to apply new thinking to the development model. Up till then our stories were developed mostly with first-time authors and illustrators. I would spend extended lengths of time working in a community through the steps of each book. Families and usually much of the community were also included in the process. The focus was on the experience for each of our contributors, and the community, the confidence-building and the further career opportunities this might lead to.

The art or photography for each story was also an intensive process where the artist and I or the photographer and I worked very closely together. Art specifications were written and even if the artist was in another state, which is often the case, during the time the art was being made, it was usually very regular extensive phone calls to support the process.

It is all labour intensive and was the fundamental reason we all have enduring friendships. The intensity and the 'overcoming all obstacles' approach, got the company up and running, but to remain viable there had to be a new model. That approach took a long time to think through, but eventually we decided if communities had a writers' kit, with elegant, friendly, subtle software, that supported the process of story-making for AEAs, teachers and communities, and using our Indij Readers stories as templates, using the ideas we developed to begin with, then that might be the way forward.

Throughout 2005 we raised the funds to research and begin development on a Community Writers' Kit and the work began in early 2006. We developed financial and site partnerships for each of the communities where the work was to take place.

The overall idea was that Indigenous communities (and later other communities as well) could develop and desk-top publish their own local stories for their own classrooms at the local school level. Given what I'd observed in communities where we'd worked, it was obvious that subject familiarity is a hook for children to enjoy the process of learning the basic skills of reading and writing. We think a critical mass of stories about the local footy team, the neighbourhood, the well-known community members, the school swimming carnival etc, will support them and their teachers as they negotiate the other skills and concepts of reading and writing. We're sure that subject familiarity helps students negotiate those skills to reading success.

We canvassed opinions from Indigenous and non Indigenous literacy consultants, teachers and academics and we were encouraged and assured that the Writers' Kit is pedagogically sound and an important project to complete and publish.

We approached Dr Robyn Ewing, of the Faculty of Education and Social Work at the University of Sydney to advise on and evaluate the process of development. Her research assistant for this work is Kathleen Rushton who is one of the writers of the Indij Readers' teachers guides.

Throughout 2006 we worked on all the aspects the writers' kit. The work took place in two sites in Melbourne, then in Dareton in far south west NSW, at Mt Druitt in western Sydney and recently in Katherine in the Northern Territory.

The research is finished, and we now move on to production and piloting. From trial and error and hours and hours of discussion and ideas, we know fairly clearly what will be required for this to be a successful initiative. We will build the kit specifically for Aboriginal Education Assistants, as they are the glue between the school and the community in most places. The kit will be adaptable for other settings, and other ethnicities. I can see teachers using this kit with say, Year Six students to make stories for the Year Ones and Twos. What lovely symmetry that will be! All the housekeeping skills those older kids have to perfect, not to mention the purpose of the work, so that they publish stories for younger children. Literacy teachers in this room have heard all this before and will know there's nothing new under the sun, eh! Just a new form. Training will have to come with the kit and we have worked out plans to roll that out across Australia. No one involved has had a moment's doubt about our ability to do this, or been daunted by the scope of the plan. We firmly believe this will impact positively and amazingly on Indigenous literacy levels right across Australia.

When produced, the Community Writers' Kit will be virtual, which is of course the only possible way to proceed. We are fortunate to live at this time, in this place, that this is all possible. We do have a couple of little ideas up our sleeve to guarantee that this works, but I'll have to keep them for another time and place until they're well in place.

So now all we have to do is raise the funds for this production, trialling and training stage. A piece of cake, eh!

It is hoped that stories developed at the local level which have a universal resonance will be published by Indij Readers. These might be in the usual way or maybe online.

In conclusion, there are other ways of going about this type of work. This is just our approach. What will be interesting to observe is how Indij Readers grows and changes over the next few years. I'd like to finish by sharing a story with you from our latest series of books. These were launched in July this year at the Melbourne Museum. All our new authors and illustrators were in attendance with family members and we had a great celebration.

There is more information about Indij Readers on our website, and of course order forms to purchase books. I do hope if your school or university curriculum resource centre or community doesn't have multiple copies of our materials, not just library copies, but in the mix of your mainstream reading resources, you might consider checking us out and hopefully remedying that situation.

This story is called *Firewood and Rabbits* and the author is Ron Jackson, an Aboriginal education assistant at Coomealla High School in Dareton, which is very close to where the Darling River joins the Murray. This was one of our research sites last year, so I spent a few months living in Dareton, which was most enjoyable. This story is informative on many levels, and of course cuts across KLAs.

3
How much can we learn from literacy assessment tasks?

Ann Daly
PhD student
Centre for Research in English and Multiliteracies Education, University of New England

This paper includes preliminary findings which are part of the author's doctoral research in affiliation with an ARC Linkage Project between the University of New England and the NSW Department of Education and Training.

Abstract

This paper is based on both observations of student test taking techniques and preliminary findings from PhD research interviews with students about their strategies for reading multimodal texts in literacy assessments. The PhD research is part of an Australian Research Council Linkage project between the University of New England and the NSW Department of Education and Training conducted by Professor Len Unsworth.

The presentation investigates factors that are related to success in reading multimodal texts based both on analysis of the texts and observation of skills exhibited by students during literacy tests and follow-up interviews. In relation to analysis of the texts, preliminary findings suggest that the degree of complexity of the verbal text can be related to the degree of difficulty in making connections between words and images. In relation to the observation of student skills, there seems to be a relationship between the level of students' reading comprehension and the complexity of their oral language and vocabulary demonstrated during the interviews. Such findings support the work of several theorists and researchers (George & Tomasello, 1984; Perera, 1984; Lemke, 1988: Gray, 1990; Hasan, 1996; Painter, 1996; Jones, 1996;

Wills, Lawrence & Gray, 2006) whose ideas and research will be discussed. These preliminary findings suggest that the explicit development of oral language needs to be a focus prior to and throughout the teaching of reading.

To elaborate the assessment context this paper will first discuss other matters that became apparent during the observation of students during reading and writing assessments and will suggest how the explicit teaching of reading and writing skills can improve students' test taking techniques and thus advantage them during assessments.

Literacy assessment – a process or an end product

State-wide literacy assessment tests in NSW provide detailed diagnostic information about children's reading and writing skills, but they only assess an end product. They do not assess the processes by which children make decisions in reading and writing tests. During the administration of writing tests, it often becomes apparent to the astute supervisor that some students take one or more of the following courses of action which disadvantage them:

- Not using the planning space – this often results in no paragraphs or poorly constructed paragraphs, whereas creating a flow chart or mind map could have assisted students to better structure their writing

- Not referring back to planning, if it was done – students need to see this process modelled during joint construction of texts

- Writing without pausing to think – this often results in spoken-like writing with everyday language rather than appropriate technical or descriptive language

- Not using the editing time to improve or even read their writing – students need to see this process modelled during joint construction of texts.

Improving students' skills during writing tests is often easily achieved by good modelling of the above techniques followed by joint construction and paired work before independent writing practice.

However, some of the poor techniques used by students during reading tests are often a factor of student personality and teachers need to monitor classroom behaviours carefully to ensure students will not develop characteristics that will cause them to make the following errors in reading tests:

- Racing to finish first, despite having plenty of time
- Not checking to see if any questions have been omitted
- Getting stuck on one question for too long and then running out of time to finish
- Reading a set of questions in the test booklet about one text and having the reading stimulus closed or open at a different text. In such circumstances the 'reading test' becomes a guessing competition

Other errors became apparent during recent case studies for an Australian Research Council (ARC) linkage project between the University of New England and the NSW Department of Education. During post-test interviews, students were asked to think aloud about the stimulus texts as they read them and then say why they chose their answers to multiple choice questions. It became apparent that in addition to the above errors students often used the following strategies which disadvantaged them:

- Reading the words only and not looking at supporting images
- Not relating text and images, for example, when asked a question about an image some students only looked at the image and not the caption describing it
- Searching the page but not knowing what they are looking for – these students need to know how to identify key words in the

- questions and then use skimming and scanning skills to locate these or similar words

- Reading and seeming to understand a text, then answering questions by relying on memory and not checking the text again to confirm answers. When asked where they found their answer, these students looked at the texts and discovered their errors.

These poor test techniques can be overcome by explicitly teaching about images and captions, key words, skimming and scanning and asking students to justify their answers.

Some students, who seemed to understand the texts while reading and thinking aloud about them, openly admitted to guessing answers in multiple choice tests. A few students could not even read the questions let alone the text, so their only choices were to omit the questions or guess. Diagnostic multiple choice tests cannot be relied on where such students guess answers or mark an answer for every question regardless of whether they can read the words. It is therefore advisable to be wary about the results of poor readers who have managed to complete the test. Teachers need to conduct an individual focussed assessment of these students' reading.

For such poor readers, analysis of the spoken language used in the ARC Linkage project interviews possibly revealed as much if not more useful diagnostic information about these readers than the reading test itself. Preliminary findings, from the recent ARC linkage project research with literacy assessments, indicate a correlation between complexity in oral language and reading comprehension assessment scores. These findings support the theories of Lemke (1988) and Gray (1990) that suggest the development of spoken language is an important factor in the ability to comprehend and produce complex text, and also the research of Painter (1996) who relates the complexity of the structure of oral language, particularly embedded clauses, to the development of thinking. However, the state-wide focus on reading and writing has resulted in pressure on teachers to spend more time on written texts and consequently spend less time on speaking and listening. There is also a need for teachers to spend more time on viewing skills in the classroom, since questions in the Basic Skills Tests which involve visual literacy are among the most difficult, having fewer correct responses. It would seem that many teachers either do not feel confident about teaching visual literacy or they do not analyse the diagnostic results and therefore do not realise that they need to focus on these aspects of texts.

PhD research into multimodal reading comprehension and oral language

In the first stage of the ARC Linkage project, multimodal reading texts and questions from the 2005 Basic Skills Test (BST) were analysed. In 2006 over 100 students, then around nine and 11 years old, were interviewed about the multimodal texts and their reading strategies when answering the questions involving image-text relations. Analysis of the texts and results showed that students had more difficulty in comprehending image-text relations that required an understanding of parts of texts characterised by high structural complexity. For the PhD research, it was considered that the analysis of the texts, student results and research interviews would provide appropriate material for testing a hypothesis relating capacity for oral complexity to the comprehension of complex sentences.

Responses to the Year 5 text *Tobwabba Art Gallery* were particularly appropriate for testing the hypothesis because there were two questions requiring understanding of image-text relations based on different parts of the text. The more difficult question, for which only 44 per cent of the state had the correct answer, involved understanding the following structurally complex part of the text to know that the dark areas represent traps and nets:

The sailfish is believed to be a cunning fish, (independent clause)
able to feed amongst the various fish traps and nets (dependent clause + ellipsis)
shown by the dark areas, (dependent embedded relative clause + ellipsis + passive voice)
without being caught. (dependent adverbial clause + passive voice)

The easier question, for which 66 per cent of the state had the correct answer, involved understanding the following simple sentence and then making connections to the image by identifying the part of the picture (top) where the artist had painted the fresh grass:

The kangaroos are feeding on the fresh grass after the rain.

This question was easier despite the fact that it had a very plausible visual 'distractor', some creek weed at the bottom of the picture, which 27per cent of children chose instead of the correct answer. The structurally complex part of this text was characterized by low lexical density, so comprehension of lexically dense terms was not an issue.

The quantity of complex language features exhibited in the interviews was expected to be low in view of the fact that formal language is not used as often in spoken language as it is in written language. As Jones (1996, p13) points out, "Written language is synoptic, about things" whereas most "spoken language is essentially dynamic, about happenings". However, when students talk about things (texts) in interviews, they will be more likely to use written-like 'synoptic' language than they would in conversational dialogue, because the language will be at the reflective end of the spoken language continuum.

The hypothesis that oral language development is related to reading comprehension will be supported if students, who had higher achievements in the 2005 BST reading comprehension tests, use grammar that has more structural complexity shown by a higher percentage of dependent clauses (adverbial and relative clauses including those that are embedded) and more instances of ellipsis or passive voice in their interviews than students with lower levels of reading comprehension. Lexical (semantic) complexity will also be examined in the form of the number of examples of non-core words, classification shifting and nominalisation. Cultural background (gender, geolocation and Aboriginality) will also be considered in the final research to see whether there are any differences for certain groups of students in view of the fact that students, who are male and/or Aboriginal and/or live in remote areas, have lower mean reading scores.

Oral language complexity and the link to comprehension

Campbell & King (2003, p53) state that, "Oracy is the pathway to solid success as a learner, and the means of feeling success as a learner. Learners must be communicators and thinkers before they can be effective readers and writers."

The hypothesis, that capacity to use complex sentence structure in oral language is related to capacity to understand complex written sentence structure, is inferred by Gray (1990, p113):

> it is doubtful if children can produce and understand written texts in any depth unless they can orally produce texts of that type themselves. We know also that children from literacy-oriented homes come to school with considerable experience in producing such texts, eg, Painter (1986), Wells (1982), Scollon & Scollon (1981), Heath (1982).

It is relevant that Gray says, "<u>can</u> orally produce texts of that type" not 'do', since one would <u>not</u> expect children to speak in a fully formal written-like mode for everyday purposes. However, as children mature their spoken language also matures and has the capacity for more complexity, so one could expect to hear some occasional evidence of more formal language structures such as complex sentences and/or nominalisations.

The reason why familiarity with complex language structure is important is that understanding of syntax (the patterns or grammatical structure of language) is one of the four basic systems for cueing meaning in text. It allows us to predict or anticipate which grammatical construction will come next in a sentence, and this is how we make sense of a text like 'Jabberwocky' even though it is full of nonsense words (Green, 2003, p115).

Perera (1984, p156) points out that some grammatical constructions are not frequently produced in oral language until adolescence and she includes the following:

- complex noun phrases (noun groups)
- adverbial clauses of place, manner, concession and hypothetical condition
- non-finite adverbial clauses (apart from those of purpose)
- some relative clauses (those introduced by a relative pronoun plus a preposition)
- some types of ellipsis
- all but the commonest sentence connectives

In regard to comprehension, Perera (1984) found that many grammatical constructions are not fully understood when a child starts school. These constructions include reversible passives and ellipsis of the verb or object in compound sentences. She also found that it is many years before children fully understand "adverbial clauses introduced by *although, unless* and *provided that*, as well as hypothetical and inferential 'if' clauses, many sentence connectives; and discourse-level ellipsis that is remote from its antecedent" (p157).

Perera (1984) goes on to argue that, "children do not acquire these constructions until they are reading fluently, and then they are more likely to use them in writing than speech" (p157). It is certainly true that, for literate students, complex grammatical constructions are more likely to be used in writing than speech. However, if one considers the claim that reading fluency precedes the acquisition of complex grammatical constructions in oral language alongside Vygotsky's (1962) observation that a child can use grammatical structures correctly before he understands their meanings, then it is important to remember that fluency and comprehension are not the same. Vygotsky (1962, p46) states, "The child may operate with subordinate clauses, with words like *because, if, when* ... long before he really grasps causal, conditional or temporal relations." It would therefore seem that ability to use complex oral language precedes comprehension of complex language structures in texts and this would support Lemke's (1988) statement that dialogue allows for "bridging between formal and colloquial language" (p140).

Scaffolding reading comprehension by speaking text meanings

The success of Brian Gray's Accelerated Literacy (AL) program (Wills, Laurence & Gray, 2006) suggests that developing students' oral language aids their reading comprehension. In AL, students with low literacy skills are taught to read while being supported (scaffolded) by a teacher who first builds the field of knowledge about the text and then preformulates questions ensuring they can be answered while unpacking the complex written language into oral chunks that can be comprehended. At the same time this process develops the literate oral language that students need to discuss and comprehend literate written texts. In the Transformations stage of the AL program, students focus closely on word choice and sentence structure by reordering the text to find out how changing the order results in different meanings and then they determine which grammatical constructions make sense until finally they understand why the author chose the structure he or she used to achieve the intended meaning.

The importance of "the child's own productive linguistic capabilities" for comprehending or "processing input" is substantiated by George & Tomasello (1984, p125) who found that even though "young children partially comprehend linguistic input somewhat above their own productive level, comprehension at an inferential level is best when input is closer to the child's own productive level". The AL scaffolding of highly literate texts unpacks the complex language which brings the texts closer to the "child's own productive level" so that the texts can be more easily comprehended. It also increases students' productive level, thus bringing it closer to the level of the text, because it "helps students fully speak their meanings, out loud" (Lemke, 1988, p140) and in this way the scaffolded dialogue is "bridging between formal and colloquial language", giving students access to the language of literate texts.

Many students from households with high levels of education have already experienced dialogue that scaffolds their understanding but many students do not experience this dialogue at home if they are from working class families (Heath, 1982), Aboriginal families (Gray, 1990) or families in low socio-economic areas (Hasan, 1996; Williams, 1998).

Williams' research was in Sydney, Heath's was in the USA. More recent research by the RAND Corporation in 65 Los Angeles neighbourhoods found that "the two factors associated most strongly with school readiness are the educational attainment of mothers and neighbourhood poverty" (Erebus, 2005, p9). The PISA study in Australia found that the between-school variance in Australia, although relatively small, was largely explained by the socio-economic status of the students. However for Indigenous students, the relationship between socio-economic status and reading achievement was much weaker, which suggests that socio-economic status is not the only factor here (Greenwood, Frigo and Hughes, 2002, p25).

Other recent studies have compared oral comprehension with reading comprehension. Beron & Farkas (2004, p125) compared oral language and reading success by using a test of *auditory processing*, which directly taps the child's ability to extract meaning from standard English speech, and they found that this skill is a key mediating variable for the effect of class and race effects on reading achievement. Other US studies by Chall & Jacobs (1996) and Biemiller (1999) also compared reading comprehension with oral comprehension or vocabulary development but none of these studies compared reading comprehension with the oral production of complex language, which is what the current study will investigate.

The theoretical basis for a hypothesis relating complexity of spoken language to the comprehension of complex written sentences comes from Olson and Torrance (1983, p145) who state that during the early school years there is an important conceptual transformation which "depends on the development of a new orientation to language, specifically, an attention to and a competence with the structure of language per se as opposed to competence with the contents, intentions or messages expressed by the language". They argue that "it has to do with learning to differentiate form from content, what is said from what is meant". They suggest "that there is a shift from attention to the beliefs and intentions of persons towards the meanings and structures of sentences" (p. 148). This shift is also evident in the structural and semantic complexity of texts along the mode continuum.

Subordinate clauses used in interviews

Initial analysis of interviews with 20 students whose reading scores placed them in the top achievement band and twenty students with reading achievement in the lowest bands in the 2005 BST for Year 3 and Year 5, showed that, students with better reading scores used more dependent clauses in their spoken language.

Year 3 Students	Percentage of dependent clauses	Year 5 students	Percentage of dependent clauses
Top 29% Band 5	From 17% to 20%	Top 21% Band 6	From 20% to 33%
Bottom 23% Bands 1 & 2	From 4% to 8%	Bottom 28% Bands 1 to 3	From 5% to 10%

A metropolitan male Aboriginal student with a reading score in the top band in the Year 5 BST had the highest percentage of dependent clauses out of the total number of clauses, and a provincial female Aboriginal student with a low reading score had the lowest percentage of dependent clauses for the Year 5 students.

For the students who sat the 2005 Year 3 BST, a metropolitan male Aboriginal student with a reading score in the top band had the highest percentage of dependent clauses while the lowest percentage was in the spoken language of a remote male non-Aboriginal student with reading achievement in the lowest band. The only students in Year 3 who used adverbial clauses preceding independent clauses in their spoken language were high scoring readers. In the 40 interviews analysed so far, some Year 3 students and one Year 5 student used no dependent clauses.

Perera (1984) notes that from the age of six the number of subordinate clauses used in spoken language stays constant then around 11 years of age it begins to increase and, from age six to 13, students use more finite adverbial clauses. As students move along the mode continuum, the use of more adverbial clauses is an important stage in learning to link related ideas within sentences. Students have to learn to use subordinate clauses in complex sentences before they can cope with lexically dense text which involves the nominalisation of ideas or the representation of ideas as single words or nominal groups instead of as whole clauses.

As Brian Gray (1990, p113) points out, "it is doubtful if children can produce and understand written texts in any depth unless they can orally produce texts of that type themselves". In order to help 'at risk' students to comprehend and "orally produce texts of that type themselves," the National Accelerated Literacy Program teaching sequence (Wills, Lawrence & Gray, 2006) includes an exploration of text structure during the High Order Book Orientation stage and attention to the impact of word order and word choice during the Transformations stage.

From the small sample taken from the PhD study it is clear that both Aboriginal and non-Aboriginal students have the capacity to achieve high reading scores and to develop complexity in their oral language. Some researchers such as Perera (1984) claim that reading fluency leads to oral complexity, however, the success of Accelerated Literacy seems to prove Gray's (1990) suggestion that understanding of written texts is probably preceded by the students' ability to "orally produce texts of that type themselves" (p113). As some students might use a working class English or Aboriginal English dialect and such dialects have some aspects of grammar that differ from standard Australian English grammar, it was decided to examine the interviews to see if any students used non-standard grammar and, if so, whether they had lower reading comprehension.

Features of non-standard English in student interviews

Few examples of non-standard English dialects such as working class or Aboriginal English were found in the interview transcripts and where they were found there were only one or two instances except for one Year 3 Aboriginal student who had five instances of non-standard verb form (the use of 'seen' for 'saw' and 'done' for 'did'). Since this student's reading score placed him in Band 5 (the top 21 per cent of students) for reading comprehension and he used 17 dependent clauses to 86 independent clauses giving him a relatively high percentage of dependent clauses, it is clear that dialectal differences in word choice did not impact on this student's ability to use grammatically complex oral language or to comprehend written text.

This example is in keeping with the findings of Daly (2006) in which no direct relation was found between reading comprehension and the use of the Aboriginal English dialect, despite earlier findings that lower scores on grammar criteria in writing and language tests were related to the use Aboriginal English.

Use of the passive voice

In the first 20 interviews analysed, only one student used the passive voice. This student was a male Aboriginal high achieving reader in Year 5. However, the interviews were not constructed in any way that would logically elicit the passive voice, which is not a common feature of conversation. Baldie (1976) posits that the ability to handle reversible transformations is a precursor to the use of the passive voice. However, Anna Trosborg (1982, p39) found that children can "to some extent produce the passive before they can make correct judgements of the equivalence of corresponding active and passive sentences". It would therefore seem that capacity in oral language precedes the ability to fully comprehend the passive voice.

Baker and Nelson (1984, p19) cite Horgan who found that no Agentive Non-Reversible passives appeared until nine years of age and no child produced both Reversible and Non-Reversible passives until age 11. The importance of scaffolding for much earlier production of passive sentences is evidenced in the research of Baker and Nelson (1984, p19) who found that, in three and four year olds, "once the passive transformation was presented to the children in input, and especially when their own utterance was recast, the children ... quickly began to use passives and soon used them with wide semantic variation."

Aspects of lexical complexity in oral language

Many researchers have noted that Western style of literacy (Australian education) is 'formal' (Harris, 1984), 'essayist' and 'decontextualised' (Scollon & Scollon, 1981) and involves "many kinds of 'secret' English which are not made explicit in schools" (Martin, 1990) and one of the features they refer to is a high level of grammatical metaphor, such as nominalisation, that occurs in lexically dense text. Ideational metaphor "produces a high level of abstraction in text, making it inaccessible to large sections of the community" (Martin, 1992), but lexically dense texts are not common in primary school, as Halliday (2004, p636) notes:

> Children are likely to meet the ideational type of metaphor when they reach the upper levels of primary school; but its full force will only appear when they begin to grapple with the specialized discourses of subject-based secondary education.

However, when one considers the gradual development of lexical density along the mode continuum, then it would be logical that a precursor of nominalisation (verbs or processes expressed as nouns) would be classification shifting (processes expressed as adjectives as part of a noun group, e.g. *the capsized boat*) and the use of 'non-core' vocabulary (more technical and formal or less everyday/colloquial words), for example, *capsize* or *indicate*, would develop before students start to use those verbs as adjectives in a noun group, as in *the capsized boat*, or turn the verb into a noun, such as *indication*. The term, non-core vocabulary (Carter, 1987, p33), is opposed to core vocabulary, that is, core items are generally seen to be the most basic or simple. Carter (1987, p35) suggests a test for core and non-core vocabulary by using syntactic substitution, such that "in the lexical set, *gobble, dine, devour, eat, stuff, gormandize* each of the words could be defined using 'eat' as a basic semantic feature but it would be inaccurate to define *eat* by reference to any other of the words in the set (i.e. *dine* entails *eat* but *eat* does not entail *dine*)." He also suggests other tests for core words including tests of antonymy, collocability, extension, summary, associationism, superordinateness and whether the term is culture-free.

When the first 40 interviews in the current PhD study were analysed, high achieving readers used more non-core words (not counting those any used in the reading text), for example, *drought*. Only one high achieving reader used classification shifting, *the capsized boat*, in his interview and nominalisations were only used by four students with high reading scores.

Conclusion

A relationship between complexity in oral language and reading comprehension is emerging in the current research. The success of Accelerated Literacy, which involves talking about literate texts before reading them, suggests that developing oral language may be crucial to reading success. The research further consolidates the clear calls by many researchers for attention to oral language development in addressing the role of grammatical understanding in enabling students to understand structural connections within texts leading to comprehension of more complex reading material (Unsworth, 2002).

To be an effective reader, a student must take on four roles; coder, participant, user and analyst. The decoding role is not just about graphophonic relationships, but an effective code breaker is someone who understands the 'fundamental features' of written texts (Freebody & Luke, 2003, p56) and grammar is one of those features. The text participant role involves understanding the ways in which written, visual and spoken texts are constructed and meanings are made, so this role also involves understanding of grammar and genre. By performing the four roles, the reader is accessing four resources which are "inter-related and interdependent" (Freebody in Healy & Honan, 2004, p1).

It seems logical that, when students use oral language to reflect on the meanings in texts and how texts are structured to achieve those meanings, the students are developing both their oral language repertoire and their comprehension of written language. For some low-achieving readers, the complexity of multimodal text negotiation appears to require the development of these students' linguistic experience as well as explicit attention to the meaning-making resources of images and image/text relations. As Lemke (1988, p136) points out, spoken language is "the medium in which we understand and comprehend". It follows that students need to use oral language, which is scaffolded by teachers or other adults, to improve their comprehension of written texts.

State-wide reading tests can only provide useful diagnostic information about students who can access textual meanings on a literal, interpretative or inferential level and who do not give up and guess.

Teachers who encourage students to have a guess if they do not know the answer are treating the reading tests like competitions, not as the diagnostic instruments they were designed to be. The state literacy assessments cannot diagnose a speech deficit or the need to scaffold spoken language for 'at risk' readers and writers. It is only by looking at the larger picture and making correlations that such a need can be deduced.

References

Baker N D, Nelson K E (1984). Recasting and related conversational techniques for triggering syntactic advances by young children. *First Language*, 5(13): 3–22.

Baldie B J (1976). The acquisition of the passive voice. *Journal of Child Language*, 3(3): 331–349.

Beron K J, Farkas G (2004). Oral Language and Reading Success: A Structural Equation Modelling Approach. *Structural Equation Modeling*, 11(1): 110–131. Lawrence Erlbaum Associates, Inc.

Biemiller A (1999). *Language and Reading Success. From Reading Research to Practice: A series for Teachers.* Toronto: Brookline Books.

Campbell R, King N (2003). Oracy: the cornerstone of effective teaching and Learning. In D Green & R Campbell (Eds), *Literacies & Learners: Current Perspectives, 2nd edition.* (pp51–67) Frenchs Forest: Pearson Education Australia.

Carter R (1987). *Vocabulary: applied linguistic perspectives.* London: Allen & Unwin.

Chall J, Jacobs V (1996). Reading, Writing and Language Connection. In J Shimron (Ed), *Literacy and Education: Essays in memory of Dina Feitelson* (pp33–48). Cresskill, NJ: Hampton Press, Inc.

Daly A (2006, March). *Assessing the literacy needs of students who speak Aboriginal English.* Paper presented at Sydney University. 'National Conference on Future Directions in Literacy', Sydney, Australia. Retrieved 4 March 2007 from:
www.edsw.usyd.edu.au/schools_teachers/prof_dev/resources/Lit_proceedings.pdf

Erebus International (2005). *Review of the Recent Literature on Socio-economic Status and Learning*. Report to the NSW Department of Education and Training. Accessed in August 2007 from www.psp.nsw.edu.au.

Freebody P, Luke A (2003). Literacy as engaging with new forms of life: The 'four roles' model. In G Bull & M Anstey (Eds), *The literacy lexicon*, 2nd *Edn* (pp52–57). Sydney: Prentice Hall.

George B L, Tomasello M (1984). The effect of variation in sentence length on young children's attention and comprehension. *First Language*, 5: 115–127.

Gray B (1990). Natural Language Learning in Aboriginal Classrooms: Reflections on Teaching and Learning Style for Empowerment in English. In C Walton & W Eggington (Eds), *LANGUAGE: Maintenance, Power and Education in Australian Aboriginal Contexts*. (pp105–139) Darwin, NT, Australia: NTU Press.

Green D (2003). Children and print: reading. In D Green & R Campbell (Eds), *Literacies & Learners: Current Perspectives, 2nd edition*. (pp113–129) Frenchs Forest: Pearson Education Australia.

Greenwood L, Frigo T, Hughes P (2002). *Messages for minority groups in Australia from international studies*. ACER Research Conference 2002.

Halliday M A K revised by Matthiessen C M (2004). *An Introduction to Functional Grammar, 3rd edition*. London: Arnold.

Harris SG (1984). Aboriginal learning styles and formal schooling. *Aboriginal Child at School*, 12(4): 3–23.

Hasan R (1996). Literacy, Everyday Talk and Society. In R Hasan & G Williams (Eds), *Literacy in Society*. (pp377–424) London: Addison Wesley Longman Ltd.

Healy A, Honan, E (Eds). (2004) *Text next: New resources for literacy learning*. Newtown: Primary English Teaching Association.

Heath S B (1982). What no bedtime story means: narratives at home and school. *Language in Society*, 11(1): 49–78.

Jones P (1996). 'Planning an oral language program'. In P Jones (Ed.), *Talking to learn*. (pp11–26) Newtown, Australia: Primary English Teaching Association.

Lemke J L (1988). Making Text Talk. *Theory into Practice*, 28(2): 136–141.

Martin J R (1990). Literacy in science: learning to handle text as technology. In F Christie (Ed.), *Literacy for a changing world*. (pp79–117) Melbourne: Australian Council for Educational Research.

Martin J R (1992). *English text: system and structure*. Amsterdam: John Benjamins.

Olson D R, Torrance N G (1983). Literacy and cognitive development: a conceptual transformation in the early school years. In S Meadows (Ed), *Developing Thinking: approaches to children's cognitive development*. (pp142–160) London: Methuen.

Painter C (1996). The development of language as a resource for thinking: a linguistic view of learning. In R Hasan and G Williams (Eds), *Literacy in Society*. (pp50–85) London: Addison Wesley Longman Ltd.

Perera K (1984). *Children's Writing and Reading: Analysing Classroom Language*. Oxford: Basil Blackwell.

Scollon R, Scollon S (1981). *Narrative, Literacy and Face in Inter-ethnic Communication*. New Jersey: Albex.

Trosborg A (1982). Reversibility and the acquisition of complex syntactic structures in 3- to 7-year-old children. *First Language*, 3(7): 29–54.

Unsworth L (2002). Reading Grammatically: Exploring the constructedness of literary texts. *L1 Educational Studies of Language and Literature*, 2(2): 121–140.

Vygotsky L (1962/1933) translated and edited by E Hanfmann and G Vakar. *Thought and Language*. Cambridge, Massachusetts: The MIT Press.

Vygotsky L (1986/1933) translated and edited by Alex Kozulin. *Thought and Language*. Cambridge, Massachusetts: The MIT Press.

Williams G (1998). Children entering literate worlds: perspectives from the study of textual practices. In F Christie and R Mission (Eds), *Literacy and Schooling* (pp18–46). London: Routledge.

Wills S, Lawrence C, Gray B (2006). In the Zone: moving from discomfort to confidence and improving literacy. Paper presented to the *2006 ALEA & AATE National Conference: Voices, Visions, Vibes*, Darwin, NT, Australia, 8–11 July. Conference Proceedings (published on CD).

4
University–school partnerships: literacy and students with additional learning needs

David Evans
Faculty of Education and Social Work, University of Sydney

Criss Moore
PhD student, Faculty of Education and Social Work, University of Sydney;
NSW Department of Education and Training

Iva Strnadova
Honorary Associate, Faculty of Education and Social Work, University of Sydney
Faculty of Education, Charles University in Prague, Czech Republic

Abstract

The National Inquiry into the Teaching of Literacy promoted debate about the teaching of reading in primary schools. The use of evidence-based research to inform the teaching of reading in schools and in the preparation of teachers was one of the report's main recommendations. This paper will highlight the outcomes of a collaborative, school-based research project for pre-service teacher education students who undertook a five-week tutoring program with children in local schools identified as having literacy difficulties.

Throughout the school-based tutoring program, university students were engaged in professional debate about evidence-based practices in the teaching of reading. These issues were the focus of their studies on campus, tutorials in schools, and linked to the planning and preparation they undertook for tutoring. Learning support staff based in schools fostered debate and guided evidence-based practices as the students worked with children.

Outcomes of the program provided evidence that the level of student professional knowledge had been enhanced. Students showed evidence through their planning, reflective journals and interviews that they were more aware of the intricacies of planning to teach reading, yet were still unsure of how this transferred into a whole class program. Further, there was strong support for the program for schools, administrators and parents. Future directions for the program was also set following discussion with students, school-base staff and reviews of the research literature.

The reception of the *Inquiry into the Teaching of Literacy* (Commonwealth of Australia, 2005) in Australia illustrated that the debate over the teaching of reading continues to be a sensitive issue in Australian education and academic circles. While the inquiry focused on the development of literacy in Australian schools, the political debate of the day focused on issues such as how reading is taught in schools, what to do about those 15 to 20 per cent of students who fail to achieve minimum standards after four years of school, what teachers are doing in their classrooms to teach reading, and how new teachers are equipped to teach reading.

As the debate focused narrowly on the teaching of reading, it regressed to the age-old 'reading wars' duality – whole-language versus phonics, or code emphasis versus meaning emphasis. This debate is not new in Australia or in other countries. Further, the report on the *Inquiry in the Teaching of Literacy* (Commonwealth of Australia, 2005) was not unique; other significant reports addressing the same issue have been released over the years (e.g. *Preventing Reading Difficulties in Young Children*, 1998; *Report of the National Reading Panel*, 2000).

The disappointing aspect of the debate that raged over the teaching of reading was the apparent failure of the differing 'camps' and the media to acknowledge the wealth of research that clearly indicates that it is not an 'either/or' debate, nor is this debate about simply combining the two approaches. (See the *Report of the National Reading Panel* for a comprehensive review of the literature.) The teaching of reading is about helping young children bring together the central elements of decoding and comprehension so they become skilled readers. This requires teachers to have expert knowledge about how students achieve this (Moats & Foorman, 2003; Snow, Griffin & Burns, 2005).

The *Inquiry into the Teaching of Literacy* (Commonwealth of Australia, 2005) made 20 recommendations about how literacy outcomes in schools could be enhanced. Four of the recommendations and accompanying discussion focused on the preparation of teachers. These recommendations were reached after the Inquiry had conducted surveys and a series of focus group interviews across the 34 teacher education institutions in Australia offering pre-service degrees and preparing teachers to teach reading and literacy skills in primary schools. Responses to a national survey of preparation courses found that "less than 10 per cent of time in compulsory subjects/units is devoted to preparing student teachers to teach reading." (p20). Further, that in half of all courses, "less than five per cent of total instructional time is devoted to this task." (p20).

In its final report, the Inquiry recommended further investigation and research into how best to prepare pre-service teachers to teach literacy, in particular, reading. This recommendation specifically made reference to pre-service teachers being knowledgeable about how to instruct beginning readers in the skills of phonemic awareness, phonics, decoding fluency, vocabulary knowledge, and text comprehension.

The preparation of teachers to teach effective reading is central to the success of children learning to read (*Australian National Inquiry into the Teaching Literacy*, 2005; Courtheart & Prior, 2007; Darling-Hammond & Bransford, 2005; *National Reading Panel Report*, 2000; Snow, Burns & Griffin, 2005; *Teaching Children to Read*, 2005). Effective teachers of reading have a rich understanding of the how children become skilled readers. It therefore requires "teacher educators to provide teachers with opportunities to gain pedagogical expertise based on a much a wider range of psychological, social, and cultural knowledge, dispositions, and practical skills for working effectively in the classroom" (Snow et al., 2005, p17).

Despite the importance of learning to read, the research about how to prepare teachers to teach reading so all children reach basic goals or outcomes in a timely manner is not abundant (Rohl & Greaves, 2005). In a study of Australian pre-service teachers, Rohl and Greaves found many pre-service teachers thought that they were "not well prepared to teach literacy and numeracy to students who find it hardest to learn" (p7). Further, Bos, Mather, Dickson, Podhajski and Chard (2001) found that pre-service teachers had "limited knowledge of phonological awareness or terminology related to language structure and phonics" (p98).

This paper will report on research undertaken within a university pre-service teacher subject. The primary focus of the subject was to prepare pre-service teachers to cater for students with difficulties learning. It provided students an opportunity to apply knowledge gained from the previous three and a half years of the program, along side specific knowledge and skills developed about the teaching of reading to children with reading difficulties. In particular, this project will identify the challenges faced by university students in developing their knowledge of the key elements of reading and the instructional pedagogy that will assist children to acquire early reading skills. In the conclusion, the nature of the program will be evaluated from the perspectives of the university students and their in-school mentors, and recommendations made for future research.

Method

Participants

Participants were students from a pre-service teacher education (primary education) course at a major research and teaching university who volunteered to be part of this project. A total of 63 students (49 female, 14 male) were enrolled in the subject. From this total enrolment, 46 students (33 female, 13 male) returned both the initial and final questionnaire and consented to be part of this project.

All students were enrolled in a compulsory Special Education subject requiring them to undertake a 15-hour fieldwork placement where they observed and/or worked with a student/s with a disability or learning difficulty (i.e. students with special education needs). This placement provides students with an opportunity to examine different education programs, facilities and support services, and the attitudes and beliefs of those persons who work with students with special education needs. As part of the course, students also complete work on-campus focusing on how to adjust programs to accommodate students with special education needs (e.g. literacy, numeracy).

In order to streamline the course (e.g. time efficiency, grounding theory in practice), plans were made to integrate the fieldwork and theoretical elements. Through links with a local learning support team, the students were able to work with children with identified difficulties in literacy, in particular, in learning to read.

Schools

Students visited one of four schools during the six-week tutoring program. The schools were located within five kilometres of the university, and enrolled students from lower to middle income families. Each of the schools was receiving services from the regional support team to assist in catering for students experiencing difficulties in reading. The support team provided assistance to the school through a range of professional learning activities (e.g. an in-class model of explicit teaching strategies, discussions about professional literature).

The tutoring program was conducted in schools where members of the learning support team were currently working as part of their caseload. Each member of the learning support team had demonstrated experience in working with students with special education needs. During the tutoring program, they scheduled their time to be in these schools so they could provide guidance to university students, and oversee the implementation of programs for targeted students with learning difficulties.

Tutoring program

Students participated in two seminars on campus on working with students who have special education needs prior to commencing the tutoring program. In the week prior to the commencement of university, students attended a one-and-a-half hour lecture where they were provided with an overview of the subject, asked to complete a questionnaire on their knowledge of teaching of reading, and participated in a discussion about how they would cater for students with reading difficulties. The first author also engaged students through a set of interview questions, to facilitate an open discussion about how they perceived the teaching of reading. The other two of the authors recorded responses.

In week one of the university semester, students spent the first tutoring session completing a two-hour workshop on campus. In this workshop, students were introduced to the expectations of the tutoring program that included participation in an in-school tutorial. Each in-school tutorial commenced with all students gathering with their tutor to receive feedback on the previous session, and participating in a discussion about an article they had been set to read. Their reading was scaffolded through a series of set questions that focused the students' attention on the key elements of learning to read. In many instances, content in the readings was directed towards the application of strategies for the teaching of reading (e.g. promoting fluency of decoding, integration of skills).

The first tutorial on-campus also focused on the assessment students were to complete with their assigned child. The set of assessments to be undertaken were from a document each student was given in the first tutorial – *Programming and Strategies Handbook* (DET, 2003). These assessments included the use of running records, the *Sutherland Phonemic Awareness Test* (Nielson, 2003), Educheck (DET, 2002), and *Johnson Word List* (DET, 2002). During the tutorial, students were shown examples of results, and how they could identify the strengths and weaknesses of students from them.

The final element of this first tutorial was focused on the necessary planning for each session. Students were guided through the use of a planning format that required them to demonstrate that they were addressing a range of elements within a balanced reading program. These elements included modelled reading, explicit teaching of skills (e.g. phonemic awareness, alphabetic principle, vocabulary, decoding fluency, comprehension), and practice of skills through games. At the end of each session, students were then required to evaluate their lesson according to these requirements, and plan for the following session. Their plans were submitted for review by the school-based learning support teacher, who provided feedback at the commencement of the next session.

Following these workshops, students were expected to attend two tutoring sessions at their allocated school. The university timetable had been arranged to ensure students were scheduled to be in schools between 9 and 12 on two mornings during the week.

Measures

Various methods for collecting data were used during the five-week tutoring program. Data were collected from students during the first lecture on their beliefs about how they would teach reading, and their attitudes toward catering for students with additional learning needs. Students were also interviewed at the conclusion of the program in smaller groups. During this time, they were asked questions about the program, including what they felt were its strengths and weaknesses, and their knowledge about the teaching of reading.

This feedback and the evaluation of the program were supported through an analysis of the journal each student submitted as part of the course assessment. These comments were assessed according to criteria such as: how well students understood how to plan a balanced reading program (including its links to the research literature), how effectively they could analyse errors made by child, the validity of decisions they made to adjust planning and instruction, their attitudes towards working with a student with learning difficulties, and how the instructional strategies from tutorial materials could be used in a whole class context.

Discussion of results

This study investigated the outcomes of a project conducted collaboratively between university staff and school-based personnel to promote the knowledge and skills of pre-service teacher education students in the area of early reading. The outcomes of the project were evaluated through records of the perceptions of students before and after the project, analysis of the planning undertaken by students to cater for children with reading difficulties, and the feedback provided by students and school-based staff.

Knowledge of teaching reading

A recurring observation in students' journals was the novelty of the material they were required to address. That is, students highlighted that they had not encountered and/or did not know concepts such as phonemic awareness, or the teaching of decoding fluency in previous classes. The introduction of these evidence-based features of effective reading programs created tensions for some students. The tension at one point boiled over in a lecture on campus, and it required some open discussion and clarification of differing points of view for this to be resolved. In the final group evaluations, this tension again arose with some students still quite anxious about the conflicting points of view they had experienced and the difficulty they faced in working through these differing perspectives on something so important to children (i.e. learning to read).

The notion of balanced reading programs was a concept named during initial students interviews. One student who claimed it as a "combination of whole-language and skills-based approaches" best depicted initial views of the concept balanced reading programs. These views were not evident in the final interview, or in the reflective journals. Students discussed, for example, the need for a balance between the differing elements (e.g. phonemic awareness, vocabulary and language development) based on the need of children. Some students went further by discussing how they analysed instructional texts to identify words useful for developing phonic skills, phonological awareness skills, and vocabulary, and then ensured that children could use these skills appropriately in their text reading. In lesson plans, this knowledge was further reinforced and maintained through implementing a series of activities or games.

The topic of effective instruction generated discussion about particular teaching activities (e.g. modelling reading, using games). At this point in their careers, students were not in a position to think beyond these activities and to consider the differing elements of instruction (i.e. what teachers do to help students achieve lesson outcomes). The elements of explicit instruction, for example, were a relatively unfamiliar concept to a number of students. Students came to this experience with the belief that students would be intrinsically motivated to learn to read, and that involvement in motivational games and activities would offer sufficient additional incentive. This finding is similar to that of Moats and Foorman (2003), especially concerning the attitudes of pre-service teacher education students. At the conclusion of the program, planning by students showed elements of wider range of instructional strategies (e.g. example selection to foster discrimination practice or maintenance), while in their reflective journals a number of students referred to adjusting their language and vocabulary to assist students. In the discussion of whole class strategies, a small number of students referred to the use of peer-assisted instruction to foster skills and knowledge of reading, and linked it to relevant literature (Swanson, 2005).

Knowledge of how to transfer the skills they learned in one-to-one tuition to the whole class context was only emerging for most students. Most students were given one opportunity to observe an experienced teacher take a whole class and use many of the principles promoted in the tutoring programs (e.g. games to practise skills, peer-assisted instruction to facilitate fluency practice, or structured literacy time where all children received purposeful instruction). While they were able to discuss in a limited manner how they could transfer strategies to the classroom, those students who did not get the chance to observe were unable to discuss how the strategies they have been using could be transferred to the whole class. Future iterations of this program will need to develop a more systematic approach to building this knowledge with students.

Students were aware that many children experience difficulties in learning to read. They attributed these difficulties to various causes including lack of practice, home background, cultural background, and type of personality. In the words of one student:

> I think it could be neurological, it could be behavioural, I think it could be the type of attention or instruction they are given at home ... it could be that they have other difficulties like hearing or seeing difficulties ... It could be a whole range of problems, I guess.

Responses from students in the initial interview highlighted a view that difficulties originating in the child or their family. Students did not indicate a position that their approach to teaching could be a factor that assisted students overcome difficulties in learning to read.

When students were asked about the steps they would undertake to assist children, they stressed the role of assessment. The words of one student highlighted a level of caution they had about their own professional knowledge, stating we would "be guided by the counsellor or Reading Recovery tutor at the school". The limited level of knowledge about the major elements of a reading program appeared to limit the ability of students to articulate what they would assess to find out "where students were at". The use of assessment protocols in the tutoring program provided a support for students to develop their knowledge about reading, and provided concrete examples that they could use in the future to assist planning. In the final interviews students strongly supported the need to be given more time to the use and development of assessment materials in the area of early reading development.

Parent-teacher links were considered by students to be a feature of assisting students with additional learning needs to learn to read. These links though, were not portrayed by students as strong ones, with an emphasis on "Encouraging parents to spend as much time with the child on different literacy activities like reading, writing or you know just exposing the child to the range of texts and that sort of thing". At the conclusion of the program some students felt that having information nights and forums would help "teach parents what to do".

Benefits of program

Feedback was attained from pre-service teacher education students, and school-based personnel as to the value and quality of the program. Senior administrative personnel, and parents of the children receiving tutoring also provided unsolicited feedback. Each type of feedback highlighted the benefit of the tutoring program.

Pre-service teacher education students were, in general, full of praise for the tutoring program. In the words of one student, and supported by their peers, it was the "best thing ever" they had completed in their course, with other students indicating that the subject should be one of the first they take as it allowed them to examine first-hand the intricacies of teaching: "I wish we had been given this earlier". While it was one-on-one, they argued that the experience was carefully scaffolded to provide explicit and direct feedback, and they were continuously experiencing success as they assisted a child to learn how to read.

A feature of the program that was considered important to its success was the contribution of the in-school support staff – "superb" in the words of one student. While there were differences between the approaches of the four in-school personnel, students highlighted key features that made their contribution so integral. Support staff were highly experienced in working with children experiencing difficulties learning, and they used this knowledge to guide students in their planning to ensure success for the children. Further, the support staff possessed expert knowledge about the teaching of reading, and were able to pass this knowledge on in the form of scaffolds and guidance. One student described the support staff as "fantastic", going on to explain that the staff member was able to model and guide them in explicit teaching strategies in a clear and manageable manner.

While there were many comments of praise, the students were also forthcoming about how they thought the program could improve. One of their concerns was that the course only ran for five weeks, and there was a requirement that they become acquainted with the tutoring program, reading content, assessments, and instructional strategies in a very short time (i.e. two workshops). This they found confusing, exhausting and frustrating. Students made suggestions for alleviating this overload of information including obtaining video of assessments so they could be partially prepared as to what to expect, providing online pre-readings for the course, and trying to get more time allocated to the first workshop (e.g. half a day).

Positive feedback was also forthcoming from other sources in the schools. On one occasion, a senior member of the area management team visited a school to work with pre-service teachers and gain first hand information about the program. This opportunity resulted in discussion with university personnel about how the program could be broadened to include more schools. One option was to consider other groups of people who could be approached to implement the tutoring program. Parents in one school provided unsolicited feedback on the success of the program, and petitioned for the program to continue due to its success in getting their children "hooked on reading".

Conclusion

The aim of this paper was to report the outcomes of a program of work conducted jointly between a university and a group of schools, and the impact that it had on the learning of pre-service teacher education students about the teaching children who showed evidence of experiencing difficulties in learning to read. The results of this project provide evidence that both parties were able to benefit from the partnership.

In promoting the notion of reading clinics, Rohl and Greaves (2005) highlighted that many pre-service teacher programs have difficulty resourcing such practices. While this program was not developed in a reading clinic model as suggested by Rohl and Greaves, it does highlight how a university program, and a local school community, benefited from sharing their resources. This program received no additional university funding, with the only provision made being in regards to timetabling. In regards to school based personnel, the program ran within the regular workloads of staff.

Students completing the course claimed that they were satisfied with the outcome of the five-week program in schools. Their satisfaction was echoed through interviews conducted at the conclusion of the program and in the reflective journals they completed. School staff, area administrators, and parents of children within the host schools also supported the benefits of the program.

The more important aspect of this program though was the reported enhancement of the students' knowledge about the teaching of reading. Students, through the interview process, indicated that they gained considerable knowledge about the teaching of reading, and in their reflective journals, some students showed evidence of how they were integrating the differing elements of reading in their pedagogy. The extent of their gains in knowledge is not examined extensively in this paper, but the authors are considering ways in which this could be directly assessed. One possible measure being examined and piloted with this group of students is one used by Moats and Foorman (2003) that evaluates levels of knowledge about phonology, language structures and programmatic links between differing aspects of literacy programs.

Ongoing research will be undertaken to refine the current tutoring model. As part of these research projects focus will be placed on how to specifically measure the knowledge of teachers about the teaching of reading. Using the work of Moats and Foorman (2003) and Snow et al. (2005), this work aims to refine the overall program to ensure pre-service teachers are better prepared to teach reading for those students most at risk. This work needs to be matched with the development of research protocols that allow for the progress of children to be evaluated. This work will be put in place during the next iteration of this model, with these outcomes guiding future research to be undertaken.
While the program does not intend or aim to make expert teachers of reading for students with reading difficulties, it is best depicted by the following commentary by one of the participating teachers:

> In conclusion and reflecting on 'reading is rocket science', I feel that this program has given me the tools and the knowledge I require to build the rocket!! First attempt may well be basic, but in time they will develop! Not quite a professional or an expert yet, but on my way.

References

Bos C, Mather N, Dickson S, Podhajski B, Chard D (2001). Perceptions and knowledge of pre-service and in-service educators about early reading instruction. *Annals of Dyslexia*, 51(1): 97–120.

Chard D, Pikulski J, Templeton S (2000). From phonemic awareness to fluency: Effective decoding instruction in a research-based reading program. www.eduplace.com/state/author/chard_pik_temp.pdf

Coulheart M, Prior M (2007). *Learning to read in Australia*. Canberra: Academy of Social Sciences in Australia.

Darling-Hammond L, Bransford J (2005). *Preparing teachers for a changing world: What teachers should learn and be able to do*. San Francisco, CA: Jossey-Bass.

NSW Department of Education and Training (2003). *Programming and strategies handbook*. Sydney: Author.

NSW Department of Education and Training (2002). *Follow-up to BST*. Sydney: Author.

House of Commons Education and Skills Committee (March, 2005). *Teaching children to read: Eighth Report of Sessions 2004-2005*. London, UK: The Stationery Office.

Moats L (1999). *Teaching reading IS rocket science: What expert teachers of reading should know and be able to do*. Washington, DC: American Federation of Teachers.

Moats L, Foorman B (2003). Measuring teachers' content knowledge of language and reading. *Annals of Dyslexia*, 53: 23–45.

National Reading Panel (2000). *Report of the National Reading Panel: Teaching children to read: An evidence-based assessment of the scientific research literature on reading and its implications for reading instruction*. Washington, DC: National Institute of Child Health and Human Development.

Neilson R (2003). *Sutherland Phonological Awareness Test-Revised*. Jamberoo: Author.

Pikulski J, Chard D (2000). Fluency: The bridge from decoding to reading comprehension. www.eduplace.com/state/author/pik_chard_fluency.pdf

Rohl M, Greaves D (2005). How are pre-service teachers in Australia being prepared for teaching literacy and numeracy to a diverse range of students. *Australian Journal of Learning Disabilities*, 10(1): 3–8.

Snow C, Burns M, Griffin P (1998). *Preventing reading difficulties in young children*. Washington, D: National Academy Press.

Snow C, Griffin P, Burns M (2005). *Knowledge to support the teaching of reading: preparing teachers for a changing world.* San Francisco, CA: Jossey-Bass.

Swanson H (2005). Searching for the best model for instructing students with learning disabilities. In T Skrtic, K Harris & J Shriner (Eds), *Special education policy and practice: Accountability, instruction and social changes.* Denver, CO: Love.

5
The entry knowledge of Australian pre-service teachers in the area of phonological awareness and phonics

Barbara J Fisher
Faculty of Education, Avondale College

Dr Merle E Bruce
Senior Honorary Research Fellow, Avondale College

Dr Cedric Greive
Faculty of Education, Avondale College

Abstract

This paper reports on part of an ongoing project in an Australian tertiary institution to pre-test primary teacher education students on their entry level phonological awareness and phonics skills, and to use the results of this test to inform the teaching of their Curriculum Studies English classes. A 25-item multiple choice test selected from the phonological and phonic knowledge outlined in the NSW *English K–6 Syllabus*, was devised by the authors. A cohort of 140 pre-service teachers undertook this test prior to commencing their class in Curriculum Studies English I. This paper analyses the results of this pre-test and discusses the implications for teaching pre-service teachers domain-specific knowledge in the area of phonological awareness and phonics.

Two recent inquiries initiated by the Australian Federal Government (DEST, 2005; House of Representatives Standing Committee on Education and Vocational Training, 2007) have highlighted concerns about the extent to which current Australian teacher education programs are adequately preparing graduates for effective teaching of reading skills. Although these concerns are wide-ranging, this paper will focus specifically on implications for early reading instruction. It will also discuss attempts by one teacher education program to address implicit suggestions in recommendations arising out of these reports that, first, beginning teachers may not have the necessary domain-specific knowledge of phonological awareness and phonics for the effective teaching of early reading skills (DEST, 2005, Recommendation 11, p20); and second, they may not have attained sufficiently high levels of personal literacy skills to enable them to promote high academic standards among their students (House of Representatives Standing Committee on Education and Vocational Training, 2007, Recommendation 4b, pxvi). Although the importance of an 'integrated' approach to the teaching of reading, involving both explicit and implicit forms of instruction (McNaughton, 2006) is recognised, this paper will focus on explicit instructional approaches as recommended in the report on Teaching Reading (DEST, 2005).

Pre-service and in-service teacher perceptions and knowledge of the metalinguistic processes associated with learning to read, has been the focus of considerable recent research, both overseas (e.g. Bos, Mather, Dickson, Podhaiski, & Chard, 2001; Cunningham, Perry, Stanovich, & Stanovich, 2004; Moats & Foorman, 2003; Spear-Swerling, Brucker, & Alfano, 2005), and in Australia (e.g. Fielding-Barnsley & Purdie, 2005; Leigh & Ryan, 2006; Louden, Rohl, Gore, Greaves, McIntoch, Wright, Siemon & House, 2004; Rennie & Harper, 2006; Rohl & Greaves, 2005). In general, this research indicates a mismatch between, on the one hand, what converging 'evidence-based' research supports as effective early reading instruction, and, on the other hand, the knowledge and skills which new teachers actually bring to the task of teaching beginning reading (Bos et al., 2001; DEST, 2005; Fielding-Barnsley & Purdie, 2005; Louden et al., 2004; Rohl & Greaves, 2005; Spear-Swerling et al., 2005).

This mismatch has manifested itself in at least two ways. First, it has been demonstrated that many pre-service and in-service teachers have limited knowledge of phonological awareness, spelling and the terminology associated with language structure and phonics (Bos et al., 2001; Cunningham et al., 2004; Fielding-Barnsley & Purdie, 2005; Moats & Foorman, 2003; Rennie & Harper, 2006; Rohl & Greaves, 2005). Consequently, these teachers may have difficulty in teaching word-level reading skills in the systematic and explicit manner which research has found to be of particular importance for students with diverse learning needs (Fielding-Barnsley & Purdue, 2005; Moats & Foorman, 2003; Rennie & Harper, 2006; Rohl & Greaves, 2005). Further, they may also confuse children with incorrect information, as for example, when a child comes to the word 'done' and they are told to sound it out (Moats & Foorman, 2003). In addition, they may have trouble interpreting screening and diagnostic assessment data (Moats & Foorman, 2003), as well as psychological and specialist reports (Fielding-Barnsley & Purdue, 2005).

Moreover, there is evidence that some teachers may over-estimate their knowledge of reading-related skills, being unaware of what they know and do not know, leading Cunningham and her colleagues (2004, p162) to conclude that, "While teachers cannot teach what they do not know ... [they] ... do not always know what they do not know". On the other hand, many pre-service and beginning teachers, while indicating positive attitudes towards explicit code instruction, have expressed frustration at their lack of knowledge and lack of preparedness for teaching phonics and other word-level early reading skills (Bos et al., 2001; Rennie & Harper, 2006). Further, pre-service teachers have expressed dissatisfaction in not being taught how and why all of the conventions of phonology and written language fit together (Rennie & Harper, 2006).

A second area of concern which may impact on teacher preparedness for literacy teaching is evidence of a decline in the academic aptitude of pre-service teachers. Research findings by Leigh and Ryan (2006) indicate that literacy and numeracy standards for students entering Australian teacher education programs had fallen from an average percentile rank of 74 in 1983 to an average of 61 in 2003. In support of this Zipin and Brennan (2006) provide anecdotal evidence, which, no doubt, could be corroborated in most Australian universities, that a significant number of teacher education students in their university struggle with attaining the required university coursework 'standards' for essay writing. Zipin and Brennan (2006) estimate that well upwards of 15 per cent of students are "weak" or "very weak" in spelling, grammar and sentence structure, while up to 50–60 per cent are "weak" or "very weak" in synthesis and analysis of the key concepts and arguments in required readings in their coursework. While the possible reasons for these findings of a drop in literacy standards of the current cohort of teacher education students are complex, and beyond the scope of this paper, the fact remains that prospective teachers who themselves struggle with academic literacies, are likely to perpetuate the cycle of low literacy standards for the next generation of readers (Zipin & Brennan, 2006).

Although the research evidence cited above indicating possible deficiencies in both the personal literacy skills and the domain-specific knowledge of language structure concepts such as phonological awareness and phonics, of pre-service and beginning teachers, represents a poor prognosis for the future teaching of reading, there are some positive implications for educational practice. Accumulating evidence exists which suggests that, given explicit instruction in phonological and orthographic information and the opportunity to practice their new-found skills in supervised, appropriately designed field-work experiences, pre-service teachers can develop the knowledge and skills necessary for effective early literacy teaching (Al Otaiba, 2005; Rohl & Greaves, 2005). Improved teacher knowledge and skills lead, in turn, to improved student outcomes in reading acquisition (Al Otaiba, 2005; de Lemos, 2005).

From this perspective, one can understand the relevance of recommendations that primary education literacy coursework should include "evidence-based ... instruction on how to teach phonemic awareness" and "phonics" (DEST, 2005, pp20,52), and that teacher education students should "undergo diagnostic testing of their literacy and numeracy skills" with a view to assisting those students with "identified deficiencies ... to develop skills to the required level" (House of Representatives Standing Committee on Education and Vocational Training, 2007, ppxvi,60). Such testing would also allow teacher educators to be aware of gaps and inaccuracies in pre-service teachers' knowledge, so that they can shape their coursework to promote the development of high standards of personal literacy and domain-specific knowledge of early reading skills for all (Rennie & Harper, 2006; Spear-Swerling et al., 2005).

The present study reports on part of an ongoing project in an Australian tertiary institution designed to pre-test primary teacher education students on their entry level phonological awareness and phonics skills, and to use the results of this test to inform the teaching of their Curriculum Studies English classes. This was a pilot study which sought to combine descriptive statistics and qualitative analysis techniques to analyse the usefulness of the test as a valid indicator of strengths and weaknesses in phonological awareness and phonics skills of beginning teachers. The study also sought to explore pre-service teacher perceptions and reactions with regard to the testing of their entry-level knowledge of phonological awareness and phonics.

Methodology

Participants

The participants were a cohort of 140 pre-service teachers, 127 of whom were undertaking a BEd (Primary) degree while the remainder were enrolled in either BEd (Early Childhood) (N=6), or a two-year, graduate-entry BTch (Primary) degree (N=7). As can be seen in Table 5.1, the group was comprised of 28 males and 112 females ranging in ages from 18 to 52. The mean age was 21.7 years and the median was 20 years. A proportionally larger number of the older students were males.

Age Range	Male	Female	Total
18 – 20	12	72	84
21 – 25	10	30	40
26 – 30	0	5	5
31 – 35	1	4	5
36 – 40	2	1	3
41 – 45	2	0	2
45 – 50	0	0	0
51 – 55	1	0	1
	28	112	140

Table 5.1: Respondents by age and sex

So as to explore the possibility that factors other than schooling may have contributed to pre-service teacher knowledge of phonics and phonological awareness, subjects were asked to complete a questionnaire indicating their pathway into the course (direct from school, transfer from another course, or after being in full-time work), and whether or not they had lived or travelled in non-English speaking country. (See Appendix One for a copy of the questionnaire.) As indicated in Table 5.2, of the 131 students who responded to this questionnaire, slightly more than half (approximately 56 per cent) had come directly from school while a further fifteen students (approximately 11 per cent) had transferred from another course. Thirty-nine of the respondents, or approximately 37 per cent, had previously worked full time, while only three students, all female, had experienced life in a country where English was not the primary language. An inspection of the data in Table 5.2 indicates that, in comparison to the females, the males were more likely to have been in full-time employment prior to entering the course, while the females were more likely to have come direct from school, or to have transferred from another course.

Background experience	Male	Female	Total
Direct from school	9	65	74
Transfer from another course	1	14	15
Travel through NES countries	0	3	3
Full-time work	16	23	39
	26	105	131

Table 5.2: Respondents by background experience and sex

Measures

A 25-item multiple choice phonics test, designed by the authors, and selected from concepts and terminology as outlined in the "Scope and Sequence of Phonological and Graphological Skills" of the NSW *English K–6 Syllabus* (Board of Studies NSW, 1998), was used to assess pre-service teacher entry-level phonological awareness and phonics skills. (See Appendix Two for a copy of the test.) For the purposes of statistical analysis the test was sub-divided into three sections, namely: 'Rules-based Items' (8 questions); 'Orthographic/Phonological Items' (8 questions); and 'Knowledge of Terminology' (9 questions).

Subsequent to completion of the test, students were asked to provide a written reflection on their reaction to the experience of undertaking the test.

Testing procedures

Testing took place during the first class period for the semester of the subject Curriculum Studies English I, which is a subject designed to familiarise pre-service teachers with the Early Stage I and Stage I sections of the NSW *English K–6 Syllabus* (Board of Studies NSW, 1998). The BEd (Primary) participants were in the second year of their degree course, while the BEd (Early Childhood) participants were in their third year, and the BTch participants were in either the first or second year of their course. None of the participants had previously undertaken a subject which focussed on early reading skills. Testing took place in two successive years (2006 and 2007) with test results from both groups being combined for the purposes of analysis.

Before commencing the test it was explained to the participants that this was part of a research project designed to help the lecturer understand and focus on those aspects of beginning literacy instruction with which they were unfamiliar. It was also emphasised that in no way would the marks from this test contribute towards their final semester grade.

Results and discussion

The phonics test

Table 5.3 displays a range of statistics that apply to the three sub-scales ('Rule-based Items', 'Orthographic/Phonological Items' and 'Knowledge of Terminology Items') and the total score. These include: the measures of central tendency; measures of spread; range; minimum and maximum scores and the quarterly percentage scores. The box plots derived from these results are shown in Figure 5.1. This reveals that the scores generated from the two sub-scales 'Rule-based Items' and 'Knowledge of Terminology Items' are uniformly spread with median measures lying approximately in the middle of the range. This indicates that, for a pre-test situation, the difficulty of the two sub-scales is about right. In contrast the scores generated from the sub-scale 'Orthographical

/Phonological Items' are skewed toward the upper end of the range, indicating that this scale is probably too easy for a pre-test.

	Rule-based Items	Orthog/Phon Items	Knowledge of Terminology	Test Total
No. of Items	8	8	9	25
Mean	5.3	6.6	4.7	16.6
Median	5	7	5	17
Mode	6	7	5	17
St. Deviation	1.42	1.23	1.53	2.82
Range	6	6	8	16
Minimum Score	2	2	1	6
Maximum Score	8	8	9	22
Quarterly % 25	4	6	3	15
75	6	8	6	19

Table 5.3: Sub-scales and test-total by measures of central tendency, standard deviation, range, maximum and minimum scores and quarterly percentiles.

The 'Total Score' is generated by the sum of the three sub-scales and has a range of 16 points out of a possible 25 points with a median measure of 17. The box plot reveals that the total score is somewhat skewed toward the upper end. This however, should be corrected if the sub-scale 'Orthographical/Phonological Items' is made more difficult.

The correlation table (Table 5.4) reveals an interesting side view of the participants in the study and pertinent information about the sub-scales. Firstly, there is a slight tendency for the males among the respondent to be older than the females ($r = -0.30$), while there were no correlations between age or sex and the sub-scales of the test. More importantly it can be seen that there is a slight tendency for those who scored well on

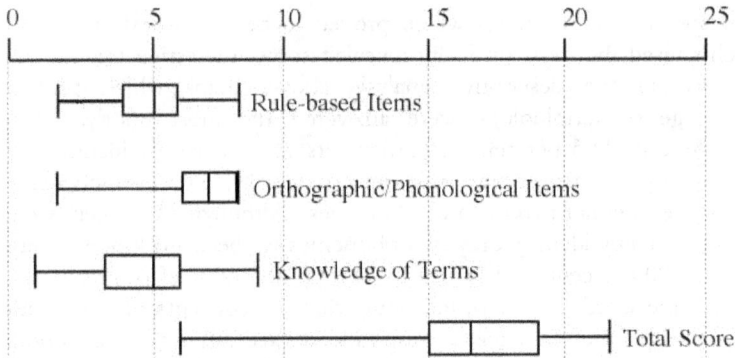
Figure 5.1: Box plots for sub-scales and total score

the sub-scale 'Rule-based Items' to also score well on the sub-scale 'Orthographic/Phonological Items' and vice versa (r = + 0.32). Despite this, with a shared variance of about 10 per cent, these two sub-scales can be regarded as having relatively little overlap. On the other hand the sub-scale 'Knowledge of Terminology' can be regarded as being independent of the other two sub-scales (r = + 0.09 and r = + 0.16 respectively). In other words, there is prima-facie evidence that all three sub-scales provide measures of different constructs. Finally, it is to be expected that correlations between the three sub-scales and the 'Total Score' would be relatively strong (r = + 0 .69, r = + 0.68 and r = + 0.66 respectively).

	Age	Sex	Rule-Based	Orthog/ Phon	Knowl. Terms	Total Score
Age	+1.0	- 0.30*	+ 0.08	- 0.02	+ 0.10	+ 0.09
Sex		+ 1.0	+ 0.20	0.00	+ 0.06	+ 0.04
Rule-Based Items			+ 1.0	+ 0.32*	+ 0.09	+ 0.69*
Orthog/Phon Items				+ 1.0	+ 0.16	+ 0.68*
Knowledge of Terms					+ 1.0	+ 0.66*
Total Score						+ 1.0

Table 5.4: Correlations for age, sex, sub-scales and total score

An inspection of the items which proved to be the easiest and those which caused the most difficulty revealed some interesting trends. As indicated in the descriptive analysis above, items which probed knowledge of terminology were answered the most poorly. For example, only 11.5 per cent of participants could correctly identify the number of phonemes in the word "black" (Item 19), with most choosing a response of either two or three phonemes. Although 83 per cent were able to correctly identify only two phonemes in the word "shoe" (Item 23), only 20 per cent could correctly identify the number of graphemes in the same word (Item 24), indicating that the concepts of phonemes and of grapheme-phoneme correspondence are not well understood. Other terminology which was not particularly well known included consonant blends (Item 11 with 44 per cent correct), homonyms (Item 21 with 45 per cent correct), and vowel digraphs (Item 25 with 46 per cent correct).

Another trend that became evident was that, although the majority displayed good phonological awareness in being able to identify individual phonemes (Items 3, 7, 8, & 13, all with approximately 95 per cent correct), and syllables (Items 12 & 22 with over 90 per cent correct) in words, many had trouble with rule-based applications of this knowledge. For example, while the majority were able to identify short vowel sounds in a one-syllable word (Item 13 with 96 per cent correct), only about half were able to identify long vowel sounds and the rules governing the spelling of long vowel sounds (Items 2, 5, 15, & 16). Again, although the majority (93 per cent) could distinguish the soft sound of 'c' in the word 'cent', when compared with words that have the hard sound of 'c' (Item 8), only 76 per cent were able to apply the spelling rule for distinguishing the soft and hard 'c' sounds (Item 18). There was also some confusion between compound and affixed words (Item 21), with only 79 per cent of participants correctly identifying the compound word.

Taken together, these results indicate that for this cohort of pre-service teachers, entry knowledge of graphological/phonological rules and terminology tends to be fragmentary, suggesting that without further instruction in domain-specific knowledge in the area of phonological awareness and phonics, they may have difficulty providing systematic and explicit beginning reading instruction. This supports findings from previous studies which found that many pre-service and in-service teachers have limited knowledge of phonological awareness and phonics (e.g. Fielding-Barnsley & Purdue, 2005; Moats & Foorman, 2003; Rennie & Harper, 2006; Rohl & Greaves, 2005).

Reflections on the test

Previous studies have reported that many beginning teachers feel frustrated by their lack of knowledge and lack of preparedness for teaching phonics and other word-level early reading skills (Bos et al., 2001; Rennie & Harper, 2006). This finding was also demonstrated in the present study. Written reflections on the experience of taking the test confirmed that many were confused with the terminology, and in most cases, resorted to guessing. Typical comments (with no attempt to correct grammatical errors) were:

> The content covered in the test had aspects and topics, which I had either never heard of in my life or had very little understanding of.

A few students, despite assurances that the marks for this test would not count towards their final grade, even expressed feelings of fear and humiliation.

> Not knowing the answer to the questions and not grasping an understanding of what the questions were asking was horrible, I felt stupid. The test was a very negative experience for me. It made me feel somewhat incompetent and it is not an experience I would want one of my students to go through.

Some students, similarly to those reported by Rennie and Harper (2006), expressed frustration that they had not been taught these things in school.

> When I attempted the test I really struggled, as when I was at school they taught what a noun, verb and syllable was but that was about it.

Some students, however, (mainly older students) felt that they had learnt these things before but had forgotten them.

> It has become real to me that I have forgotten many things that I was originally taught when I was younger, and at several times throughout the test I felt like I knew an answer, or I had come across several terms before, but could not remember what to do. This test in itself has really opened up my eyes on what is needed to be learned to be a successful teacher of English.

Some comments also reflected a tendency for some students to have previously had an inflated idea of their degree of understanding of English phonology, as suggested by Cunningham et al. (2004), with observations such as:

> Now I know how much I really have to learn! The test was a real wake-up call because I had considered English as being straightforward to teach. I know that the test was probably full of 'basics', but I was so lost!

Some students expressed appreciation of being shown how much they had yet to learn, and of the importance of the knowledge of such concepts in beginning reading instruction. For example:

> The test made me realise I have a lot to learn before I am ready to be thrown into a classroom. Its given me something to learn from so I can have the ability and confidence to teach a class full of children how to read .... Its good to see that the things we are being taught in this class will actually have practical use in a classroom.

While the majority of students, as noted above, viewed the whole exercise positively, as a chance to highlight what they still needed to know, three students expressed the view that they considered the learning of terminology associated with basic literacy skills to be irrelevant and a waste of time.

> I feel it is beyond the level of knowledge a student doing this particular course is required to know. So far on prac my teachers have never mentioned those words when teaching or in preparing lessons. If they were to come up in books a teacher reads well there is always the dictionary. Some words I agree are useful to learn, however lots of this I feel is not using our time wisely and it is unnecessary.

Such comments reflect the polarisation between code-based and meaning-based approaches to literacy instruction, which currently exists in the Australian educational community, and the need to find a proper balance between the two (de Lemos, 2005; Harris, 2006; McNaughton, 2006). While this paper acknowledges the importance of an integrated approach, it has focussed on pre-service teacher knowledge and understanding of code-based instruction because of converging research evidence that many beginning teachers have deficiencies in this area (DEST, 2005; Louden et al., 2004; Rennie & Harper, 2006). The written comments have also highlighted, unintentionally, the fact that a number of the pre-service teachers in the present study, like those in reported by Zipin and Brennan (2006), showed deficiencies in personal literacy skills with regard to grammar, punctuation and sentence structure. The development of a diagnostic test of personal literacy skills could be the focus of future research.

Conclusion

The present study has reported on part of an ongoing project in an Australian tertiary institution to pre-test primary teacher education students on their entry level phonological awareness and phonics skills, and to use the results of this test to inform the teaching of their Curriculum Studies English I class. This project, which commenced in 2006, has, in a sense, anticipated a recommendation of the Report on the Inquiry into Teacher Education (House of Representatives Standing Committee on Education and Vocational Training, 2007), albeit on a limited scale, that teacher education students should undergo diagnostic testing in literacy and numeracy at the beginning of their coursework with a view to assisting them to develop skills to the required level.

The phonics test reported on in this paper proved to be useful, even in its original form, for highlighting gaps in the entry knowledge of pre-service teachers in the area of phonological awareness and phonics. This information has enabled the lecturer (the lead author) to be more informed and more intentional in her instruction in systematic and explicit beginning literacy knowledge and skills as recommended by the Report and Recommendations on Teaching Reading (DEST, 2005). Consequently, the participants showed an overall mean gain in scores on a similar, but more difficult, test in their final examinations. Based on the findings of the present study the original test has now been modified so as to increase the difficulty of the Orthographic/Phonological subscale, and the modified version is currently being trialled with a view to using it as a pre-, post- and maintenance test for research with future cohorts of pre-service teachers. The final goal of this project is that, with enhanced knowledge and understanding of phonological awareness and phonics, together with instruction in other aspects of literacy which form part of the undergraduate coursework of this institution, pre-service teachers will be better equipped for effective teaching of reading in the early years of schooling.

References

Al Otaiba S (2005). How effective is code-based reading tutoring in English for English learners and preservice teacher-tutors? *Remedial and Special Education*, 26(4): 245–254.

Board of Studies NSW (1998). *English K–6 Syllabus*. Sydney: Board of Studies NSW.

Bos C, Mather N, Dickson S, Podhajski B, Chard D (2001). Perception and knowledge of preservice and inservice educators about early reading instruction. *Annals of Dyslexia*, 51(1): 97–119.

Cunningham A E, Perry K E, Stanovich K E, & Stanovich P J (2004). Disciplinary knowledge of K–3 teachers and their knowledge calibration in the domain of early literacy. *Annals of Dyslexia*, 54(1): 139–166.

de Lemos M (2005). Effective strategies for the teaching of reading: What works, and why. *Australian Journal of Learning Disabilities*, 10(3,4): 11–17.

DEST (2005). *Teaching reading: Report and recommendations.* National Inquiry into the Teaching of Literacy. Canberra: Department of Education, Science and Training. Retrieved 11 February 2007, from www.dest.gov.au/nitl/report.htm

Fielding-Barnsley R, Purdie N (2005). Teachers' attitude to and knowledge of metalinguistics in the process of learning to read. *Asia-Pacific Journal of Teacher Education,* 33(1): 65–76.

Harris P (2006). *Probing relationships between literacy research, policy development and classroom practice.* Paper presented at and appearing in the refereed proceedings of the Future Directions for Literacy Conference, 3–4 March 2006, University of Sydney. Retrieved 27 March 2007, from www.literacyeducators.com.au/docs/Harris_Paper.pdf

House of Representatives Standing Committee on Education and Vocational Training (2007). *Top of the class: Report on the inquiry into teacher education.* Canberra, ACT: House of Representatives Publishing Unit. Retrieved 3 April 2007, from www.aph.gov.au/house/committee/evt/teachereduc/report/fullreport.pdf

Leigh A, Ryan C (2006). *How and why has teacher quality changed in Australia?* Australian National University CEPR Discussion Paper 534, Canberra, ACT: ANU. Retrieved 22 May 2007, from www.rsss.anu.edu.au/themes/TQConf_Ryan.pdf

Louden W, Rohl M, Gore J, Greaves D, McIntosh A, Wright R, Siemon D, House H (2004). *Prepared to teach: An investigation into the preparation of teachers to teach literacy and numeracy.* Canberra: Department of Education, Science and Training. Retrieved 3 April 2007 from www.dest.gov.au/NR/rdonlyres/8F448021-C7BC-4741-870F-66EE1A9ACDE2/10111/Prepared_to_Teach_FINAL_for_web.pdf

McNaughton S (2006). *Effective literacy instruction and culturally and linguistically diverse students: Or having the 'tail' wag the dog.* Keynote address to 'Future Directions in Literacy' Conference, 3–4 March 2006, University of Sydney.

Moats L C, Foorman B R (2003). Measuring teachers' content knowledge of language and reading. *Annals of Dyslexia,* 53(1): 23–45.

Rennie J, Harper H (2006). *KAL that counts: An investigative study into preservice teachers' knowledge about language.* Paper presented and published in proceedings at the 2006 Australian Teacher Education Conference, Fremantle, WA, 7–9 July. Retrieved 8 May 2007, from www.atea.edu.au/ConfPapers/2006/rennie.pdf

Rohl M, Greaves D (2005). How are pre-service teachers in Australia being prepared for teaching literacy and numeracy to a diverse range of students? *Australian Journal of Learning Disabilities,* 10(1): 3–8.

Spear-Swerling L, Brucker P O, Alfano M P (2005). Teachers' literacy-related knowledge and self-perceptions in relation to preparation and experience. *Annals of Dyslexia,* 54(2): 266–296.

Zipin L, Brennan M (2006). Meeting literacy needs of pre-service cohorts: Ethical dilemmas for socially just teacher educators. *Asia-Pacific Journal of Teacher Education,* 34(3): 333–351.

APPENDIX ONE

QUESTIONNAIRE FOR PHONICS TEST

Date_____

Name_____

Age_____

Gender: Male   Female

1. Have you studied linguistics prior to studying at Avondale College? Circle one of the following:
                    Yes   No

2. Have you engaged in any teacher-related experiences prior to studying at Avondale College? Circle one of the following:
                    Yes   No

Elaborate_____

_____

3. Circle your current course at Avondale:
   a) B.Ed
   b) B.Tch
   c) Early Childhood
   d) Other_____

4. Experience prior to commencing Curriculum Studies - English I. Circle one of the following. Did you:
   a) come direct from high school;
   b) transfer from another tertiary course;
   c) travel overseas to a non-English speaking country;
   d) take part in paid full-time work;

5. If you have been employed then list fields of employment and time spent at each job.

Example- Forklift driver – 3 months

Employment   Duration

_____

_____

_____

_____

_____

6. Any other relative comments you wish to include.

_____

_____

APPENDIX TWO
PHONICS TEST FOR PRE-SERVICE TEACHERS

Name_____   Date_____

1. If the letter *"i"* were inserted after the *"a"* in *"pad", "man"* and *"pants"*, the *"a"* would be:
   a. long *"a"*
   b. short *"a"*
   c. silent *"a"*
   d. *r*-controlled

2. If *"daper"* were a word, the *"a"* would probably be:
   a. long *"a"*
   b. short *"a"*
   c. silent *"v"*
   d. *"r"*-controlled

3. The vowel sound in *"rare"* sounds like the vowel sound in:
   a. *ate*
   b. *are*
   c. *there*
   d. *ball*

4. The sound of *"a"* in the sound pattern *"ance"* or *"adge"* is usually:
   a. long
   b. short
   c. silent
   d. schwa

5. If a word contains two vowels, one of which is a final *"e"*, the first vowel sound is probably:
   a. long
   b. short
   c. silent
   d. schwa

6. Which one of the following consonants influences the sound of vowels?
   a. *"b"*
   b. *"r"*
   c. *"m"*
   d. *"j"*

7. Which word has a different ending sound?
   a. crab
   b. comb
   c. grab
   d. rub

8. Which word has a different beginning sound?
   a. cat
   b. cent
   c. cut
   d. cook

9. Which word has a different sound represented by *"ch"*?
   a. chaperone
   b. chef
   c. chalet
   d. charcoal

10. When two *"d's"* appear together in a word, as in *"daddy"*, *"middle"* and *"puddle"*:
    a. both "d's" are heard
    b. the first "*d*" is heard and other one is silent
    c. the second "*d*" is heard and the first one is silent
    d. both "*d's*" are silent

11. Which of the following consonant clusters is not a consonant blend?
    a. *"cl"*
    b. *"cr"*
    c. *"ch"*
    d. *"br"*

12. Which of the following words has two syllables?
    a. asked
    b. acted
    c. turned
    d. watched

13. The short sound of "*i*" is heard in:
    a. hid
    b. hide
    c. tie
    d. high

14. Which of the following consonant combinations is not a consonant digraph?
    a. "*ch*"
    b. "*sh*"
    c. "*th*"
    d. "*rh*"

15. Which of the following words has a long vowel sound?
    a. watch
    b. cheer
    c. fur
    d. feed

16. Which of the following words has a long "*oo*" sound?
    a. book
    b. boot
    c. hood
    d. pull

17. "*dis*" is an example of a:
    a. synonym
    b. diphthong
    c. prefix
    d. suffix

18. The letter *"c"* followed by *"e"*, *"i"*, or *"y"* usually has the sound of:

    a. *"ch"*
    b. *"ck"*
    c. *"s"*
    d. *"sh"*

19. How many phonemes are in the word *"black"*?

    a. 2
    b. 3
    c. 4
    d. 5

20. Which of the following is a compound word?

    a. truthful
    b. campground
    c. likeable
    d. trusting

21. The words *"sale"* and *"sail"* are:

    a. homonyms
    b. synonyms
    c. antonyms
    d. rhyming words

22. How many syllables in the word *"responsibility"*

    a. 6
    b. 8
    c. 10
    d. 14

23. How many phonemes are in the word *"shoe"*?

    a. 2
    b. 3
    c. 4
    d. 5

24. How many graphemes in the word *"shoe"*?

   a. 2
   b. 3
   c. 4
   d. 5

25. *"ea"* is an example of a/an:

   a. diphthong
   b. onset-rime
   c. vowel digraph
   d. blend

6
Building literacy education: pasts, futures, and "the sum of effort"

Peter Freebody
Professorial Research Fellow
Faculty of Education and Social Work, University of Sydney

Introduction: What is *the future?*

In a famous remark about education, Antonio Gramsci pointed to the urgent need to understand schools through the lens of "an historical conception of the world that understands movement and change, and that appreciates the sum of effort and sacrifice which the present has cost the past, and which the future is costing the present" (Gramsci, 1971, p34). While 'futuring' has been an enthusiasm for literacy educators, even more so since the turn of the millennium, the serious costs to be borne now for present conditions to be maintained, and the even more dramatic cost of adapting to rapid changes in the communicational environment, are not notions that have been at the front of most speculations. In this paper, I argue that we need to develop ways of theorising the future explicitly. More specifically, a point here is to see the future of 'literacy education' as part of broader patterns of social and institutional futures, and to have a 'moral analysis' of the future. This amounts to a recognition that choices facing societies such as ours, even choices about the apparently technical matters of educating our youngsters to read and write, call for moral rationalities to do with equity and excellence, the relative status of the 200 or so languages spoken in Australia, and the affordances and limits of the technologies that are reshaping our educational, work, civil, and domestic lives.

A useful starting point for articulating issues that bear on the future of education is offered by Kress (2003) who presented four questions related to high-speed changes that should preoccupy educators:

- What are the economic structures and opportunities open to school-leavers in an information-driven economy?
- What are the forms and modalities of communication, and what might be the educational implications of a move away from the dominance of written language toward the use of images?
- What are the emerging social structures and relations of social power?
- What are the technologies of communication, in particular, what are the implications of a move away from the single dominance of paper-texts toward digital-screen-online-texts?

Clearly all of these have serious implications for literacy educators in view of the significance for their educational, work, civil, and domestic lives of the level and qualities of literacy education that schools offer young people. For over a decade commentators have continued to put in front of educators the changing conditions of work places in late-industrial societies such as Australia in an effort to have the basic organisational structures of curriculum (materials, pedagogies, and assessments) revisited (e.g. Gee, Hull, & Lankshear, 1996). These revisitations are often disruptive activities, troubling the professional status of teachers and the community's trust in that professionalism, teachers' confidence in their practices and in their potentially conflicting accountabilities to students, parents, communities, and jurisdictions.

So literacy becomes a troublesome topic when we consider the future of the relationship between, on the one hand, the conventions of schooling and, on the other, life after and outside of school. Equally interesting, from the point of view of exploring pasts, futures, and the costs of transitions, is the future of schooling itself. Most deeply schooled people, such as me, generally carry on as if schools always were and always will be more or less as they are, and that one of the things that makes 'developing' countries 'developing' is that they are beginning to have more and more serious schooling. It is salutary to consider just how recent formal, mass schooling is and how potentially fragile it is. More specifically for our purposes, it is salutary to consider lessons from the history of literacy and literacy education, and the ways in which those lessons inform and detail the contradictions underpinning current educational practices that have remained unresolved since the formalisation of schooling in the middle industrial period.

For example, one of the key lessons from history provided by Graff (2001) is that literacy development, for individuals and collectives, has taken multiple paths. In the less thoroughly schooled past, there was more of an understanding that people could become effective literate participants in society through many different means and at different rates, and an appreciation of those differences. The central place occupied by literacy in school-education has meant that schools' heavy reliance on age-grading essentially makes variations in the reading and writing performance of young people into serious problems for systems, schools, teachers, students, and families. Clearly the leveling, filtering and sorting functions of schooling can and do work directly against official rhetoric advocating equity. That we discuss literacy education as if we have forgotten that contradiction impacts on the lives of many students. It is a highly consequential instance of collective professional amnesia:

> Missing from our common operational and legitimising myths and legacies ... is the informality and possibility of elementary and higher learning without the lock-step enforced march of age-grading and wholesale psychologies of human cognition and learning based on their simplistic presumptions ... for a great many persons, traditional alphabetic literacy of reading and sometimes writing was acquired in the widest variety of informal, as well as formal circumstances, and at a wide range of chronological ages ... at ages sometimes younger but far more commonly older than the limited span of childhood and early adolescence that came to be defined as the 'critical period'. Modernisation of schooling into mass systems rested in part on the denial of previously common courses or paths. (Graff, 2001, pp17–18)

Human beings have long learned skills such as literacy without schooling or in sites that might accompany schooling, such that some anthropologists refer quite specifically to 'school-literacy' to demarcate it from other daily activities (e.g. Street, 2005). In the modern minority world, literacy is linked inextricably with schooling, and many of the effects attributed to literacy learning have been shown to be in fact effects of schooling (Scribner & Cole, 1981). So in considering the future of literacy we can consider the future of schooling and then wonder what it is over and above school-knowing that literacy education might have to offer.

The most considered and patiently developed models of the future of schooling have been provided by the Center for Educational Research and Innovation at the Organization for Economic and Cultural Development (OECD). The OECD has built up three categories encompassing a total of six scenarios for the global future of schools on the basis of trends in its member nations. These are:

1. Attempting to maintain the status quo

- Bureaucratic School Systems Continue

2. Diverse, dynamic schooling following deep reforms ('re-schooling')

- Schools as Focused Learning Organisations
- Schools as Core Social Centres

3. Pursuit of alternatives as systems disband/disintegrate ('de-schooling')

- Extending the Market Model
- Learning Networks and the Network Society
- Teacher Exodus and System Meltdown

Some of the key features of each of these scenarios are noted here (the interested reader is referred to the OECD website, noted in the reference list, for a fuller discussion including an outline of the bases for these characteristics).

1. Try to maintain the status quo

- powerful bureaucratic systems will continue to operate, and continue to be resistant to deep change;
- schools will be knitted together into state/national systems governed by complex administrative arrangements;

- political and media commentaries will frequently be critical in tone about schools, teachers, and teacher education;
- there will be no major increases in overall funding for schools, and the continual extension of schools' duties further will stretch resources;
- the use of ICTs will continue to grow without changing schools' main organisational structures or operating principles;
- there will remain a distinct teacher corps, sometimes with the status of a civil service; and with strong unions/associations, but also with dubious or contested professional status.

2a. Reschooling #1: Schools as focussed learning organisations

- schools will be revitalised around a strong knowledge agenda, in a culture of high quality, experimentation, diversity, and innovation;
- new forms of evaluation and assessment will be developed and implemented;
- there will be strong links to the tertiary education sector;
- substantial investments will be made, especially in disadvantaged communities, to develop flexible, state-of-the-art facilities, in which ICTs feature extensively;
- equality of opportunity will be the norm, and will not be considered to be in conflict with 'quality' agenda;
- highly motivated teachers will work in favourable working conditions, with high levels of access to research and development;
- there will be high levels of professional development, group activities, networking, and mobility in and out of teaching.

2b. Reschooling #2: Schools as core social centres

- Schools will come to be seen as an effective bulwark against social and cultural fragmentation in society and the family;

- Curriculum will be strongly defined by collective and community tasks;
- Extensive shared responsibilities between schools and other community bodies, sources of expertise, and tertiary education will be in evidence;
- A wide range of organisational forms and settings will be in operation, with a strong emphasis on non-formal learning;
- There will be high esteem for teachers and schools;
- ICTs will be used extensively, especially for communication and networking;
- Schools will employ a core of high-status teaching professionals, with varied arrangements and conditions; but there will also be many others, 'paraprofessionals', around that core.

3a. Deschooling #1: Radical extension of the market model

- market features will be extended as governments encourage diversification and as they withdraw from much of their direct involvement, pushed by dissatisfaction among 'strategic consumers';
- many new providers will enter the learning market, with radical reforms in funding structures, incentives and regulation, so there will be diversity of provision, even though schools will survive;
- the notion of 'choice' will play a key role, choice for those buying educational services, and for those, such as employers, giving market value to different learning pathways;
- there will be a strong focus on cognitive outcomes, but possibly on 'values';
- indicators and accreditation arrangements will displace direct public monitoring and curriculum regulation (e.g. exams);

- innovation will abound as will painful transitions and inequalities;
- new learning professionals – public, private; full-time, part-time – will be created in the learning markets.

3b. Deschooling #2: Learning networks and the network society

- there will be such widespread dissatisfaction with schools that new possibilities for learning will lead to schools being abandoned;
- learner networks will form part of the broader 'network society';
- networks will be based on diverse parental, cultural, religious and community interests – some very local in character, others using distance and cross-border networking;
- small group, home schooling, and individualised arrangements will become widespread, and a substantial reduction of existing patterns of governance and accountability will be evident;
- there will be widespread exploitation of powerful, inexpensive ICTs;
- demarcations – between teacher and student, parent and teacher, education and community – will blur and break down, such that new learning professionals will emerge.

3c. Deschooling #3: teacher exodus and system meltdown

- a major crisis of teacher shortage will develop that proves highly resistant to conventional policy responses;
- crisis will be triggered by a rapidly ageing profession, exacerbated by low teacher morale and buoyant opportunities in more attractive graduate jobs;
- the large size of the teaching force will mean long lead times before policy measures show tangible results on overall teacher numbers;

- wide disparities will arise in the depth of the crisis associated with socio-geographic, as well as curriculum-subject, areas;

- different possible pathways will arise in response to 'meltdown' – a vicious circle of retrenchment and conflict or emergency strategies will spur radical innovation and change.

One of the considerable benefits of futures modeling such as that conducted by OECD is that we are led to keep in mind that schooling has numerous facets – organisational, economic, cultural, and technological. This can keep us from over-investing in single causes of change, imagining, for instance, that technological or curricular changes will of themselves produce changes in schools and that these changes will have only positive effects and only on teaching and learning. Vectors of change such as digital technologies operate on literacy learning and teaching but only within the context of other vectors, some of which hold in place aspects of schooling that may militate against the positive potentials of technological change. Warschauer makes this point in terms of the contradictions built into formal mass schooling from the start that have stayed with us 130 years after schools were made compulsory in Australia:

> The future of learning is digital ... What constitutes learning in the 21st century will be contested terrain as our society strives towards post-industrial forms of knowledge acquisition and production without having yet overcome the educational contradictions and failings of the industrial age. (Warschauer, 2007, p41)

So what might be some of those 'contradictions and failings' that hold us back? We can begin with four that have direct implications for literacy education:

- Our definitions of literacy

- Our attitudes about 'under-performing' students, families and schools

- Our magical beliefs about technology and learning

- Our naïveté about the allocation of responsibility for learning literacy.

These form the bases of the discussion that follows, and I briefly discuss each of them in terms of imagining the future. The most general expression of my point here is that literacy education needs to be discussed in terms of a moment in history in which the future of schooling – organised teaching and learning, formal and informal – is being pushed and pulled, imagined in radically different ways by different sectors and ideological interests in OECD-style countries, presenting us with very old challenges, often in completely new settings.

What is *literacy*?

Our definitions of a phenomenon set limits around our imagination and direct our research attention. Definitions of literacy have differed dramatically over the years, across the disciplines that have systematically addressed it, and in various policy statements. If the nature of literacy practices is changing – the material modes of production, the genres, the technologies of production and dissemination, the readerships, the sociocultural purposes, and so on – then we would expect these changes to be reflected in changing definitions and, more specifically, in the breadth and flexibility built into definitions in current use. A definition that I find useful, that takes account of changing conditions of production, use, and dissemination, and that, purely coincidentally, was co-authored by me, is the following:

> Literacy is the flexible and sustainable mastery of a repertoire of practices with the texts of traditional and new communications technologies via spoken language, print and multi-media. (Luke, Freebody & Land, 2000, p14)

This does not look like many other definitions in that it does not privilege psychological, sociological, linguistic or ideological approaches to literacy, but rather aims to invite attention from scholars and practitioners with interests and dispositions from all of those areas. This definition builds change, flexibility and repertoire into the core business of understanding literacy as the activities and materials coming under its purview are changed by and in turn themselves change other social, economic, cultural, and technological developments.

The term literacy is currently too tightly defined and too loosely used: definitions often narrow the focus to a knowledge of grapho-phonemic correspondences, or extracting 'meaning' from print. At the same time the term is used to connote or even substitute for the efficacy of school systems, the cultural level of individuals or societies, employability, the capacity for logical thinking, or even the capacity for democratic engagement – indeed all the 'literacy myths' that Graff (2001) has explored so thoroughly. The concept of literacy has developed a celebrity and political life of its own (Freebody, 2005), taken to hint at dark, deep system problems and to justify radical and apparently counter-productive policy measures (e.g. as reported in Fuller and others, 2007).

What is *underperformance in literacy*?

One intriguing aspect of literacy achievement, however it has been assessed in recent decades, is its resolute correlation with demographics such as socio-economic status, gender, first-language status and ethnicity. Estimates vary over times and places, but the durability especially of SES and literacy has been striking, and what might and can be done about that is an interesting and consequential question to ask of the future. According to international comparisons, Australian students' literacy achievement reflect 'high-performing, low equity' school systems (McGaw, 2007a), and they point to the need to explore more deeply our understandings and assumptions about the relationship between literacy and equity and the ways in which our assumptions about categories of students and their backgrounds continue to hinder our literacy efforts. For instance, Freebody, Forrest, & Gunn (2001) conducted an intensive interview study of the views of teachers who taught in schools in socio-economically disadvantaged areas. Among the conclusions were:

i. SES is a highly 'generative' category: Teachers attach a rich set of attributions to the category 'low SES', including attributions about experiences, language, exposure to literacy, adequate parenting, and so on. A selection of statements from Year 1–3 teachers working in schools serving disadvantaged communities conveys something of this richness:

> we're very acutely aware of the fact that we are servicing children, who do not experience what you could call mainstream life experiences. And as I said before, a lot of our kids come from refugee camps where they are deficient in

experiences in their mother tongue. We have to try to teach them literacy in English as well. We realise that many of them come from disadvantaged homes or least-advantaged homes that are pretty poor, that are ... do not have proper role models. That do not give children the experiences on which they can build, their own language and um literacy levels.

I had a third of the class were in families that had two adults within the home for starters and that was just two adults whether it be biological parents, step parents or just the latest relationship and a lot, I saw a lot of children who couldn't come to school just through the fact that they had been bashed, that they had been, that they were victims of alcoholism, that they were malnourished, shocking sort of scabies, lice, that sort of thing and I'm not meaning that that happens in every low socio-economic situation but I think the parents in the low socio-economic situation have so many pressures on them, or a single mum may have that or someone may have lost their job and you just, just all of these outside pressures that affect the parents, affect the children and then you have them coming to school so tired because they've been upset the night before.

Just because you're rich doesn't mean that you're going to have a child that's quite bright. But, they've got more access to resources at home, and the low socio-economic status means maybe if the parents haven't got ... they might not necessarily be well educated themselves, and they don't have the skills to know what to do with their kids when they're at that early age, when they're developing literacy skills.

ii. Educators' understandings of literacy and SES often function to exonerate them from the SES-achievement cycle: the strong tendency among teachers in the early years in schools in low SES areas, along with many other categories of people, is to focus their descriptions of the students' difficulties on the home and the family as a learning environment. In this sense, many teachers chartacterise such families as 'failures'. The culture of the home life, as attributed to low SES families, is the source of the problems in literacy and thus sets the limits on what educators can come to see as possible for students in these settings. The school seems to be left with few options, swimming, however valiantly, against the stream:

> I think that puts a lot of pressure on them. And maybe because the parents aren't spending as much time with the children, that the kids get the feeling that maybe school isn't that important as, you know, 'cause mum and dad, or mum – whoever's there – dad, is not interested and they haven't checked my homework for the last three weeks. Well then they're not interested in school. Therefore school isn't important. That sort of mentality.

> Children coming to school have a very low level of literacy on entry into primary school or pre-school even. They umm, things like: 'What's a book?' 'Never seen one' sort of thing which I found very hard to comprehend when I first got here. Umm and the parents ... the same way because of the fact that they failed, they don't value education, school as a institution of learning. They value it more as a institution of baby sitting. Well, it's convenient. They have to send their kids so why not? And umm, any days when they can't send their kids they're upset about the fact, but they, I think themselves they failed at school so to them school's not a place to go for a positive thing.

iii. Material resources are often related to cultural and intellectual resources requisite for success in school. In societies such as ours, there are elaborate and well-understood procedures for automatically converting material disadvantage to educational disadvantage, among members of the culture generally, and among school teachers, many of whom, myself included, have come from families who regarded teaching as an aspiration, an attainable entrée into the middle, semi-professional class. Some of the key conversion procedures in this process involve literacy:

> I suppose the money's not there to get them interested in books.

> There isn't the money to be spent on what you would call a normal upbringing.

Some accounts are better developed, with a grounding in the absence of learning materials or skills. But much of it also, as in many of the statements above, and as developed more fully in Freebody, Forrest, & Gunn (2001), is about moral relations between classes, acted out as irresponsibility or a failure of 'values':

> A lot of children in these classes are from low socio-economic families so that their background especially where literacy is concerned is very materially poor, so that they don't have the books, the reading material at home to give them a book awareness, or the fact that they needed school to begin their literacy development. A lot of the parents, well not a lot, no, some of the parents here are illiterate themselves, so that they don't have the skills to teach their children before they get here, how to read and how to write, or even make them aware that, umm, it is important that they learn reading and writing.

In an earlier report of these findings, we concluded:

> we found classroom activities conducted in 'disadvantaged' schools to differ from those in the 'non-disadvantaged' school in our sample. What is perhaps even more striking is the richness and fine detail of these educators' accounts of the relationships between poverty and achievement. In the descriptions and explanations given by the educators interviewed for this study, poverty, as a group attribute, brings with it a complex and confidently drawn mosaic of associations to do with much more than material resources: A heavily-weighted baggage of moral, intellectual, social, physical, cultural, and motivational dispositions is readily attached to poor people. Educators, like all of us, are members of a classed society. (Freebody, Ludwig, & Gunn, 1995, p204, Vol. 2)

This deep-seated attachment of educational deficiencies is one of the legacies, to which Warschauer referred, of 19th and 20th century educational practice, organisation, and even policy that urgently needs to be made explicit and undone. One helpful heuristic point to begin with is this: Why do we not assume that, precisely because of their material disadvantages, and the particular forms of social fragmentation of experience that can sometimes accompany those disadvantages, children form lower SES settings probably bring to school more cognitive capability and flexibility, more determined motivation to succeed, and more responsiveness to genuine offers of help from educated adults? Why do we not act on the premise that the century-old legacy of schooling's legitimation of social structure should lead us to an understanding of the practices of selective privileging, rather than to itemising, with evermore forensic precision, the deficient skills and dispositions of disadvantaged families?

There have, of course, been several systematic studies of how the conversion of material disadvantage into educational disadvantage, through differentially effective literacy teaching, can be disrupted. A good example is reported in Langer (2001), the results of a five-year longitudinal research study on 'beating the odds' in literacy learning. Briefly, Langer examined the literacy education work of 44 teachers, 88 classes, 2640 students, and 528 additional 'student informants' drawn from 25 schools asking the simple question: What features of instruction make a difference in student learning, as demonstrated in high-stakes reading and writing tests? Here is an (unreasonably) abridged summary of the features of schools that she found were 'beating the odds':

- They systematically used a range of instruction (so-called "teacher- and student-focused") rather than being dominated by one approach to literacy education; that is, they were focused on materials, strategies, and organised activities that seemed effective, rather than on debates about 'ideal-types' of literacy teaching and learning

- They undertook regular assessments that were explicitly integrated into ongoing goals, curriculum activities, and lessons structures, rather than stand-alone bouts of testing.

- They made overt, cumulative connections between knowledge and skills across multiple curriculum areas, termed by Langer "connectedness and continuity in learning", rather than hoping that the students would all figure that kind of horizontal continuity out for themselves.

- They engaged students in interactive learning to develop depth and complexity of understanding in literacy, rather than relying heavily on students' working alone; there was lots of talk about literacy knowledge, texts, topics, and interpretations.

As the OECD futures scenarios indicate, a priority on equity in the distribution of precious communication skills such as literacy is in the balance as systems proactively evolve or hang on regardless. Langer's study and others like it (see Freebody, 2007) give optimism to teachers and policy-makers with respect to possibilities for literacy development. Importantly, Langer's conclusions also frame those possibilities in terms of literacy's connections to broader curriculum activities and its special role in strengthening both the vertical (across time) and horizontal (across subject domains) aspects of continuity in students' learning experiences in school.

What is *online literacy*?

Any discussion of future directions for literacy education would seem strangely incomplete without some mention of new technologies. While highly consequential demographic, cultural, and linguistic changes swirl around educators, it seems that it is technological changes that have snared the millennial 'new times' tag most comprehensively. Increasing its share of attention in literacy research, theory, and policy over the 40 years since Chall's landmark study of reading teaching have been the newer digital and online forms of reading and writing in and around school. In a substantial review of the research on the Internet and schooling over the period 1997–2003, Kuiper, Volman, and Terwel (2005), for instance, have drawn the following conclusions about 'future directions' for literacy and literacy research:

- Students often have difficulty locating relevant and useful information, and often lack skills in exploring websites, resulting in a focus on trying to find one answer to their question.

- Students rarely look at the reliability or authority of the information they locate and use.

- The vast amount of information on the web results in access to information, but skills to decipher, weigh up, analyse, and compare that information with other sources is lacking in the research literature.

Students, in short, according to Kuiper and colleagues, are competent with, but not literate in online communications. Similarly, the particular demands presented by online work have not yet stimulated a body of systematic research that can offer teachers some guidance on what to do about the shortfalls established in this and comparable reviews. Notwithstanding the weight of history bearing on literacy researchers, it seems that here is a distinctive 'future direction' now directed at them, with a short timeframe on it, as digital and online work increases in schools.

Conclusions: Whose problem is *the future*?

In his 2007 Australia Day address, entitled "A different kind of hero", given at Parliament House, Victoria, Glyn Davis, the Vice-Chancellor of the University of Melbourne, surprised his audience by singling out the heroism of teachers:

> [they are] the unacknowledged legislators of every generation, unlikely candidates who get little recognition for their contribution ... people who find themselves regularly pilloried in public discussion, despite their importance in our Australian story ... next time a public speaker takes a cheap shot at school teachers, reflect for a moment on just how much our political system, our way of associating, our peaceful streets and national consensus about the norms of public life, are learned from teachers.

... pilloried in public discussions about literacy in particular. At a recent 'summit' on literacy education held in Hobart, I was pulled out of a presentation by Professor Barry McGaw (2007b) on the PISA results by a film crew from a commercial TV channel. They wanted to interview me about literacy. Professor McGaw had been spelling out the state-by-state analyses of Australian 15-year-old students in the 2000 and 2003 PISA studies. He showed how, in terms of statistically reliable differences, Australian students came in the second grouping. More particularly, he was in the process of indicating that Tasmanian students had in 2003 performed at a statistically equal level to Queensland and Victoria, as well as to Sweden, the Netherlands, Belgium, Norway,

Switzerland, Japan, Poland and France, and had beaten the USA, Denmark, Iceland, Germany, and many other countries. Statistically, Tasmania was beaten by only four countries – New Zealand, Canada, Korea, and Finland. I walked from this straight in front of a TV camera and was asked: "So who is to blame for the disgraceful literacy levels among Tasmanian students?" I was good at school, so I reckoned I knew the 'right answer' to this, but I worked my way instead from McGaw's findings, eliminating various potential culprits, and stepping gradually toward the kinds of interests the media had displayed in literacy, and the kinds of 'facts' they had installed in the public consciousness over the years on this matter. Eventually, in fact, I wound up, driven on partly by distemper, at the conclusion that "you – the media are responsible".

This was the 'wrong answer'. Also it was not a good conclusion, and the path leading to it was shaky at best from a purely logical point of view. There are, however, significant lessons for future directions in literacy education that can be drawn from encounters like this (which, needless to say, was never beamed out to Tasmania's unsuspecting viewing public). One significant point concerns the need for a sharper understanding of how communities can and should discuss literacy education. The opposite of an educative society is a punitive society. Punitive societies dedicate effort to refining allocations of blame; educative societies dedicate effort to refining opportunities for supporting and improving learning.

A second lesson, comes from turning the question around and asking who might take responsibility for the strengths of Australian education. It is here that we see that literacy education is the responsibility of a community, a teaching force, a school staff, and individual teachers. Most discussions of 'solutions' and improvement are focused only on individual teachers, but students are influenced individually and collectively, they go through our schools moving from one teacher to another, and, therefore, there is a collective responsibility, shared by families, researchers, teacher educators, school leaders, teachers, policy-makers, curriculum developers, the media, and so on. There is, moreover, a responsibility to work hard to develop some more formal theoretical and practical continuity among these groups of people around the question of literacy across the school years and across the school subjects. Activist Jean Anyon is unequivocal on this matter, and on its importance in the current political settings of countries such as ours:

> education policy cannot remain closeted in schools, classrooms, and educational bureaucracies. It must join the world of communities, families, and students; it must advocate for them and emerge from their urgent realities. (Anyon 2005, p199)

Students in traditional 'target equity groups', along with their teachers, have most at stake in how whole-heartedly this collective approach to education can be implemented and sustained.

References

Anyon J (2005). *Radical possibilities: Public policy, urban education, and a new social movement.* London: Routledge.

Davis G (2007). *A different kind of hero?* Australia Day Address to the Victoria Parliament, Melbourne. Retrieved 9 December 2007, from www.unimelb.edu.au/speeches/transcripts/davis2007126

Freebody P (2005). Critical literacy. In R Beach, J Green, M Michael, & T Shanahan (Eds) *Multidisciplinary Perspectives on Literacy Research, 2nd Edn* (pp433–454). Cresskill, NJ: Hampton Press.

Freebody P (2007). *Literacy education in schools: Research perspectives from the past, for the future.* Camberwell, Vic: Australian Council for Educational Research.

Freebody P, Forrest T, Gunn S (2001). Accounting and silencing in interviews: Smooth running through "the problem of schooling the disadvantaged". In P Freebody, S Muspratt, & B Dwyer (Eds) *Difference, silence, and textual practice: Studies in critical literacy* (pp119–151). Cresskill, NJ: Hampton Press.

Freebody P, Ludwig C, Gunn S (1995). *Everyday literacy practices in and out of schools in low socio-economic urban communities.* Canberra: Report to the Commonwealth Department of Employment, Education and Training, Curriculum Corporation.

Fuller B, Wright J, Gesicki K, Kang E (2007). Gauging Growth: How to Judge No Child Left Behind? *Educational Researcher*, 36, 268–278.

Gee J P, Hull L, Lankshear C (1996). *The new work order: Behind the language of the new capitalism*. Boulder, CO: Westview.

Gramsci A (1971). "On Education", in *Selections from the Prison Notebooks*. (trans by Q Hoare and G Smith) NY: International Publishers.

Kress G (2003). *Literacy in the new media age*. London: Routledge.

Kuiper E, Volman M, Terwel J (2005). The web as an information resource in K–12 education: strategies for supporting students in searching and processing information. *Review of Educational Research*, 75(3): 285–328.

Langer J (2001). Beating the odds: teaching middle and high school students to read and write well. *American Educational Research Journal*, 38(4): 837–880.

Luke A, Freebody P, Land R (2000). *Literate futures: Review of literacy education*. Brisbane, Queensland: Education Queensland.

McGaw B (2007a). Foreword to P Freebody, *Literacy education in schools: Research perspectives from the past, for the future*. Camberwell, Vic: Australian Council for Educational Research.

McGaw B (2007b). *Why literacy matters to the community*. Plenary address to the Tasmanian Literacy Summit, Hobart, June.

OECD *Futures For Schooling*. Retrieved 2 September 2007, from www.oecd.org/document/42/0,2340,en_2649_34521_35413930_1_1_1_1,00.html

Scribner S, Cole M (1981). *The Psychology of Literacy*. Cambridge, MA: Harvard University Press.

Street B (Ed) (2005). *Literacies across Educational Contexts: Mediating, learning and teaching*. Philadephia: Caslon Press.

Warschauer M (2007). The paradoxical future of digital learning. *Learning Inquiry*, 1(1): 41–49.

7
Conversations across borders: interactions between literacy research, policy and practice

Pauline Harris
Faculty of Education, University of Wollongong

Abstract
This discussion paper critically examines the nexus of literacy research, policy and practice from two key theoretical perspectives – frame analysis and sensemaking theory.

The nexus of literacy research, policy and practice is problematic and conversations and ongoing dialogue based on understanding the complex ways in which these three fields interact are much needed. Driven by this concern, the Literacies Research Initiative team at the University of Wollongong initiated an inquiry into the nexus of literacy research, policy and practice (Harris, Derewianka, Chen, Fitzsimmons, Kervin, Turbill, Cruickshank, McKenzie & Konza, 2006). This paper explores this nexus from two key theoretical perspectives used in this inquiry: frame analysis (Goffman, 1974) and sensemaking theory (Weick, 1995). Frame analysis and sensemaking theory work synergistically together to illuminate the three fields and the interactions among them; and elucidate directions for conversations and issues that might be explored. The purpose of this discussion is twofold: to provoke thinking and dialogue about the issues that it presents; and to identify ways that this nexus might be enhanced by conversations between the three fields.

Frame analysis
Originating from the work of Erving Goffman (1974), frame analysis concerns itself with the organisation of experience. Of particular relevance to understanding the nexus of literacy research, policy and practice is the use of frames through which ideas are produced and people are entreated to take action. Frames refer to 'schemata of

interpretation' through which individuals or groups 'locate, perceive, identify, and label' events and phenomena' (Goffman, 1974, p21).

Frame analysis is particularly pertinent to understanding policy development and its relationship to practice and research. For the purposes of this paper, 'policy' is defined as documents of legislation and regulation that are intended to govern practice. 'Policy' is distinct from 'policy messages', which concern what is conveyed about policy through means such as press releases, newsletters, forums, debates, professional development sessions and conferences.

In policy development, frames are used strategically to invoke a particular idea and accomplish desired action. For example, a central frame of the recent policy reform document, *Teaching Reading* (DEST, 2005), is the idea of literacy success for 'all children'. The merit and inclusivity of this idea is undeniable among literacy educators and strongly appeals to parents and other key stakeholders in children's education. The implications of this salient frame, however, transcend its obvious merit and appeal. It strategically positions the authors and associates of the proposed policy reforms as benefactors or 'heroes' – in much the same way as Lakoff (2003) argues that the frame 'tax relief' positions politicians as 'heroes' who will free their constituency from tax burdens; or the Federal government in Australia used 'work choices' to frame industrial relations and workplace reforms. In so doing, the 'all children' frame is ironically anything but inclusive, as will be explored below.

Problematisation and representation in frame analysis

From the standpoint of frame analysis, policy development is conceived as an act of problematisation, particularly in the context of policy reform:

> 'Policy problems do not exist as a social fact awaiting discovery. Rather, these problems are socially constructed as policymakers and constituents identify and interpret some aspect of the social world as problematic.' (Coburn, 2006, p343)

The problematisation of literacy by policy reformers is a case in point. The recent *Teaching Reading* Report (DEST, 2005a) and its related documents have explicitly problematised literacy and the efficacy of reading instruction for 'all children', citing data on poor literacy standards. This problematisation is not neutral – its implications further position the authors and associates of the proposed reform as the 'heroes' who will rescue the situation, while positioning those responsible for the status quo as the 'villains'.

Once a phenomenon has been problematised, representation of the problem is significant yet inevitably incomplete, given the complex nature of social phenomena in our world (Weiss, 1989). The *Teaching Reading* Report, for example, highlights certain aspects of the situation while de-emphasising or ignoring others. In so doing, the report aligns itself with other recent reports (e.g. de Lemos, 2002; Ellis, 2005) that share a similar worldview. Together, these reports overtly adopt a narrow approach to literacy that prioritises:

- Reading at the expense of writing, multiliteracies and the relationship between reading and writing;
- Beginning reading at the expense of literacy development throughout the school years;
- Decoding skills at the expense of a more comprehensive view of literacy that includes making meaning, using texts for social purposes, critical literacy and diverse contexts in which literacy is learned and used; and
- Students with decoding difficulties at the expense of students with no such problems or with literacy problems that fall outside decoding practices (Turbill, 2006).

The *Teaching Reading* Report acknowledges the four reading resources model (Luke and Freebody, 1999) that has been widely adopted in Australia and which provides a comprehensive account of reading practices that includes but is not limited to decoding practices. However, the Report marginalises the model by alleging its 'lack of supporting evidence-based research' (DEST, 2005b, p25), overlooking the extensive research literature review on which this model was based and continues to be developed. The Report's critique significantly recontextualises the model by juxtaposing it against the 'evidence' the Report cites on the primacy of decoding skills for learning to read and the lack of teachers' expertise in teaching these skills. In so doing, the Report is brought back into its preferred frame of reading as basic skills (phonemic awareness, phonics, reading fluency, vocabulary and reading comprehension strategies) and teaching as 'direct instruction'.

Representation of constructivist approaches likewise is incomplete and oversimplified. The Report aligns Vygotsky, Piaget and whole language approaches under the umbrella term of constructivism and solely interprets the constructivist view of the teacher as a 'facilitator of learning rather than a director' (DEST, 2005a, p29). Yet, a Vygotskian perspective portrays the teacher as expert and instructor who explicitly and systematically leads children in educational dialogue – the teacher is not merely a facilitator (Bodrova & Leong, 2007). Indeed, profound differences on this matter exist between Vygotskian and Piagetian perspectives on learning and development – differences overlooked in the *Teaching Reading* Report, to the detriment of acknowledging the contributions of different constructivist approaches to understanding teaching/learning processes and the research base on which such approaches stand. This incompleteness aids the problematisation of the very approaches that the Report rejects.

Three kinds of problem framing processes

The way a policy problem is framed is significant not only in terms of its completeness and accuracy, but also because it "assigns responsibility ... and creates rationales that authorize some policy solutions and not others" (Coburn, 2006, p344). There are three processes involved in problem framing.

One kind of framing is diagnostic framing that involves policymakers in defining problems and attributing blame (Benford & Snow, 2000; Snow & Benford, 1992). As explored above, this kind of framing tends to be incomplete, given the complexity of social phenomena, and not altogether neutral as worldviews and agendas come into play. In the *Teaching Reading* Report, the problem of failing literacy standards is attributed to practices that allegedly are not 'evidence-based' – in particular, constructivist approaches. Consequently such approaches are negatively framed and their removal from classroom practices is explicitly recommended.

A second kind of framing is prognostic framing that involves proposing solution/s to the problem that include goals and strategies (Benford & Snow, 2000; Cress & Snow, 2000; Snow & Benford, 1992). The *Teaching Reading* Report (DEST, 2005a), for example, identifies 20 recommendations that are clustered under evidence-based approaches to teaching reading; role of parents; school leadership and management; standards for teaching; assessment; preparation of teachers; and ongoing professional development. A recurring frame for these solutions is evidence-based practices, specifically direct instruction – and the call for teacher education and professional development to be based on the same.

A third kind of framing is motivational framing that serves as a call to arms (Snow & Benford, 1992). The *Teaching Reading* Report's literature review (DEST, 2005b) comprises part of this motivational framing – providing a rationale for action. Yet this review is carefully and selectively constructed. Criteria for the selection of literature are identified stating that the review 'summarises key findings from evidence-based research' (DEST, 2005b, p16) that the Report defines as:

> the application of rigorous, objective methods to obtain valid answers to clearly specified questions ... systematic, empirical methods that draw on observation and/or experiment designed to minimise threats to validity; (2) relies on sound measurement; (3) involves rigorous data analyses and statistical modelling of data that are commensurate with the stated research questions; and (4) is subject to expert scientific review. (DEST, 2005a, p85).

The recurring use of the 'all children' frame adds motivational weight, too, in calling on educators to ensure that no child is left behind, to invoke a similar frame from the *Teaching Reading* report's US counterpart, the *No Child Left Behind Act* (US Congress, 2002).

Consequences of problem framing

How a problem is framed validates some courses of action and not others (Coburn, 2006). For example, in the *Teaching Reading* Report, research and pedagogies (e.g. code-based direct instruction) that fall within the 'evidence based' frame are validated, while research and pedagogies (e.g. whole language and constructivist approaches) that fall outside this frame are explicitly invalidated.

Further consequences of problem framing in regard to authorisation of people to carry out solutions are brought into question – for example:
- What individuals and groups are authorised to lead, inform and monitor solutions, as opposed to those for whom it is mandated that they enact the solutions?
- Through what means, and how overtly/covertly?
- What are the consequences for cohesion of literacy education and interactions within and amongst literacy research, policy and practice?

This last question does not concern itself with all speaking as one voice – intellectual tensions and multiple perspectives are beneficial for literacy education, particularly when they lead to re-examining our own positions and strengthening our arguments (Freebody, 2005). What is a concern, however, is the disquiet that results when policy framing polarises people and sees players jostling for position, voice and funding. Texts that polarise and dichotomise literacy education undermine connections between literacy research, policy and practice: teachers do not necessarily view literacy instruction in such terms and do not engage with dichotomies that have resurfaced in current proposed policy reforms (Harris, 2006; Broadley et al., 2000; Johnson, 2002; Mills, 2005).

Contestation, of course, is an inevitable consequence of policy. Counter-frames can and do emerge, which provide alternative portrayals of the situation and its solutions, along with different implications for roles, responsibilities and resources (Benford & Snow, 2000). Such disputes can give rise to reframing, however, the extent to which frames can be negotiated is shaped by structures of power and authority.

Aligning frames and evoking resonance

Given the ever-present spectre of contestation and the need to mobilise policy implementation, it is not surprising that policymakers work to align their frames with the interests, values and beliefs of those they seek to take action (Benford & Snow, 2000). The *Teaching Reading* Report's use of an 'evidence-based research' frame is a case in point. Its definition and privileging of evidence-based research, as previously cited, resonates with other recent reports on literacy in Australia (e.g. de Lemos, 2002, Ellis, 2005) and overseas (e.g. 'No Child Left Behind', 2002) – thereby aligning the *Teaching Reading* Report with these other reports. Moreover, this research definition is aligned with particular definitions of literacy that focus on basic reading skills and exclude other aspects of reading and literacy, as previously seen in this paper. In proceeding with this frame to put forward recommendations for evidence-based practices, alternative research paradigms are delegitimised and so, too, are associated classroom practices aligned with such research.

Indeed, the power of alignment rests in its ability to not only marshal and empower people and resources in desired directions but also to weaken those associated with undesirable directions. For example, this paper previously highlighted an apparent confusion in the *Teaching Reading* Report, between Vygotskian and Piagetian approaches that are grouped under the same heading of constructivist approaches to teaching – mistakenly assigning the Piagetian notion of 'teacher as facilitator' to a Vygotskian approach. Yet, this so-called confusion has the effect of aligning undesirable approaches together so that they may be collectively knocked down – even if the perceived faults (e.g. teacher as a facilitator) do not apply in each case.

However, frame alignment is only as effective as the degree to which a frame resonates with individuals and mobilises them into action (Williams & Kubal, 1999). While the texts of current policy reform, such as the *Teaching Reading* report, clearly align with particular groups of researchers and practitioners who share similar views, they do not align with other groups who also have a contribution to make to reform – such as researchers whose work in other paradigms reveal rich and complex insights into key matters such as the diversity of children's literacy experiences and implications for practices in catering to diverse needs at school.

Nor do current policy reform texts necessarily align with the ultimate audience of such reforms – teachers who are to put proposed changes into place. Indeed, when policymakers single-mindedly advocate particular methods for 'all children' and exclude others, they fail to take stock of teachers' perspectives (Hammond & Macken-Horarik, 2001; Kamler & Comber, 2004). Teachers commonly are concerned with implementing practices that they find work for *their students* (Anstey & Bull, 2003) as opposed to 'all children'. In so doing, teachers typically draw on a broad range of instructional practices.

Such choices by teachers have been dismissed by current reform documents as the *Teaching Reading* Report that states:

> 'Many teaching approaches used in schools are not informed by findings from evidence-based research, and that too many teachers do not have a clear understanding of why, how, what and when to use particular strategies' (DEST, 2005a, p14).

The criticism of teachers' competences notwithstanding, exhaustive and inclusive reviews of the research literature have revealed that no reading research has uncovered literacy pedagogies that work for 'all children' (Allington & Johnston, 2001).

The effectiveness of frame alignment in current policy reform documents is also brought into question in regard to groups and individuals who mediate teachers' policy implementation. These people include non-system actors such as researchers, teacher educators, professional development providers, professional associations and publishers. These groups have been found to have significant impact on ways in which teachers interpret and implement policy:

> On the one hand ... many non-system actors have a greater capacity than policy actors to reach teachers in ways that are substantive, sustained, and situated in their day-to-day work in the classroom. On the other hand, non-system actors ... tend to transform messages as they carry them to teachers. As a result non-system actors are a powerful yet not entirely

controllable mechanism for reaching teachers. (Coburn, 2005, pp44–45).

Key questions that arise from this discussion of frame alignment and resonance include:

- In what ways are the frames of current policy reforms designed to try to align with the values, interests and beliefs of teachers, researchers, professional development providers and literacy consultants?
- To what degree do these frames resonate with these individuals and groups and why?
- To what extent do these frames create dissonance, with whom and why?

Considering questions like these brings us into the realm of sensemaking – a key factor that mediates between policy and practice, as explored below.

Sensemaking theory

Arising from the seminal work of Weick (1995), sensemaking theory is concerned with the interpersonal interaction and dialogue with messages from the environment through which understandings, norms and routines are socially constructed. People's actions are based on how individuals notice and interpret information in their environment – such as policy messages in a teacher's school environment. Sensemaking theory thus positions teachers' interpretations as a critical factor that mediates between policy and practice. This theory recognises, too, that teachers' interpretations are influenced by their worldviews and practices that, in turn, are rooted in a teacher's history of connections with and responses to past messages from the institutional environment (Coburn, 2006).

Drawing on sensemaking theory, there are four key factors that shape teachers' response to and implementation of policy and related messages:

- Congruence in terms of teachers' perceptions of correspondence between the message and their own world views and pre-existing practice;

- Intensity in terms of the degree to which teachers have opportunities to engage with the message in sustained ways;
- Pervasiveness in terms of the degree to which teachers encounter messages and/or pressure in multiple and overlapping ways; and
- Voluntariness in terms of the degree to which messages are stating recommendations or mandating that certain actions be done (Coburn, 2004).

Sensemaking and framing in the field of practice

There is a deep complementarity between sensemaking and frame analysis that further illuminates the policy/practice relationship. According to Klein, Moon and Hoffman (2006), sensemaking involves both fitting data into a frame and fitting a frame around the data. Just as policy makers select frames through which they produce ideas and entreat people to take action, so too do teachers use frames to make choices about their implementation of policy. The question thus arises: What frames does a teacher draw on?

To explore this question, consider the case study of one teacher, Sandra (a pseudonym), whom I observed in her Kindergarten classroom for one year. Sandra worked in a metropolitan school, where a high percentage of students were from Chinese backgrounds. The large majority of Sandra's students were new arrivals from China, having been raised by grandparents in their prior-to-school years. These children's needs included acclimatising to a new sociocultural setting; learning English as a second language; and making the transition into school where behavioural expectations, social experiences and ways of learning differed substantially from their previous experiences.

Sandra's literacy instruction fell into two broad categories. One category consisted of core practices, which were undertaken on a daily basis; they included modelled reading with the whole class, guided reading with levelled readers in reading groups, and home readers. Sandra's school setting and its established norms and routines for literacy learning in the early years largely determined these practices. The second category consisted of Sandra's non-core practices, which supported the core literacy program but were given less priority in terms of teaching time, resources and assessment focus. These practices included experiences such as drama, cooking and free play. Despite their less frequent occurrence in her classroom, these experiences were amongst Sandra's preferred practices for teaching literacy and resonated most strongly with her teaching philosophy and beliefs about children's literacy learning.

Myriad and often conflicting texts converged on what Smith and Lovatt (2003) would refer to as her operational space. These texts formed a complex network of intertextual frames through which Sandra deliberated on, selected and prioritised her literacy instructional practices. Specifically, these texts and frames were:

- Sandra's teaching philosophy – 'This is what I believe and value' text, framed by an emphasis on children's enjoyment of learning, motivation, happiness, meaningfulness of teaching/learning experiences, engagement, learning through cooperation and interactions in group settings. This frame shaped Sandra's written statement of her philosophy in her program, as well as her general approach to the children.
- Mandatory NSW *English K–6 Syllabus* (Board of Studies NSW, 1998) – 'This is what children should be learning' text, framed by specific learning outcomes that direct instructional foci and are criteria for assessment at particular stages of schooling. This frame shaped instructional priorities and choices in Sandra's literacy program.
- Parents' expectations – 'Moving up and getting ahead' text, framed by parents' expectations and requests conveyed in conversations with the teacher, for structured homework, levelled home readers, with aspirations for seeing their children move up to the next reading level and positioning children for school success, later life chances and career opportunities.
- Kindergarten teachers' collective conversations and practices – 'This is what we can do' text, framed by the teachers' alliances of solidarity in the face of resource shortages and challenges presented by tensions among resource availability, mandatory outcomes, children's needs and parents' expectations.
- Children's words and actions, making up myriad 'This is me' texts, framed by children's ways of behaving and interacting

with others, their interests, achievements, struggles, predispositions, resources, with recurring predispositions towards solitary pursuits and technical excellence that were overtly nurtured by their parents.

- School values – 'This is what we stand for' text, manifest, for example, in written school policies on school values and how they were to be upheld, framed by appreciation of diversity, focus on home-school partnerships, and a formalised Home Reading Program.
- Direct instruction – 'This is what needs to be taught and how' text, framed by systematic teacher-directed instruction of material, broken down into small and sequential steps, monitoring student understanding and eliciting their successful participation, and assessing measurable outcomes. This was particularly manifest in the Reading Recovery Program and Benchmark Kits, implemented through guided reading of levelled readers in ability-based reading groups and assessment through running records.
- Developmentally appropriate practices – 'This is who I am teaching' text, framed by child-centred instruction, facilitating children's learning through practices that are matched to the child's age-indicated developmental needs, their individual needs and interests and sociocultural backgrounds. This was manifest in Sandra's inclusion of play, cooking and drama as vehicles of literacy learning.
- Learning through interactions and shared understanding – 'This is what we think and mean' text framed by assisting children's learning through negotiating shared understandings and scaffolding children's participation in their zone of proximal development, between their actual and potential capabilities.
- Socialisation into school – 'These are the social resources needed at school' text framed by the view that learning at school involves functioning in group settings and learning to share, cooperate, take turns, consider others and listen to one another. This was manifest in Sandra's interactions with children where she emphasised these social aspects of their behaviour.

These frames were mobilised in the face of the realities Sandra faced – for example, the resources and predispositions of children that focused on solitary pursuits mobilised a 'socialisation into school' frame through which she focused on group learning and cooperation. Both consistency and contradiction existed amongst these frames – for example, the 'developmentally appropriate' frame was at odds with the 'direct instruction' frame, but congruent with the 'teacher's philosophy' frame. Such is the complexity of teaching. Through these various frames, Sandra continued to negotiate her complex classroom realities and implemented curriculum policy in ways that 'made sense' in her situation – as teachers do when they deliberate on matters of policy implementation.

Sandra is not atypical. Teachers constantly engage with and transform messages from policy and research as well as from key informants and data sources in their setting – not least of all, the children they teach (Broadley et al., 2000; Coburn, 2001; Johnson, 2002). In so doing, teachers build and produce professional knowledge (Cochran-Smith & Lytle, 1993). In this, their professional judgment is critical (Pearson, 2003).

On interpreting and implementing policy, Coburn (2001), in her indepth study of reading policy reform in California, unearthed findings that strongly resonate with Sandra's experiences:

- Teachers construct their understandings through their interactions with colleagues, in both formal and informal settings. Sandra's interactions with her colleagues, particularly her Kindergarten colleagues, were a vital part of the choices she made, and provided a means through which she filtered and reconciled messages from various frames about teaching approaches and materials.
- As teachers continue to work closely together, their worldviews and practices tend to converge as they develop shared understandings. Sandra and her Kindergarten colleagues clearly had developed a like-mindedness about their instructional practices that had a strong connection with their perceived need for solidarity in the face of challenges they faced (such as the

need to share readers on a rotational basis across their classrooms, as there were not enough materials for each classroom at the same time).
- Teachers' professional communities play a gate-keeping role in filtering myriad and often conflicting policy messages. Sandra and her colleagues, for example, made choices about what aspects of the NSW *English K–6 Syllabus* (Board of Studies NSW, 1998) they would prioritise with their Kindergarten children.
- Various factors account for teachers' judgment about how to implement policy. These include relevance to the grade level a teacher is teaching; difficulty level for the children being taught; philosophical opposition; perceived inappropriateness; lack of 'fit' with existing classroom structures and practices; and teachers' sense of their own lack of understanding. These were all key considerations for Sandra, too.
- Negotiating technical and practical details are part and parcel of teachers implementing policy in their classrooms – putting their policy interpretations into action was far from straightforward. Teachers negotiated details with colleagues on how to put abstract ideas into practice. This negotiation saw various considerations come into play – for example, how to use aspects of a textbook series in the context of the teacher's program; timing, format and record keeping for assessment; grouping students; and what kind of paper to use for a particular activity. Ultimately, the choices teachers made were shaped by their worldviews, pre-existing practices and structural constraints at the school level. In Sandra's case, the need to rotate an inadequate supply of reading materials around the Kindergarten classrooms was one such ongoing practical consideration; as was Sandra's negotiation of timing and balance so she could incorporate play, cooking and drama in her literacy program.
- School principals also influenced teachers' enactments of policy. They did so by shaping access to policy ideas; participating in the social process of interpretation and adaptation; and creating substantively different conditions for teacher learning in schools. These actions in turn are influenced

by principals' understandings about reading instruction and teacher learning. A key influence from Sandra's school principal was an emphasis on home-school partnerships and the Home Reading Program based on levelled readers. This emphasis was a support in some ways for Sandra, enabling her to work to meet parents' expectations for children's reading. At the same time, tensions arose as parents were ever-keen to see children move up in the levelled readers they took home.

As teachers such as Sandra draw on different frames to make sense of policy and shape their practice, they may be likened to what Lévi-Strauss (1974) called bricoleurs. Defined as individuals who use materials at hand to create new structures from "limited possibilities" (Lévi-Strauss, 1974, p21), teachers make choices from possibilities and options that they see available (Smith-Lovatt, 2003). They improvise and assemble class literacy programs from available resources and ideas. As they do, they may adapt ideas through processes of addition, deletion, substitution and transposition – all processes that make up the practice of bricolage (Nöth, 1990). In so doing, teachers have a pivotal role in the judgments they make and the decisions they enact as they interpret and implement policy.

Identifying lines of conversation

Frame analysis and sensemaking theory illuminate processes and issues related to the nexus of research, policy and practice; they also provide a basis for identifying some strategies for enhancing the nexus. These strategies are identified below in terms of directions for conversations with and amongst researchers, policymakers and teachers, along with issues that might be explored.

One such direction concerns policymakers and researchers tuning in to what teachers say about policy – the messages they notice, how they interpret them, and where/how teachers access policy and related messages. Teachers' reasons behind the choices they make when implementing policy in their classrooms is worthy of authentic dialogue between teachers, researchers and policymakers. Such conversations would do well, too, to tune into the gate-keeping choices that teachers make when deciding what messages from research and policy they choose to incorporate and what to exclude; details teachers find themselves negotiating on their own and with other teachers on ways of putting policy into practice; and factors that influence teachers' actions, including their worldviews, pre-existing practices, shared understandings, structural constraints and classroom realities that they develop with their colleagues.

A second direction for conversation concerns connections with research. While policymakers are currently urging teachers to use evidence-based practices, exactly what does 'evidence-based' mean and to whom? Current reform documents such as *Teaching Reading* define such research as empirical quantitative inquiry, yet this is not a view or an approach shared by everyone in literacy education. Avenues to explore in conversations within and amongst the fields of literacy research, policy and practice include: Whose definitions of evidence-based research hold sway and why? What other forms of research should be admissible for informing policy and practice? What research messages do teachers notice and select? How do teachers access research and how? What ways (if any) do teachers implement research in their classrooms? Similar issues arise, too, for teachers' connections with research as they do for policy: gate-keeping choices teachers exercise when it comes to including or ignoring messages from research; details they negotiate on their own and with other teachers; and factors influencing their interpretations and enactments of research messages.

Another direction concerns teachers' interactions with colleagues about policy and research interpretation and implementation, in formal and informal settings, and the degree to which collaborative cultures are created in teachers' settings to support interpretation and implementation of research and policy. These are conversations that occur on a day-to-day basis and have a significant role in shaping teachers' choices and understandings. Teachers' social networks are of interest too, as is the role of executive in policy reform leadership.

Another course for discussion focuses on the role of school executive staff in providing access to policy and to research. Issues that such conversations could explore include: what gets privileged and why; how are collaborative cultures for interpreting and enacting policy and research created; what opportunities are provided for teachers to develop understandings and pathways for implementing policy a research; how are these experiences structured; and how do executive staff frame messages about policy and research policy messages and research messages in ways that shape interpretations and mobilise actions.

Tuning into perspectives among policymakers, conversation could explore influences on their work, such as their worldviews, pre-existing practices and structural constraints; policymakers' professional conversations and social networks and how these influence their policy work; policymakers' interpretations of research and 'research messages'; their gate-keeping choices about what research to put in or leave out in the documents they produce; and their role in creating collaborative cultures to support policy implementation in ways that 'make sense'. It would also be fruitful to understand how policymakers go about framing problems under focus: the means by which they come to understand a problem exists or there is a need for policy reform; the frames they choose to represent a problem and its solutions; and how they position these frames to align with the values, belief and interest of their projected audience.

Non-system actors play a significant role in the nexus of literacy research, policy and practice – teacher educators, researchers, consultants, professional associations and professional development providers. Bringing these groups into the conversation, lines of discussion could explore issues of resonance and dissonance with current policy documents and reforms, and alternative ways they see for portraying problems and solutions under focus. In exploring these alternative frames, implications for roles, resources and responsibilities could be discussed; as could be individuals' and groups' sense of the degree to which they feel they can negotiate and inform policy in light of extant power and authority structures.

In closing

Framing and sensemaking are processes that take time and involve interactions among people. Clearly, policymakers engage in framing processes as they recontextualise research and align their frames with others of like minds and worldviews. Teachers, too, engage in framing and collective sensemaking as they make sense of how to put policy into action in their classrooms, against the backdrop of their worldviews, pre-existing practices, structural constraints and classrooms realities.

What continues to be needed are conversations between literacy research, policy and practice, and between groups within each of these fields. Avenues that could be explored in these conversations have been suggested and are being pursued in our own project (Harris et al., 2006), with a view to sustaining authentic dialogue over time.

The goal of such dialogue is not to reach consensus – if it was, it would be a futile, naïve and even counter-productive goal. Rather, the goal ideally is to inform and enrich our perspectives of literacy education by tuning into others' points of views, especially those who have opposing views and ideas, or who work in quite different fields and situations from our own. At a time when policy reformers are erecting border-patrols that allow some groups and individuals 'in' and keep others 'out' of the research/policy/practice nexus, it appears imperative to traverse the borders that divide literacy education and engage in dialogue in ways that authentically and collectively 'make sense'.

References

Allington R L, Johnston P H (2001). What do we know about effective fourth-grade teachers and their classrooms? In C Roller (Ed), *Learning to teach reading: setting the research agenda* (pp150–165). International Reading Association, Newark: DE.

Anstey M, Bull G (2003). *The literacy labyrinth*, 2nd Edn. Sydney: Prentice-Hall.

Benford R D, Snow D A (2000). Framing processes and social movements: an overview and assessment. *Annual Review of Sociology*, 26: 611–639.

Bernstein B (1990). *The structuring of pedagogic discourse*. London: Routledge.

Board of Studies NSW (1998). *English K–6 Syllabus*. Sydney: Board of Studies NSW.

Bodrova E, Leong D J (2007). *Tools of the mind: the Vygotskian approach to early childhood education*. Upper Saddle River, NJ: Pearson Merrill/Prentice Hall.

Broadley G, Broadley K, Chapman J, Jackson W, Ryan H, Shepherd H, Tunmer B (2000). What matters to teachers? Let's listen. *Australian Journal of Language and Literacy*, 23(2): 128–138.

Coburn C E (2001). Collective sensemaking about reading: how teachers mediate reading policy in their professional communities, *Educational Evaluation and Policy Analysis*, 23(2): 145–170.

Coburn C E (2004). Beyond decoupling: rethinking the relationship between the institutional environment and the classroom. *Sociology of Education*, 77(3): 211–244.

Coburn C E (2005) The role of nonsystem actors in the relationship between policy and practice: the case of reading instruction in California. *Educational evaluation and policy analysis*, 27(1): 23–52.

Coburn C E (2006). Framing the problem of reading instruction: Using frame analysis to uncover the microprocesses of policy implementation in schools. *American Educational Research Journal*, 43(3): 343–379.

Cochran-Smith M, Lytle S (1993). *Inside/outside: teacher research and knowledge*. Teachers College Press, New York.

Cress D N, Snow D A (2000). The outcomes of homeless mobilization: the influence of organization, disruption, political mediation and framing. *American Journal of Sociology*, 105(4): 1063–1104.

De Lemos M (2002). *Closing the gap between research and practice: foundations for the acquisition of literacy*. Camberwell, Vic: ACER.

DEST (2005a). *Teaching Reading – Report and Recommendations*. Canberra: Department of Employment, Science and Training.

DEST (2005b). *Teaching Reading – Literature Review*. Canberra: Department of Employment, Science and Training.

Ellis L A (2005). Balancing approaches: revisiting the educational psychology research on teaching students with learning difficulties. *Australian Education Review*, (48) Canberra: ACER.

Freebody P (2005). Foreword to Balancing approaches: revisiting the educational psychology research on teaching students with learning difficulties. *Australian Education Review*, (48) Canberra: ACER.

Goffman H (1974). *Frame analysis: an essay on the organization of experience.* Boston: Northeastern University Press.

Hammond J, Macken-Horarik M (2001). Teachers' voices, teachers' practices: insider perspectives on literacy education. *Australian Journal of Language and Literacy*, 24(2): 112–132.

Harris P (2006). Hearing teachers' voices and capturing their visions: exploring perspectives of literacies in the early years. *ALEA/AATE Annual Conference Proceedings*. Darwin: Australian Association for the Teaching of English/Australian Literacy Educators' Association.

Harris P, Derewianka B, Chen H, Fitzsimmons P, Kervin L, Turbill J, Cruickshank K, McKenzie B, Konza D (2006). Towards a literacy research agenda: investigating the relationship between literacy teaching, research and policy. *ARC Discovery Grant Application*, Faculty of Education, University of Wollongong.

Johnson G (2002). Moving towards critical literacies in conversations about the teaching of English. *Australian Journal of Language and Literacy*, 25(1): 49–61.

Kamler B, Comber B (2004). The new English teacher: re-designing pedagogy. *English in Australia*, 12(1): 131–142.

Klein G, Moon B, Hoffman R F (2006). Making sense of sensemaking II: a macrocognitive model. *IEEE Intelligent Systems*, 21(5): 88–92

Lakoff G (2003). Framing the Dems: How conservatives control political debate and how progressives can take it back. *The American Prospect*, 14(8) www.prospect.org/print/V14/8/lakoff-g.html

Lévi-Strauss (1974). *The Savage Mind.* London: Weidenfeld & Nicolson.

Luke A, Freebody P (1999). Further notes on the four resources model. *Reading Online.* www.readingonline.org

Mills K (2005). Deconstructing binary oppositions in literacy discourse and pedagogy. *Australian Journal of Language and Literacy*, 28(1): 67–78.

Nöth W (1990). *Handbook of Semiotics*. Bloomington, IN: Indiana University Press

Pearson P D (2003). The role of professional knowledge in reading reform. *Language Arts*, 81(1): 14–15.

Singh P (2002). Pedagogising knowledge: Bernstein's theory of the pedagogic device. *British Journal of Sociology of Education*, 23(4): 571–582.

Smith D L, Lovatt T J (2003). *Curriculum – action on reflection, 4th Edn*. Tuggerah, NSW: Social Science Press.

Snow D A, Benford R D (1992). Master frames and cycles of protest. In A Morris & C Mueller (Eds) *Frontiers in social movement theory* (pp135–155). New Haven, CT: Yale University Press.

Turbill J (2006). Invited Presentation at the ACSA Conference (Australian Curriculum Studies Association), February, Melbourne University

United States Congress (2002). Public Law 107–110, 107th Congress [*The No Child Left Behind Act of 2001*]. Washington, DC.

Weick K (1995). *Sensemaking in Organizations*. Thousand Oaks, CA: Sage.

Weiss J A (1989). The powers of problem definition: the case of government paperwork. *Policy Sciences*, 22(2): 97–121.

Williams R H, Kubal T J (1999). Movement frames and the cultural environment: resonance, failure and the boundaries of the legitimate. *Research in Social Movements, Conflicts and Change*, 21: 225–248.

8
Catching the reading bug: looking at how to immerse children in the literary experience using visual and textual literacy

Jacqueline Hicks
University of Sydney

Abstract

This paper will explore the explosion of children's picture books, and the manner in which it may be exploited in the literary classroom.

Introduction

I started out writing this paper armed with a number of references, and good academic practice. Off I went to research the process of how visual and textual literature, predominantly in the form of picture books, counted towards the development of good reading practice. However, there is more to this than an academic argument. That would be a dry and reasoned perspective on the process. Let's get emotional instead. It may not be reasoned, and former Federal Education Minister, Dr Nelson, and his determined successor, Julie Bishop, would probably, if they could start it, drive a Mac truck through the holes.

What I firmly believe comes from a collage of personal experiences. One of them was leaning against the wall in my overcrowded training room listening to a colleague expound why a particular reading scheme was a bad trip for a proto-literate child, especially one from a EAL (English as an Additional Language) background. After an interesting sidetrack into clothing and culture, we went with her for a walk through *Dog in, Cat out*, and why it was a predictive classic, helping those same kids contextualise the reality of reading strategies in a western cultural classroom.

Next comes the reality for me, as a 16-year-old going with my father to the wool sales, and having to fill out the paperwork on a form. On the same day I stuck the L plates on the car for the first time, I learned something else as well. My wonderful, strong, hard-working farmer father, was functionally illiterate. He had managed to survive a sniper's bullet in Bougainville, but he had failed to survive the literacy process in the school classroom. Like our son, and probably for similar reasons, he struggled with that light bulb moment on the way to literacy. Our son, Sam, too, always appeared a square peg in a round hole, labelled, by the colour of his basal reader, as one of the dummies, and bullied because of it. His passage through school was fraught with tensions, days off, long phone conversations with senior masters, and, finally, an early escape from school into an apprenticeship.

Our daughter, on the other hand, slipped seamlessly into the process, meeting the reading challenge head on, burying herself in books of all shapes and sizes, and eating up the MS Readathon, to my great financial detriment. What was the difference? One aspect was undoubtedly the amazing dedication of her teacher, as well as Sophie's natural, voracious curiosity. To me, however, a major issue was that her classroom was crowded with picture books, both old familiar friends, and new ones to tempt her imagination.

The next image is of the day I started writing this paper. The hide of me, I suddenly thought. I haven't been in a classroom since Terry Metherell was Minister for Education, in the NSW Coalition Government in the late 1980s. What do I know about the reading process, catching the bug or sliding kids into literacy? What I do know is what I see every day, as students find their way into the Curriculum unit where I work, often very vague about how they need to go about the process of building up their own teaching practice, and uninitiated into the diversity of literary choices at their disposal. I regularly ask the Primary and Secondary English teaching students, when they come to classes, if they have read a book in the last week they identify as a children's book. Few hands go up. By the time they graduate, I know I will get a very different response.

So what makes the difference?

Explosion of children's literature picture books
It is really not giving anybody information to say that there has been an explosion of picture books published in the last few years. It is no

surprise either to know that many of them court controversy. Many are clearly not written with shared bed-time or early literacy needs in mind. Picture books are now an experience for all ages. It is an issue that Shaun Tan (2001) grapples with when he argues that there is no barrier to the age group reading such a text, or enjoying it, nor should a picture book be created with a given audience in mind. Coupled with this, is the revived interest in graphic novels as a textual experience. Allyson Lyga argues that graphic novels are a workout, as the brain is "bombarded simultaneously with the graphic novel's character, setting, plot, and action" (Lyga, 2006, p58). The same applies to the narrative constructions of the picture book. These developments are symptomatic of the way in which children are soaked in visual, textual and verbal messages needing to be received, filtered and understood, mostly in a very different classroom environment to that of the majority of their teachers and parents.

All this has meant that our approaches to picture books, especially, and literature in the classroom in general, has undergone a process of navel gazing. If we want kids to catch the reading bug through picture books, we need to provide a diversity of texts. There are those which offer, as does *Dog in, Cat Out*, a way in to decoding and meaning making for even the smallest kindergarten participant if there are successful engagement strategies employed. There are others, such as *The Watertower*, which have opened up a new discourse within the secondary classroom. Still others, such as the *Red Tree* or *The Lost Thing* offer a strongly visual narrative experience, dominating and often subverting the text. Texts such as *Voices in the Park* have become a convenient hanger for a postmodernist cloak in the secondary environment. The whimsically melancholic *John Brown, Rose and the Midnight Cat* has acted as a flag carrier for a number of books which approach the question of death and grief, from *The Very Best of Friends* to *Lucy's Bay* and *Let the Celebrations Begin*.

This explosion of texts has offered an increasingly exciting perspective for children in the classroom to develop much needed multiliteracy skills. These are the skills necessary to contend with the bombardment of visual and textual information forced on them through media outlets and daily life. It has also meant that strategies for decoding, for meaning making, and for analysing text and images have increased in importance.

Skills learnt in developing literacy experiences within the picture book genres can then be transferred to other media, such as film, advertising, print media and the virtual world. This means that the skills we encourage in the classroom can be developed into creating a socially more aware and astute observer, from pre-school to adulthood, with the strategies necessary for dealing with information overload. The student who has conquered the multimodal reading process has the skills to assess the information on a website, navigate the intricacies of Graeme Base's *The Waterhole*, and critically assess the veracity of the seemingly never ending collection of electioneering material currently arriving unsolicited via unsuspecting Australian letterboxes and television screens.

When I began my career as a librarian and a teacher, (back, as my daughter says, before the last ice age) picture books were undergoing a metamorphosis based on new printing techniques which allowed illustrators and authors to explore a wider visual experience. There was still a perception that picture books were for proto-literacy development and a shared-reading experience, conjuring up images of children snuggling down for sleep with cuddly books such as *Goodnight Moon* or wonderful rhythms such as *Hairy Maclary from Donaldson's Dairy*. A wise lecturer at Teachers College observed that a copy of *Where the Wild Things Are* should be given out with every child's birth certificate. *Rosie's Walk* and *A Very Hungry Caterpillar* were encouraged as reading tools in the Infants classroom, especially for those children whose first language was not English, whose needs were never entirely addressed by my training. We were a long way from *Woolvs in the Sitee*, *Way Home* or *My Hiroshima*. As the perspective of what makes a picture book has developed, so too have the differences of opinions on what is appropriate to be included, and how such a text would be used in the classroom.

I am coming to this topic as a teacher librarian, long Metherellised out of the classroom.[3] My evangelism now rests with students starting out on their teaching careers, within both the primary and secondary spheres.

---

[3] For those who may not have encountered the reforms led by the then Minister of Education in NSW, the period between 1988 and 1990 were a time of major upheaval and constant restructuring within both school and vocational education.

As such, I have both a captive audience, and one which has not had to weather the debate on the postmodern, and accusations of teaching nothing but cultural studies. These students also have missed out on the more acrimonious elements of the 'grammar wars' surrounding the initial changes to the NSW English Syllabus in the mid-'90s. This means that many cannot see what the fuss is about when the current NSW Stage 6 English Syllabus is discussed.

Reading through what has been written about teaching with picture books in the literacy classroom, over the time I have been Curriculum Librarian, demonstrates that, in the early '90s, our approach to teaching, and the literature with which we could indulge our students, gained an enormous boost through the adventurous spirit of authors and illustrators, especially in Australia. Seminal critical analysis of the picture book as a genre also found something of a high water mark at that point. This has allowed us, as professionals in the literary environment, to be spoilt for choice when looking for visual and textual narratives with which to work.

Parallel to the debate about the nature of the picture book, and intended audience, is the recent discussion about the nature of reading teaching. That this debate has created a number of tensions, not least of which have been around the use of sequenced reading schemes, has highlighted one of the dichotomies facing the classroom teacher, and the teacher librarian. Many of you will have listened to a constructive discussion delivered by Professor Derrick Armstrong (2006) and Professor Brian Cambourne (2006a), at the 2006 National Conference on Future Directions in Literacy (Simpson, 2006), in relation to the *Nelson Report*, and the tensions created by its findings (DEST, 2005). There is no news in saying that approaches to teaching reading, and in immersing students in a literature rich classroom, are areas fraught with challenges. As the mother of a child with learning difficulties, the greatest challenge was encouraging and maintaining his interest in what he saw as a losing battle to conquer reading. What the debates around phonics versus whole language, picture book versus reader, does is strengthen my resolve that there are many paths to literacy, just as every student will find different maps to get there. That this view is one shared with many others, is reinforcement of 'real' literature's importance.

The need to immerse children of all ages in a visual and textual soup of picture books and graphic texts was reinforced to me by watching one of my colleagues proselytise about the need to use good literature. By this, she meant literature that engaged the spirit and fed the imagination of the reader, not textual food which had been created to a bland recipe of unchallenging repetition and uninviting visual prozac. The iconic story recounted by Margaret Meek, of her student, Ben's, first meeting with *Rosie's Walk*, says volumes about engagement with a text which invites identification from the child (Meek, 1988, p11). Where picture books are concerned, I have to embrace the comment made by Maurice Saxby that "the best picture books are those that have the power to slide into a child's imagination" (Saxby, 1997, p185). When discussing with a student what texts are worthwhile, my litmus test is focused on whether the student feels he or she could reread it constantly. Is it still going to be the focus of a lesson or unit of work which excites them when they teach it the next time around, and then the next? If the answer is no, then perhaps it should stay on the shelf. When a new group of students comes through for a library orientation, this test wins through. They will reflect back on the titles which enticed their own childhood reading, reinforcing the manner in which they too have slid into books. To defer again to Meek, she argues convincingly for "the textual variety of children's picture books" against the reading scheme which "offers no excitement, no challenge, no real help" (Meek, 1988, p19).

Multitude of visual and literary experiences

So where does this place the visual and literary feast now available for inclusion in classroom practice? There are picture books which should entice the most reluctant reader into the literary experience, in the right hands and with the right approach. As is reinforced above, that could mean 26 right approaches for 26 different kids with 26 different learning styles. Despite the potential for teachers to be heavily criticised for their teaching practice in our current political climate, this is exactly what can be seen in most classrooms everyday. So the issue is to find the right germ to slide open the imagination. It also indicates that there is really nothing new under the sun. We are still dealing with Meek's need for textual variety, and we are still engaging with *Rosie's Walk*.

Our daughter Sophie's reading opportunities offered this textual variety. They also offered a visual smorgasbord which challenged and made it possible for her to engage in a different narrative experience. The recent awarding of the Premier's prize to Shaun Tan's *The Arrival* indicates how much more adventurous our explorations of these narratives have become. Any survey of picture books published in the last decade will demonstrate the diversity of texts. We have gone from struggling with defining the role of picture books to allowing ourselves to enjoy them on a number of levels. Dr Seuss's *The Butter Battle Book* and Raymond Briggs' *The Tin-pot Foreign General and the Old Iron Woman* may give pause to an adult's justification of war, and there is no escaping the message in David Miller's *Refugees*. These are picture books with a message, and have attracted criticism as well as praise. Their place in the classroom may occasionally cause comment. Contextualising the experiences of those who have come through war and escape, however, can have a positive effect on understanding, while helping to promote an inclusive environment.

The rich visual narrative of *An Ordinary Day* allows the reader/viewer to look at the manner in which a visual narrative subverts the textual one, just as the four focalisations in *Voices in the Park* offers an exploration of the manner in which meaning making is very dependent on point of view. Anthony Browne's wonderful habit of providing a metafictive conversation, such as including well known works of art, and intertextual play, gives participants the opportunity to explore the surreal, and look for hidden meaning set up in juxtaposition with the text.

The manner in which *First Light* plays the visual against the textual narrative with a sense of impending danger, with the sinister subtext of the boy's relationship with his father, demonstrates the manner in which text and visual can work to create, or undermine perceptions. The same can be said about *We're Going On a Bear Hunt*, where the illustrator, Helen Oxenbury, subverted the intentions of the author by discarding the knights and ladies of his original vision, and substituted them with a family jaunt through imagination and long grass. Oxenbury and her editor talked about this at length at the 2006 Australian Children's Book Council Conference (Oxenbury, 2006).

Develop the will to read

The most important issue is the will to read. The question has to be asked. What are the triggers that will build the will to immerse the child in the reading environment, make them savvy to the skills they need to extract meaning, enjoyment and knowledge, and engage them in the multiliterate community? While the Federal report into reading focuses on very specific skills, Cambourne argues against the toxicity of focusing exclusively on phonics before meaning making (Cambourne, 2006b, p33). What is important is to encourage in readers the sense that reading is fun, enticing and engaging, a skill for many purposes and a door into a number of different worlds, that "engaged reading has it own intrinsic rewards beyond test scores"(Bremner & Dufficy, 2006, p73). What comes through the discussion fostered by Meek and others is that the natural desire to read will be enhanced by the reinforcement of enjoyment. As we all know, by making reading a chore, or by creating laborious tasks, the thrill of reading is lost in the need to complete tedious or repetitive assessments. This is not new. As Jo-Anne Reid points out, this was recognised as an issue in 1922, when a classroom teacher, Miss Archibald, is quoted as reinforcing the need to foster a love of reading (Reid, 2006, p21).

So what is needed is to ask ourselves, what gets inside a child's mind?

Open a mirror on the child's world

Jon Callow and Margery Hertzberg argue strongly for the choice of culturally and linguistically appropriate texts (Callow & Hertzberg, 2006, p46) while Meek's aged but much valued arguments on reading development indicate the importance of predictive and contextualised texts such as *Rosie's Walk*. The opportunity to develop an awareness of book conventions, using *Rosie's Walk, Dog In, Cat Out* or *The Stinky Cheese Man*, has been understood for many years. Indulging children in contextualised reading, as demonstrated by Callow and Hertzberg's case study example, quoted in *Beyond the Reading Wars*, is crucial to the development of the reading process (Callow & Hertzberg, 2006, p44). When such an experience works, it is because there are visual hints, conventions to prompt the movement of the eye from the given to the new, and hooks to pull the child further into the process. *The Stinky*

Cheese Man, on the other hand, works because it is metafictive, highlighting the textual strategies we usually take for granted, such as the little red hen's fury at the "ISBN guy". It works with those in the know because they get the intertextual jokes. It also works with those beginning the literacy journey as a wonderful way to introduce the conventions of the book.

There is also a reinforcement of the need for cultural contextualisation. Scieszka and Smith's *Really Ugly Duckling* went off with a whimper not a bang when I read it in our workroom because my highly educated Mandarin and Cantonese speaking colleagues had never been exposed in childhood to the traditional telling of the same story (Scieszka & Smith, 1992). In the same way, choosing *Enora and the Black Crane* to read with a predominantly Wiradjuri class, while enjoyable, demonstrated that for children brought up distant from that particular culture, the contextual and cultural familiarity was missing. Town children, with different experiences, would, however, have gained pride from the Indij Readers, especially, amongst an AFL mad group, *All the questions you ever wanted to ask Adam Goodes.*

Mary Ryan and Michelle Anstey draw attention to the manner in which, what they refer to as Lifeworld and School-Based world, connect and intersect in their discussion of classroom readings of *The Rabbits* (Ryan & Anstey, 2003). Over the course of time spent working with the text, the meaning making or semantic skills dominated. When prompted for critical analysis, however, the students began to read the subliminal messages within the text, that of the European presence in Australia. Ryan and Anstey observes that "all literacy practices are a reflection of the sociocultural processes and knowledge of the learner" (Ryan & Anstey, 2003, p11). The redoubtable Miss Archibald would have agreed, having argued that there needed to be a "definite connection between the child's spoken language ... and the new written language" encountered in the school environment (Reid, 2006, p21).

Miss Archibald cannot have foreseen the arrival of syllabus documents calling for the study of picture books from the beginning of schooling till at least Year 10. The skills required to create meaningful learning may be challenging for both student and teacher, especially for those for whom a visual literacy is a new and unscaffolded encounter. For them, the meeting of text, which, semiotically, carries a special set of signs, with the visual, which offers an entirely different set, may challenge preconceptions of textual competency. As I came originally from a Fine Arts background, I have always been attracted to the visual, and find the language offered by Kress and van Leeuwen a bonus when discussing the visual narrative. The lusciousness of Anne Spudvilas' illustrations for *Woolvs in the Sitee*, or those of Donna Rawlins in *Digging to China*, strike a chord, as does the delicate whimsy of *The Nativity* illustrated by Julie Vivas. I could go on all day. Having the privilege of watching both Julie Vivas and Donna Rawlins work has been one of my life highlights. Every bit as much as Shaun Tan, these two, and many other gifted illustrators, utilise a talent one has to be born with. Constructing a textual narrative to complement and enhance the visual one becomes an awesome responsibility. Using such a complex medium in the classroom environment should extend the imaginative and creative processes of reading across the stages.

Awareness of how visual narratives develop

Exploiting the visual elements in the narrative to draw the reader/viewer into the reading experience, by using literature that is enticing, both visually and verbally, is a way of tapping into the child's enjoyment. While Rosie, and Max with his wild things, follow a predictive pattern, texts such as *The Stinky Cheese Man* offer a metafictive exploration of what makes a book work, exploiting and subverting the concepts of given and new, and textual protocols.

I see the issue as very much one of creating meaning makers with skills to interpret across a wide range of visual and textual media from web pages to picture books to advertisements. For this reason, the past decade's development of picture books which push boundaries have been a crucial part of my work with the students using our collection. Jane Torr argues "the fact that picture books are complex works of literature where the written text and illustrations together combine to construct the overall meaning allows for multiple interpretations and personal associations to be stimulated in the reader" (Torr, 2003, p12). Torr is discussing a preschool class. Mark Howie and Prue Greene offer a similar perspective, but in this case, their target group is a low ability

Year 9 class looking at *Gorilla*. Howie and Greene make the point that illustrated text has been around since the Middle Ages, illuminating meaning with beautifully embossed calligraphic visuals. What the students do is grapple with "literary theory and critical literacy in a most accessible way" (Howie & Greene, 2003, p7). What is coming through is the issue highlighted by Clare Bradford, when she quotes David Lewis, that "picture books are 'inescapably plural'" and that this involves 'the use of signs' (Bradford, 1993, p10). As Bradford goes on to discuss, these signs convey meanings made complex by the combination of image and text, so that the deceptively simple text can create "subtle and layered works" accessible at different levels to different reader/viewers (Bradford, 1993, p13).

In conclusion, it would seem to me that there are endless possibilities for harnessing "the plurality of the picture book" (Grieve, 1993, p16), not just as a cuddly experience before bed, in a shared reading, or DEAR (Drop Everything and Read) program, but throughout the school experience. Each reader/viewer gains and contributes a complex perception. The crucial skill is to be able to scaffold from one experience to the next, a meaningful relationship with the visual and textual product in front of them. The preoccupation in the classroom with meeting the need to learn and make meaning, is one which will shape the way in which picture books come into play, especially in the English classroom. Gunther Kress and Theo Van Leeuwen have greatly assisted the rise of a vocabulary to work with picture books, and to assist in developing a critical literary theory (Kress & van Leeuwen, 1996). A language or rhetoric for the study of picture books inside and outside the classroom has been around for some years. I see my role as participating in the identification of picture books which encourages that act of sliding into the child's imagination. For this to happen, we need to treasure and nurture our picture book creators, and the reader/viewer whose reading experience is enriched because of them.

References

Armstrong D (2006). *Opening Address*. Paper presented at the Future Directions in Literacy Conference, University of Sydney.

Bradford C (1993). The Picture Book: Some Postmodern Tensions. *Papers: explorations into children's literature*, 4(3): 10–14.

Bremner S, Dufficy P (2006). Meeting diverse reading needs in a multilingual classroom. In R Ewing (Ed), *Beyond the Reading Wars* (pp71–81). Newtown, NSW: Primary English Teaching Association.

Callow J, Hertzberg M (2006). Helping Children to Learn. In R Ewing (Ed), *Beyond the Reading Wars* (pp41–53). Newtown, NSW: Primary English Teaching Association.

Cambourne B (2006a). Confusing the role of phonics in *Becoming Literate in Alphabetic Scripts* with the role of phonics in *Learning to Read Alphabetic Scripts*: Implications of the National Inquiry into the Teaching of Literacy. In A Simpson (Ed), *Proceedings of the National Conference on Future Directions in Literacy* (pp11-20). University of Sydney: Division of Professional Learning Education and Social Work.

Cambourne B (2006b). Playing 'Chinese whispers' with the pedagogy of literacy. In R Ewing (Ed), *Beyond the Reading Wars* (pp27–39). Newtown, NSW: Primary English Teaching Association.

DEST (2005). *Teaching Reading: Report and Recommendations: National Inquiry into the Teaching of Literacy*. Canberra: Department of Education, Science and Training.

Grieve A (1993). Postmodernism in Picture Books. *Papers: explorations in children's literature*, 4(3): 15–25.

Howie M, Greene P (2003). Teaching the visual in English: the grammar of visual design and critical literacy. *Idiom*, 39(2): 5–10.

Kress G, van Leeuwen T (1996). *Reading Images*. Victoria: Deakin University Press.

Lyga A A W (2006). GRaPHiC NOVELS for (REaLLY) YOUNG REaDERS. *School Library Journal*, 52(3): 56–61.

Meek M (1988). *How texts teach what readers learn.* South Woodchester, Glos: The Thimble Press.

Oxenbury H (2006). *In Conversation* Paper presented at the CBCA 8th National Conference Sydney.

Reid J-A (2006). Reading stories: understanding our professional history as teachers of reading. In R Ewing (Ed), *Beyond the Reading Wars* (pp15–25). Newtown, NSW: Primary English Teaching Association.

Ryan M, Anstey M (2003). Identity and text : developing self-conscious readers. *Australian Journal of Language and Literacy*, 26(1): 9–22.

Saxby H M (1997). *Books in the life of a child : bridges to literature and learning.* South Melbourne: Macmillan Education Australia.

Scieszka J, Smith L (1992). *The Stinky Cheese Man and other fairly stupid tales.* New York, NY, USA: Viking.

Simpson A (Ed) (2006). *Proceedings of the National Conference on Future Directions in Literacy.* Sydney: University of Sydney Faculty of Education and Social Work Division of Professional Learning.

Tan S (2001). Picturebooks: who are they for? In *Leading Literate Lives : AATE/ALEA Joint National Conference*, Hobart 12–15 July 2001. Hobart: AATE/ALEA.

Torr J (2003). Talking about picture books. *Professional Educator*, 2(3): 12–13.

Appendix - Picture books cited in the text

Base G (1986). *Animalia*. Ringwood, Vic: Viking Kestrel.

Base G (2003). *The Waterhole*. Camberwell, Vic: Puffin Books.

Briggs R (1984). *The Tin-pot Foreign General and the Old Iron Woman*. London H Hamilton.

Brown M W (1947). *Goodnight Moon*. New York: Harper.

Browne A (1998). *Voices in the Park, 1st Edn*. New York: DK Pub.

Carle E (1970). *The Very Hungry Caterpillar*. London: Hamish Hamilton.

Crew G (1993). *First light*. Port Melbourne: Lothian.

Crew G (1994). *The Watertower*. Flinders Park, SA: Era Publications.

Crew G, Rogers G (1992). *Lucy's bay*. Nundah, Qld: Jam Roll Press.

Dodd L (1983). *Hairy Maclary from Donaldson's Dairy*. Barnstaple: Spindlewood.

Gleeson L, Greder A (2001). *An Ordinary Day*. Sydney: Scholastic Press.

Hathorn E (1994). *Way Home*. Milsons Point, NSW: Random House Australia.

Hutchins P (1968). *Rosie's Walk*. London: Bodley Head.

Hutchins P (1970). *Rosie's Walk*. Harmondsworth: Puffin in association with Bodley Head.

Marsden J, Tan S (1998). *The Rabbits*. Port Melbourne, Vic: Lothian Books.

Meeks, A R (1991). *Enora and the Black Crane*. Sydney: Ashton Scholastic.

Miller D (2003). *Refugees*. South Melbourne: Lothian.

Morimoto J (1987). *My Hiroshima*. Sydney: Collins.

Rawlins D (1988). *Digging to China*. Sydney: Ashton Scholastic.

Rosen M, Oxenbury H (1989). *We're Going on a Bear Hunt*. London: Walker Books.

Rubinstein G (1991). *Dog in, Cat out*. Norwood, SA: Omnibus Books.

Scieszka J, Smith L (1992). *The Stinky Cheese Man and other fairly stupid tales*. New York, NY, USA: Viking.

Sendak M (1967). *Where the Wild Things Are*. London: Bodley Head.

Seuss (1984). *The Butter Battle Book*. New York: Random House.

Tan S (2000). *The Lost Thing*. Port Melbourne: Lothian.

Tan S (2001). *The red tree*. Port Melbourne: Lothian.

Tan S (2006). *The arrival*. South Melbourne: Lothian Books.

Van Allsburg C (1981). *Jumanji*. Boston: Houghton Mifflin Co.

Vivas J (1986). *The Nativity*. Adelaide Omnibus Books in association with Penguin Books.

Wagner J (1977). *John Brown, Rose and the Midnight Cat*. Harmondsworth: Penguin.

Wild M (1989). *The Very Best of Friends*. Sydney: Margaret Hamilton.

Wild M, Spudvilas A (2006). *Woolvs in the S itee*. Camberwell, Vic: Penguin.

Williams J (2003). *All the questions you ever wanted to ask Adam Goodes*. Sydney: Indij Readers Ltd.

Yolen J (1992). *Encounter, 1st Edn*. San Diego: Harcourt Brace Jovanovich.

9
Literacy meets technology in the primary school: symbiosis of literacy and technology

Karen McLean
Australian Catholic University

Abstract

This paper suggests that there exists a symbiotic relationship between literacy and technology. By symbiotic we mean a mutually beneficial relationship. Furthermore, this paper examines the discourse surrounding current political debate and curriculum reform in schools using the Victorian system as a case in point. In particular, it considers the integration of information and communications technology (ICT) into the English curriculum. Also, this paper describes the use of technology in the literacy programs of school based primary education. Traditionally literacy and technology have been considered pedagogically opposed, but this paper suggests that through the symbiosis of literacy and technology, the pedagogies surrounding the teaching of literacy and technology are mutually inclusive. Finally, the paper looks at the relationship between literacy and technology from both a research and practical perspective. It highlights the need for further research in this area, in order to explore implications of pedagogical practice supporting literacy development in the context of our rapidly changing and technologically advancing world.

Introduction

The purpose of this paper is to share insights into the symbiotic nature of the relationship between literacy and technology in the early years of schooling. As noted by Locke and Andrews (2004) "while changes in technology have a role to play in the transformation of literacy, so new literate practices can serve to transform technology use" (p126). In the marine world small fish can be found taking shelter among jellyfish tentacles. These tentacles offer safe haven for the smaller fish who in turn act as bait for larger fish. In this example symbiosis has mutual advantages. This paper suggests that we need to look at symbiosis between literacy and technology and the potential of this relationship to transform learning.

Arguments to explore symbiosis are not new. In fact the impetus for this paper stems from research into archives of literacy and technology discourse throughout the 1990s. In 1992 Bigum and Green drew attention to the tensions between prevalent literacy and technology pedagogies. In a political climate of economic rationalist viewpoints, literacy and technology were tied to employment opportunities and work. Bigum and Green (1992) argued for:

> a cultural-critical perspective on both literacy and technology and a holistic view of the nexus between literacy pedagogy and the new technologies (p24).

Reference was given to three literacy paradigms; functional, critical and cultural. Lankshear, Snyder and Green (2000) describe a view of functional literacy that is tied to skill development:

> being literate has been seen as a matter of cracking the alphabetic code, word formation skills, phonics, grammar and comprehension skills (p27).

This view of literacy puts forward that once essential skills have been mastered they can be used for employment and work. The second paradigm mentioned is critical literacy. Luke (1993) notes "literacy is about the distribution of knowledge and power in contemporary society" (p4). A critical literacy perspective embraces a paradigm that explores the power relationships existing between literacy and knowledge in society. Comber (2001) in reference to critical literacy emphasises that teachers in the early years of schooling can be troubled by the political nature of critical literacy as they already feel burdened by responsibility for literacy acquisition. The final paradigm mentioned is cultural literacy. Cultural literacy perspectives acknowledge the influence culture and community have on literacy learning. Lankshear, Snyder and Green (2000) state:

> reading and writing can be understood and acquired only within the context of the social, cultural, political, economic and historical practices to which they are integral (p26).

A cultural literacy paradigm acknowledges diversity of cultural contexts and experiences that influence literacy development in children. Of these three literacy paradigms Bigum and Green noted that functional literacy prevailed as the literacy paradigm providing the strongest nexus between literacy and prescriptive technological discourses, through measurable outcomes and skill based content well suited to a 'culture of compliance' (p7).

By 2000, the need for a metalanguage for evolving multiliteracies was apparent (Unsworth, 2002) and the concept of critical literacy was expanded to multiliteracies through the work of The New London Group and others who recognised the "plurality of literacies" (Comber, 2001, p168). Prominent discourse continued to suggest evolving paradigms should include cultural–critical perspectives with due consideration to the notion of changing literacies and the changing dimensions of literacy (Lankshear & Knobel, 1997; Unsworth, 2002; Kalantzis, Cope & Harvey, 2003). In short, the rhetoric advocated the need to reconceptualise literacy (Kalantzis, Cope & Harvey, 2003; Zammit & Downes, 2002; Beavis & Durrant, 2001; Unsworth, 2002) and transform curriculum (Kalantzis, Cope & The Learning Design Group, 2005; Zammit & Downes, 2002) to meet the needs of the emerging knowledge society. Globalisation and continued advancements in information and communications technology (ICT) gave rise to new literacies; visual and digital literacies (Kalantzis et al., 2003; Lankshear & Knobel, 2006; Labbo, 2006). These new literacies required new skills and understanding, such as the ability to add a hyperlink to a web page, play an electronic game or read increasingly visual messages presented in different media forms.

It is clear that being literate today has changed, as a literate person needs to have control over a broad range of communication practices. Currently it seems there is mismatch between the old basics; reading, writing and arithmetic, and the technology revolution that has extended the boundaries of literacy to include multiliteracies and the new basics (Kalantzis, Cope & Learning by Design Group, 2005). Zammit and Downes (2002) state:

> learning environments that encompass these new texts and technologies require the modification of existing teaching and learning practices and the generation of new practices (p27).

There seems to be no doubt that old basics remain important but there is also an urgent need to consider expanding notions of text and implications for pedagogical practice. Comber (2001) argues that schools should not offer "the simplistic and reductive" (p177) in the early years of schooling in a belief that children will have exposure and access to other literacies later. It seems timely that curriculum be transformed to address mismatch between old basics and the technology revolution by incorporating new basics and thereby encompassing communication practices beyond reading and writing.

Current directions

In 2007, are we any closer to embracing pedagogical practices with the potential to transform learning through a holistic nexus of literacy and technology in what some might call the new basics or communication practices? Are we pioneering new doorways to literacy through pedagogical reform? Literature provides evidence that the educational community has picked up on the rhetoric but it would seem that in practice there is still some way to go. Throughout this paper I am attempting to pull together these threads to conceptualise a study.

The Victorian Essential Learning Standards (VELS) could be described as the face of the State Government of Victoria's curriculum reform. In essence, VELS provides a framework for curriculum planning in schools. One of the key aims of this reform is to prepare students for:

> a world which is complex, rapidly changing, rich in information and communications technology, demanding higher order knowledge and understanding, and increasingly global in its outlook and influences (Victorian Curriculum Assessment Authority, 2004, p2).

Within this curriculum document English is identified as a disciplinary strand of which traditional disciplines are a part. Technology, however, is labelled as an interdisciplinary strand; functioning within other disciplines and beyond the school (Victorian Curriculum Assessment Authority, 2005). The clear distinction between the placement of English and technology in separate strands highlights key government strategy to interweave technology across the curriculum. Paradoxically, assessment and reporting by schools to the Department of Education and Training in Victoria remains skills and content generated in the form of continued Achievement and Improvement Monitoring (AIM) testing. The contradictions are abounding in government documents. The fact that the strand is called English instead of Literacy or Language highlights our confusion with current jargon. English maintains a traditional skill based, functional underpinning which some may argue is highlighting limitations in Victorian Government thinking. Literacy or Language implies broader communication and social practices more in line with the current discourse. Kalantzis, Cope & Harvey (2003) draw our attention to the need to reframe English to encompass communication practices, reminding us that by our choice of words literacy can mean "something new, something appropriate to new learning" (p22), or something old, something inappropriate. It should be acknowledged that the notion of English as it is commonly viewed carries an aesthetic interpretation and some would argue that replacing 'English' with 'literacies' is reductionist. Others such as Comber (2001) point out that by acquiring a range of literacies "aesthetic, ethical, cultural, moral stances, views about knowledge, ways of working, organizing, thinking and interacting" (p177) makes learning significant. It is not the purpose of this paper to explore this notion but it is important to recognise that alternative viewpoints exist.

In Victoria, in 2007, what is the evidence that schools are adopting holistic approaches to the infusion of technology in the literacy program? In this paper the use of the term 'holistic approaches' refers to approaches to teaching and learning that encompass all areas of literacy; 'old basics' and 'new basics' within an integrated framework whereby meaningful learning occurs across all fields. Furthermore, the infusion of technology in the literacy curriculum implies an approach whereby technology is seamlessly a natural part of meaningful literacy learning experiences. This is the kind of pedagogical shift that is sought but not necessarily attained through current curriculum reform.

Despite the current rhetoric and push in the direction of curriculum reform – Locke and Andrews (2004) remind us that literacy and technology transform each other through symbiosis – it appears that in reality technology continues to be implemented as an 'add on' rather than an ingredient of literacy in the classroom. In fact, for schools and educational institutions in Victoria, the current rhetoric has made evident that transformative curriculum requires more than government mandates: it requires a change in pedagogical approach through the implementation of supportive frameworks and professional learning that develop teacher understanding of the symbiosis of literacy and technology. Kalantzis, Cope and The Learning Design Group (2005) remind us: "transformative curriculum, attempts to cater more consciously, directly and systematically to difference amongst learners" (p60). In practice, technology as part of teaching repertoire is essential, as the lifeworld experiences of the learner go beyond textbooks to incorporate many multimodal texts and other forms of communication. In order to cater for difference amongst learners, connections between lifeworld experiences and 'English' must be made, to be truly described as transformative curriculum (Kalantzis, Cope and The Learning design Group, 2005).

In 1992 Bigum and Green alluded to the preoccupation of schools to spend large budgets on the purchase of technology:

> the willingness of schools to purchase more products and to continually and regularly upgrade both hardware and software, something that would be unimaginable in any other area of school expenditure (p9).

As each year progresses we must consider whether schools have moved beyond this, and are strategically putting resources into addressing the urgent necessity to explore notions of transformative learning through pedagogical shift; embracing the potential of a mutually beneficial relationship between literacy and technology.

My experience suggests that this much needed pedagogical shift is yet to occur on a large scale in the Victorian education system. Old pedagogy views technology as an 'add on' whereas new pedagogy views technology as central to all learning. Current literature on the symbiosis of literacy and technology suggests there is good reason for a continued focus on old pedagogical approaches. One problem already alluded to is the need for schools to reconsider the allocation of resources to staff support and ongoing professional development. Other writers suggest further complexities associated with the current lack of uptake. Labbo (2006) describes a need for learning communities to be established; such communities would include principal, staff and university researcher. Andrews (2004a) also argues that the establishment of effective learning communities is more important than the technology itself. It would seem that a commitment by schools to work together with technology in a learning community would encourage pedagogical reform to occur at the school level as teacher ideologies and practice seem to matter more than access to current technology (Andrews, 2004a). Thus, educators need support to move beyond the use of technology to support literacy programs towards embracing the symbiotic relationship between the two. Again, it is not about the money spent on technology; innovation on old technology can be transformative as can innovation on new. If transformative literacy education is the goal then the emphasis should be on the development of pedagogical frameworks and practices that will evolve and adapt to the ever changing technological world that we live in and enable educators to experience the mind shift that is necessary to embrace and infuse the literacy curriculum with technology. Writers suggest literacy practices in new learning environments should develop through the merging of existing teaching and learning practice with new (Zammit & Downes, 2002). Also, as we experience the push in this direction, the use of technology needs to support new and enhance old literacies, until holistic alignment between theory, practice, policy and assessment occurs (Labbo, 2006).

Insights

This paper argues that we need to look closer at the transformative nature of the symbiotic relationship between literacy and technology in the early years of schooling because of the potential of this relationship to engage students in learning. Insights gained stem from an initial interest in pushing the perceived boundaries of literacy and technology in the early years classroom with respect to emerging themes in current literature. It has been my experience that teachers in early years classrooms in Victoria have tended to use technology in the literacy session only in so far as it provides a learning centre activity, phonics or literacy skill practice. Research has suggested similar findings across other primary schools (Andrews, 2004; Labbo, 2006). My concern with this approach to technology in the literacy program is that the technology was used to support the literacy program as a tool, but did not go beyond this to harness the symbiotic relationship between literacy and technology and transform learning. Alarmingly, in classrooms where technology was used merely as a support tool for literacy development a mismatch between the uses of technology at school and at home was evident. This cultural disparity has been highlighted by other researchers in this field (Beavis, 2003; Kalantzis & Cope, 2005; Unsworth, 2001; Hurrell, Sommer & Sarev, 2001; Lankshear, & Knobel, 1997) whereby school use of computers is criticised as being limiting and controlled, in contrast to home and community use of computers which is considered to be exploratory and fun.

In an effort to harness some of the natural curiosity that students have for technology outside of school and bring this into the literacy program I initiated a partnership with a like minded colleague who had a similar interest in this area. Through a project approach we sought answers to the following question:

How can technology be a doorway to literacy in the early years?

My teaching background in technology and literacy coupled with reading of current literature in this area, challenged me to initiate further exploration of the symbiotic relationship between literacy and technology. Kalantzis, Cope & the Learning Design Group (2005) describe a need to actively harness the potential of digitised technologies in new learning environments; the view being that digitised technologies will become central to all learning. It would seem that students learn or perceive now differently to and from traditional ways. This may eventually require us to consider methods of assessment and reporting that are aligned to new learning paradigms but this is a topic for further study. Through reading current literature we could see that the answers we were seeking would only be found if we were to push the boundaries of our current understandings and use of technology in the literacy session. To get to the essence of insights gained through this project I would like to present two case studies. Locality and names have been altered for research purposes.

Case Study 1

The focus of this case study was a Year 2 boy who was tuning out of the literacy session on a regular basis, through non-attendance, and the use of behavioural and avoidance strategies. The challenge for the partnership was to engage him in literacy learning using technology. Our definition of engagement has been encompassed by the Fair Go Project; a joint research initiative by the NSW Department of Education and Training and the University of Western Sydney who describe engagement as occurring on an operative, cognitive and affective level:

> Student engagement operates at cognitive (thinking), affective (feeling) and operative (doing) levels ... It is not just students doing things but it is something happening inside their heads ... when students are strongly engaged they are successfully involved in tasks of high intellectual quality and they have passionate, positive feelings about these tasks. (NSW Department of Education and Training, 2006, p10)

If in our partnership we could engage Jake in literacy at an operative, affective and cognitive level using an approach that harnessed the symbiotic relationship between literacy and technology then we would gain valuable insights into its potential to act as a doorway to literacy.

Jake's history

From the first day of school it was clear that Jake would rather be somewhere else; he chose to sit away from his peers and did not participate in classroom activities. In Victoria at this time, the Early Years literacy program was implemented in all state schools (Department of Education, Employment and Training, 1999). Jake entered the Reading Recovery program in year one and also received level 2 government funding for a teacher aide in his second year of schooling. In Year 2 his literacy levels were deemed to be well below that of his peers. At the beginning of this project Jake was often absent from school and when in attendance the classroom teacher had great difficulty in getting him to read or write anything.

Preparation

At this point of the project I was part of a team that had taken teacher professional leave to explore the potential of electronic whiteboards in the classroom. Applying key considerations from this action research project (McLean, McKay, Baltetsch, Ottrey, 2006) we set up an electronic whiteboard in the classroom. In an effort to maximise the learning potential the board was set up in a part of the room that could be used for whole group, small group, individual and paired work. In short, it was not the focal point of the classroom.

The project

As noted above Jake's learning needs were evident from the beginning. We believed we needed to engage him in literacy learning. More immediately we needed to get him reading and writing anything. Our first insight came early in the project. Jake had observed his teacher using the electronic whiteboard and was eager to play with it himself. It is important to note at this point that Jake did not have a computer in his home and his access to modern technology outside of school was limited compared to that of his peers. Our experience told us that Jake's minimal interaction with others and sitting alone indicated a lack of involvement with his peers, so we allowed him to use the board on his own whilst the rest of the class worked on other tasks. Initially it appeared Jake just wanted to write on it. He wrote his name and asked the teacher to convert it to text. The program did not recognise his name because he did not form the letters correctly. We expected this to deter him from continuing but on the contrary he was determined to have the program recognise his handwriting and convert it to text. Perhaps the teacher modeling this process had captured his attention and desire to achieve success. After many more unsuccessful and undeterred attempts we used the recording device on the electronic whiteboard to record the letter formations accurately. Jake then copied the model as it replayed over and over until he could form the letter. He then asked to exit the recording program so that he could try and record his name again. This time it worked and oh what joy! Here was a child who had been at school for over two years and could not write his name accurately. In less than 10 minutes he was able to achieve a small piece of literary success! What was also surprising about this result was Jake's ability to remember and work through the steps needed to get text recognition:

Step 1 – Write his name

Step 2 – Put the pen down and click the select tool

Step 3 – Select the handwritten text

Step 4 – Click on the down arrow

Step 5 – Look down the list of options and identify correct conversion

Step 6 – Select the correct conversion

Previously, a recommended strategy for assisting this child with learning was to keep instructions and steps to a minimum. With motivation and engagement Jake was able to remember and repeat at least six steps in sequence.

This small breakthrough for Jake gave us the impetus to expand the use of technology in the literacy session. What was evident from this incidental moment was the use of technology in an authentic context. Durrant and Green (2000) emphasise the importance of authentic context, form and purpose of learning when using technology in the classroom. In this example Jake was motivated to write his name because he wanted to use the new technology. Repetition of this task using pen and paper in the classroom had been unsuccessful; there was no authentic purpose behind it as he could recognise his recording as his name. Technology in this instance provided motivation, appropriate form and interaction; consistent reinforcement and confirmation that he could do it. There was finally a purpose behind the task as Jake had to improve his handwriting so that the technology would work.

Building on his initial motivation we set out to enrapture Jake in literacy learning. The next step was to immerse him in reading, writing, listening and speaking with technology. One possibility was to bring language experience and the Reading Recovery strategy of the cut up sentence to life on the electronic whiteboard. The students in the class had recently visited Sovereign Hill in Ballarat and were busily making class books to share their experiences. We decided to develop an electronic cut up sentence and an e-page with Jake. Using the electronic whiteboard Jake selected his photograph and inserted it into the electronic whiteboard program. The teacher scribed his sentence for him and he converted it to text. In the next stage of the sentence building process Jake copied the sentence word by word underneath the teacher model. After each word he converted it to text so that these words could be manipulated on the page. Once he had completed this task he was able to shuffle up the words himself, reassemble and read aloud his sentence, with and without the teacher model to direct him. It should be noted that Jake had undertaken physical manipulation of words on paper in the Reading Recovery program and classroom with limited success.

Following this activity Jake worked with the teacher in PowerPoint to insert a Quick Time movie of himself at Sovereign Hill, a voice recording, another photograph and a hyperlink to his electronic cut up sentence. With the click of a button a colour copy of Jake's work was printed out in duplicate, providing one copy to display and one to share with his family.

Could Jake's learning have been achieved any other way? I would suggest that the answer to this question is no. What was evident here was authenticity of learning in a workable time frame. In this example authenticity refers to having a purpose that is considered real and relevant by the learner. For instance, the activity described has been carried out before with pen and paper and Jake's attempts were unsuccessful. This sentence making activity enabled Jake to engage in learning in a multimodal way, using audio, image and interactivity. This level of multimodality was not typical of usual sentence work and vital to his level of engagement in the task. Some of Jake's motivation and encouragement was related to the mystery of technology; but engagement was through psychomotor skills for manipulation, affective through his enjoyment, and cognitive to follow steps and problem solve. It would seem that technology provided the speed, memory and automation necessary for the student to achieve success. In short, multimodality and the way the technology was integrated provided for student learning.

At the conclusion of this session Jake was eager to share his work with his classmates. In a rare moment, not even the recess bell could deter him from sharing his work with his peers. Using technology with authentic purpose and context Jake was able to read, write, speak in front of his peers, listen and respond to questions about his work. This was quite an achievement! Following his class presentation Jake's attitude to learning changed. He began to attend school on a regular basis and to display a real interest in learning. For our partnership the significance of the infusion of technology into the literacy session was apparent. It provided real context for technology underpinned with notions of literacy as communication practices. As Durrant and Green (2000) remind us: "the importance of the word and the printed page remains, but such importance is being transformed in relation to new technologies, new cultures and new forms of life" (p95). Jake had provided us with an insight into what this transformation looks like in the early years classroom.

Case study 2

Further insights into technology as a doorway to literacy were gained through a second project. My partner teacher had been a participant in another research project; Partnerships in Information and Communications Technology Learning (PICTL). The PICTL project in Victoria aimed to expand teachers' (and pre-service teachers') knowledge, understanding and skills in ICT in education through partnerships (McNamara, McLean, Jones, 2006). Key findings from this project and others with a similar focus (Lee, 2006) suggest that teachers need to be able to focus on curriculum and the learning needs of children, with technology being a natural part of this rather than an add on. A similar view is put forward by Labbo (2006): "It is clear that new technologies will not automatically transform classrooms if teachers are not comfortable using them for educational purposes" (p206). Through her involvement using the supportive partnerships model used in the PICTL project the partner teacher developed an openness and willingness to embrace technology and continue to build on her existing understandings.

The Victorian PICTL project identified the following principles for successful technology professional development partnerships:

- Partnerships work better if partners are of a similar ICT skill level
- Learning should begin where the partnership is at on the learning continuum
- Critical reflective practice is important
- Authentic context for partnership learning and student learning is essential
- A framework supports pedagogical growth and development.

In planning for the infusion of ICT into the literacy session we decided to apply these principles to our partnership.

For the purposes of this paper I have chosen to detail one perspective. Boys and literacy have been an ongoing concern for educators at all levels of the schooling system and in the Year 2 classroom engagement of boys in literacy continued to be an issue. In our partnership we decided to explore the potential of technology to provide doorways to literacy with a group of Year 2 boys. The genre focus in the classroom was fairy tales and the teaching and learning unit was to culminate with the presentation of a class book of fairy tales. For some of the boys in particular, creative writing and fairy tales were not a popular choice. However, residing in the classroom was a family of stick insects. The alien appearance of these insects had provided scientific interest for a group of boys. We wanted to harness this level of interest in the literacy program, so we decided to use the stick insects in the children's fairy tales. The children were placed in groups of three and using a storyboarding technique with cut out characters, settings and objects they created a fairy tale. The story boards were organised into beginning, middle and end and a template for the recording process was given to each group. Once this task was completed orally the children recorded it using the electronic whiteboard. A screen capture of the electronic whiteboard story board is provided in Figure 9.3 below.

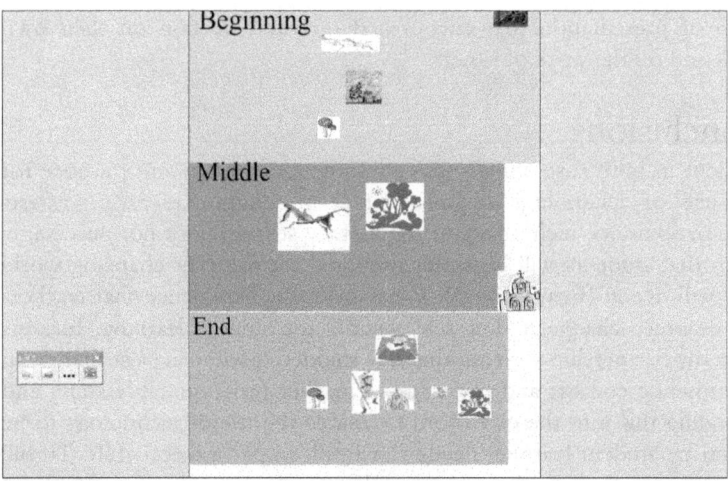

Figure 9.1: Screen capture of story boarding activity

The children recorded their voices and manipulations of objects on the story boards as each student told their story. When each group had completed this task a share time was provided. Children listened to each group presentation and provided feedback to each other on the task. What was evident from this activity was the high levels of motivation displayed by the children, to not only complete this task, but to do it to the best of their ability. With regard to the formal literacy objectives the activity provided evidence that all groups had successfully developed narrative structure; beginning, middle and end, and the peer feedback suggested a further need to add appropriate vocabulary to the fairy tales to make them more interesting. The presentations became a catalyst for deeper learning, as students were given the opportunity to critically reflect on their own contribution and that of others. Holistic approaches to social learning were inherent in the task. The time element was also present again in this example technology integration. With the practicalities of the task integrated into a technological framework, time was not wasted dealing with peripherals and organisational details. In particular, provision for peer feedback and affirmation were important aspects for building on student learning. Ownership of the task and control of the technology was placed in the hands of the students. Given this level of control over the task development and presentation, students were provided with an authentic context and purpose and a form of presentation that encouraged critical reflection on their own work and on the work of others.

Conclusions

Evident in both case studies was an authentic context and purpose for the use of technology in the literacy program. Research suggests systematic use of technology in the literacy session does not necessarily mean that students will be better prepared for the ever changing world they will live in (Beavis, 2003). It has been my experience that teachers will embrace change if they see benefits for student learning. Insights from my partnership with another like minded teacher suggest that given an authentic context and purpose for teacher professional learning and extending this into the classroom to enable the use of technology to be driven by student learning needs can result in pedagogical shift. Turbill (2003) notes the ongoing concern that teachers in the early years of schooling are not embracing technology in the classroom. My experiences would support this concern, but the insights gained from reading literature in this area and my involvement in small scale action research projects suggests that if professional development for educators focused on deepening teacher understanding of the symbiosis of literacy and technology the pedagogical shift is possible.

References

Andrews R (2003). ICT and Literacies: A new kind of research is needed. *Literacy Learning in the Middle Years*, 11(1): 9–12.

Andrews R (Ed) (2004). *The Impact of ICT on Literacy Education*. London: RoutledgeFarmer.

Andrews R (2004a). Where next in research on ICT and literacies? *English in Australia Number 139, Literacy Learning: the Middle Years*, 12(1): 58–67.

Beavis C (2001). Expanding notions of text. In C Durrant & C Beavis (Eds), *P(ICT)ures of English: Teachers, Learners and Technology*, (pp145–161) Kent Town, SA: Wakefield Press.

Beavis C (2003). Critical engagement: ICTs, literacy and curriculum. *Practically Primary*, 8(1): 39–44.

Bigum C, Green B (1992). Technologizing literacy: The dark side of dreaming. *Discourse*, 12(2): 4–28.

Comber B (2001). Critical literacy: Power and pleasure with language in the early years. *The Australian Journal of Language and Literacy*, 24(3): 168–181.

Durrant C, Green B (2000). Literacy and the new technologies in school education: Meeting the l(IT)eracy challenge? *The Australian Journal of Language and Literacy*, 23(2): 89–108.

Durrant C, Beavis C (2001). A p(IC)ture is worth ... In C Durrant & C Beavis (Eds), *P(IC)tures of English*, (pp1–11). Kent Town: Wakefield Press.

Durrant C, Beavis C (Eds) (2001). *P(ICT)ures of English: Teachers, Learners and Technology*. AATE Interface Series. Kent Town: Wakefield Press.

Early Years of Schooling Branch, DoE, Employment and Training (1999). Early Years Literacy Program. EaT Department of Education, Victoria, Longman.

Hurrell G, Sommer P, Sarev J (2001). Cyber English and the new classroom aliens. In C Durrant, C Beavis (Eds), *P(IC)tures of English. Teachers, Learners and Technology*, (pp175–190). Kent Town: Wakefield Press.

Kalantzis M, Cope B, Harvey A (2003). Assessing multiliteracies and the new basics. *Assessment in Education*, 10(1): 15–26.

Kalantzis M, Cope B, Learning Design Group (2005). *Learning by Design*. Melbourne: Victorian Schools Innovation Commission in association with Common Ground Publishing Pty Ltd.

Labbo L (2006). Literacy pedagogy and computer technologies: Toward solving the puzzle of current and future classroom practices. *Australian Journal of Language and Literacy*, 29(3): 199–209.

Lankshear C, Gee J P, Knobel M, Searle C (1997). *Changing Literacies*. Buckingham: Open University Press.

Lankshear C, Knobel M (1997). Literacies, texts and difference in the electronic age. In C Lankshear, J P Gee, M Knobel, C Searle (Eds), *Changing Literacies*, (pp133–163). Buckingham: Open University Press.

Lankshear C, Knobel M (2006). *New Literacies: Everyday Practices and Classroom Learning, 2nd Edn*. Berkshire, England: Open University Press.

Lankshear C, Snyder I, Green B (2000). *Teachers and Technoliteracy: Managing Literacy, Technology and Learning in Schools*. St Leonard's: Allen and Unwin.

Lee K (2006). Online learning in primary schools: Designing for school culture and change. *Educational Media International*, 43(2): 91–106.

Locke T, Andrews R (2004). ICT and literature: A Faustian compact. In R Andrews (Ed), *The Impact of ICT on Literacy Education*, (pp124–152). London: RoutledgeFalmer.

Luke A (1993). The social construction of literacy in the primary school. In L Unsworth (Ed). *Literacy Learning and Teaching: Language as Social Practice in the Primary School*, (pp1–92). South Melbourne: Macmillan Education Australia Pty Ltd.

McLean K, McKay C, Baltetsch R, Ottrey A (2006). *E-Learning – Interactive Whiteboards. Knowledge Bank Report for Teacher Professional Leave*. Melbourne: Department of Education and Training.

McNamara S, McLean K, Jones M (2006). *Partnerships for Information and Communications Technology in Learning Final Report. Stories in ICT Professional Development: A Victorian Case Study*. Canberra: Department of Education, Science and Training.

NSW Department of Education and Training & University of West Sydney (2006). *School is for me: Pathways to student engagement. Fair Go Project*. Sydney: University of West Sydney.

The New London Group (1996). A pedagogy of multiliteracies: Designing social futures. *Harvard Educational Review*, 66(1): 60–92.

Turbill J (2003). Exploring the Potential of the Digital Language Experience Approach in Australian Classrooms. *Reading Online*. Available at www.readingonline.org/international/turbill7/

Unsworth L (2001). *Teaching Multilieracies across the Curriculum: Changing Dimensions of Text and Image in Classroom Practice.* Buckingham: Open University Press.

Unsworth L (2002). Changing dimensions of school literacies. *Australian Journal of Language and Literacy,* 25(1): 62–77.

Victorian Curriculum and Assessment Authority (2005). Victorian Essential Learning Standards Overview. Melbourne: Victorian Curriculum and Assessment Authority.

Victorian Curriculum and Assessment Authority (2004). Introducing the Victorian Essential Learning Standards. Melbourne: Victorian Curriculum and Assessment Authority.

Walsh M, Asha J, Sprainger N (2007). Reading digital texts. *Australian Journal of Language and Literacy,* 30(1): 40–53.

Zammit K, Downes T (2002). New learning environments and the multiliterate individual: a framework for educators. *Australian Journal of Language and Literacy,* 25(2): 24–36.

10
Looking for clarity amongst the challenges faced by teachers as they consider the role of ICT in classroom literacy learning experiences

Jessica Mantei and Dr Lisa Kervin
University of Wollongong

Primary school teachers today operate within a climate of great change with the rapid infusion of Information and Communication Technologies (ICT) into schools with the expectation that these be included within classroom experiences. Many schools purchased computer hardware and software and have provided professional development for teachers with the expectation that the technology will be put to use. Studies show, however, that many teachers continue to feel ill-equipped to use technology to support learning in spite of these in-service opportunities. Further studies identify the classroom teacher as the major factor in determining whether ICT are an important component of daily learning experiences; teachers who use ICT to meet their personal needs such as planning a school program, downloading music for leisure or paying bills on the Internet are more likely to utilise ICT for learning and teaching than those who find little use for such technologies in their daily lives.

This paper explores the challenges reported by a variety of teachers from Kindergarten to Year 6 from a range of schools across systems as they attempt to use ICT to support their students' literacy learning. Data were analysed through coding of interview transcripts, field notes and video/audio footage and emerging themes identified. Findings of this study reveal common challenges between teachers of differing ages and experience in a variety of school settings. The ensuing discussion identifies current issues and makes recommendations for teachers using ICT to support literacy learning.

Teachers are under increasing pressure to include new technologies in classroom learning experiences as they consider how to best present curricula content in ways that are meaningful to, and connect with, the needs of contemporary learners. The enormous advances in technology have impacted on literacy practices, rendering the tools of reading and writing that learners used in the past, although still necessary, insufficient (Anstey & Bull, 2006). As literacy educators we need to broaden our understanding of texts to include those that are multimodal and screen-based. Further, we need to shift from a philosophy of literacy learning as the accumulation of context knowledge in school to one that fosters the understanding and implementation of a range of skills, strategies and processes that support students to make meaning from their literacy experiences. While these understandings are evident for many teachers, our research has revealed that there are still many tensions and challenges faced by teachers as they consider how to best incorporate ICT into classroom literacy experiences.

This paper begins by reviewing the findings in the literature in two areas of interest:

- Challenges for teachers incorporating ICT into classrooms
- Implications for the teaching and learning of literacy

These areas provide a platform upon which the experiences of our focus teachers can be laid. Each teacher reported on within this paper has been involved in a research project with the researchers where they have looked to incorporate ICT into their classroom literacy practices.

Challenges for teachers incorporating ICT into classrooms

Descriptions of children as 'digital natives' (Prensky, 2001), 'clickerati kids' (Hill, 2004) and the 'Net Generation' (Oblinger, 2005) portray children as familiar and competent using ICT to achieve their aims. Prensky (2001) highlights the divide between 'natives' (school children) and 'immigrants' (their teachers), positioning teachers as 'struggling to teach a population that speaks an entirely new language' because of the 'outdated language (that of the pre-digital age)' that they use (Prensky,

2001, p2). Oblinger observed that primary school aged children access more than eight hours of "media messages," each day; much of the time participating in multiple simultaneous activities, for example, surfing the Internet while listening to music (Roberts, Foehr & Ride-Out, 2005, in Oblinger, 2005, p69). Although Leu (2002a) and McCombs (2000) argue that children are intrinsically motivated to learn with ICT, and that allowing children some control over their learning will further motivate them to complete tasks, Johnson (2005) warns that ICT alone may be insufficient for true engagement of learners. The literature argues that learners have changed and, therefore, the learning environment must too; this review turns now to investigate the changing nature of the learning environment of the primary school classroom.

The introduction of any new technology seems to be veiled with the notion of 'promise' – what it will do to revolutionise the classroom, how it will change the work of a teacher and how it will support and contribute to student learning. The apparent 'push' to incorporate technologies into classroom experiences is not a new phenomenon. Indeed, the introduction of technologies of 'old' into classrooms – chalkboards, books, pencils, pens, overhead projectors – were surrounded by similar tensions as we see today with the incorporation of ICT, associated peripherals and mobile technologies. There appears an ever-increasing range of technologies to incorporate within classroom learning experiences.

Just as Johnson (2005) asserts that the presence of technology fails to assure student engagement, Abas and Khalid (2007) observe similarly that the purchase and installation of technology is no guarantee that teachers will use it to facilitate learning. It is necessary for teachers to be realistic about what may happen with technology use and how its introduction, implementation and evaluation can be carefully planned for.

Information and Communication Technologies (ICT) have enabled teachers to bring global information and events into classrooms in a way that no previous technology has allowed, delivering a broad range of texts to the 'fingertips' of the learner (Leu, 2001) along with the potential to engage with local, national and international audiences (Kankaanranta,

2005) in both the creation and consumption of text. While it is the case that there are risks for children in the location of appropriate material and the need to critique the information that they find (Sangiuliano, 2005), there is no longer a question over whether schools should use ICT – this is given; the focus now is on which contexts and purposes are best supported through the use of technology (Abas & Khalid, 2007). Although the ideal is for all schools to have full Internet connection capabilities with sufficient computer access for all students, the reality is different. Many Australian classrooms require upgrading to carry the extra load required by ICT and reflect pedagogies of the past, with rooms not conducive to collaboration and child driven learning (Frazel & Souza, 2003). Reinking, Labbo and McKenna (2000) concede that schools and the broader community will comprise a blend of print and screen based texts for a long time to come, challenging schools to provide for the needs of learners in a climate where the literacy demands of the future are not known.

While it is recognised that teachers should incorporate ICT in their regular teaching practice, it is vital that teachers are acknowledged for the considerable knowledge they have about their profession – what constitutes 'good' pedagogy, the nature of learning and ways to engage students in the classroom. Roblyer (2006) describes, "technology is, above all, a channel for helping teachers communicate better with students. It can make good teaching even better, but it cannot make bad teaching good" (pv). Technology is not a substitute for good classroom practice. As such, it is vital for educators to have a clear rationale and purpose for integration of technology in classrooms in connection with curriculum goals, student learning gains and our own personal philosophies.

Implications for the teaching and learning of literacy

Lewin (1999) argues that without mastery of fundamental reading and writing processes, a child will be unable to successfully manipulate the Internet and other digital technologies because such texts demand faster, more efficient reading and writing skills for sifting through a larger amount of information than was previously required. Broadening this view, Harste (2003) asserts that the transmission of core knowledge has become a less important function of modern schooling, replaced by a focus on the development of a child's ability to think creatively, to solve problems and to understand the power of texts to position readers in certain ways. Allington's (2002) findings provide a further perspective of literacy, identifying the most important element of successful teaching not as any single commercially available product, but good, effective teachers who make decisions based on sound theoretical understandings about the ways children best learn. Recent changes to schooling are both complex and diverse; nevertheless, in preference to shrinking from the challenge, Leu (2000, p424) asserts that in order to prepare learners for the "futures they deserve", teachers must embrace new information technologies in supporting literacy learning.

Teachers are identified in the literature as the main barriers to successful integration of computer-based technologies in the classroom, but related issues around connectivity and a shifting paradigm also influence the use of ICT to support literacy learning.

The teacher decides whether ICT are used in classroom literacy learning. Teacher reluctance to embrace new technology has been cited as the main hindrance to successful integration of ICT into classrooms (Holland, 1996; Durrant & Green, 2000; Turbill, 2003) because the teacher has the power to allow or forbid access in their classroom. Use (or non-use) of ICT have been linked in the literature to the ways that teachers use technology in their own lives; teachers who use technology to fulfil personal needs are more likely to recognise the benefits and potential and therefore provide opportunities for children to use ICT in their learning (Kuhn, 2001; Leu, 2002b; Lankshear & Knobel, 2003). With experience, teachers develop an informal set of criteria about which practices and experiences will or will not work in classrooms and they design their learning experiences according to this criteria (Snyder, 1999). For a teacher reluctant to use ICT to support literacy learning, breaking down and broadening these beliefs is key to bringing about change.

Teachers are reported to continue to feel ill-equipped to use ICT in their classroom, despite professional development opportunities. Professional development and ongoing technical support are identified as critical factors in determining successful integration of ICT into classroom learning and teaching experiences (Kuhn, 2001; Leu, 2002b; Macleod, 2006). Perceived lack of professional development is problematic in broadening pedagogies for the computer-based climate because teachers who do use ICT in their classrooms tend to use new tools in old ways (Labbo, Reinking & McKenna, 1998).

While such arguments exist, it is important to acknowledge that teachers are experts in pedagogy, not necessarily technology. As such, it is vital to consider how the incorporation of technology supports and connects with understanding of both learning theory and teaching practice; more simply, why is it that teachers do what they do in their classrooms. Technologies need to be incorporated for the goal of supporting specific teaching and learning needs within the cohort of students in a specific context. Educators are in an enormous position of power, as "enlightened shapers of our future. Each teacher must help to articulate the vision for what the future of education should look like" (Robyler, 2006, pv). The role played by information technologies within education is a significant part of this future.

In exploring the role of ICT in literacy learning, Moreillon (2001) observes that rather than making a shift in literacy teaching, teachers are using ICT to conduct school as usual. Such an approach, where teachers draw on traditional literacy practices to reach out to newly emerging skills in reading, writing, viewing and communicating provides a comfortable place to start integrating technology into daily practice (Leu, 2002b; Leu, Mallette, Karchmer and Kara-Soteriou, 2005; Shambaugh, 2000). Rather than labelling such practice an inhibitor to the integration of ICT in literacy learning, Labbo (2005) makes connection to Vygotsky's (1978) zone of proximal development, arguing that the 'zone of proximal comfort', where teachers extend their own knowledge and skills by building on what they know about teaching and learning, is a valid place to start to embrace the challenges of the literacy paradigm of the digital age.

But it is not enough for teachers to remain in this zone. For children to learn to understand and think creatively about the real problems faced by their communities, they require learning experiences that are an authentic reflection of this community (Jonassen, 2003). Herrington, Oliver and Reeves (2003) identify authentic learning tasks as valuable in being able to engage students in the experience because of their relevance to real world situations and the opportunities they afford the learner to pursue avenues of personal interest along paths of preferred learning towards a diverse range of acceptable outcomes.

This complex and somewhat overwhelming state of play led us to ask:
- What are the challenges identified by teachers?
- How are ICT used to support literacy learning?
- What tensions exist between teacher beliefs, classroom practices and professional expectations?

Methodology

Data collected between 2005 and 2007 have been analysed and reported on in this paper. The teachers were each part of projects with one or both of the researchers investigating the ways teachers use technology to support learning in their classrooms. Data were collected through interview, observation and analysis of artefacts throughout each of the periods of data collection. Analysis of data was ongoing throughout each period of data collection. Further analysis of data was conducted following final data collection, follow up interviews and at the culmination of all projects. Data were analysed through coding of transcripts from interview, field notes and recordings and emerging themes identified. Table 10.1 demonstrates the varied relationships the researchers had with the teachers, the projects that they were involved in and the ways that data were collected and analysed.

Teacher pseudonym	Joshua
Project	iPod Pedagogy: Using the technology of millennial learners in primary classrooms
Description of the research project	The class teacher introduced 12x30GB 5th Generation Video iPods into his Grade 4 classroom. From the period of May to November 2006 (term 2 to mid term 4) the students in this class engaged with a range of tasks that incorporated the iPods within their classroom learning experiences, with emphasis on Talking and Listening. These tasks were planned, implemented and evaluated as the teacher worked through an action research (Kemmis & McTaggart, 1988; Stringer, 1996) process. The students and the teacher were interviewed at regular intervals throughout this period. Work samples were collected and analysed.
Data collection period	Term 2 – mid Term 4, weekly visits, 90 minutes per session (2006)
Teacher pseudonym	Madeleine and Rhonda
Project	An investigation of the process Stage 1 children engage with in their construction of non-linear texts.
Description of the research project	The second named researcher worked with these Grades 1 and 2 teachers for ninety minutes each week over a period of twenty weeks. During these visits the researcher worked with a focus group of students who were identified by the teachers as needing 'extension' with literacy. The researcher collected data with a focus on the process the students engaged with as they constructed their text using computer-based technologies. Data included the use of researcher observations, semi-structured interviews with the teacher, group focus interviews with the students and the collection of student work samples.
Data collection period	Term 2 and Term 3, 90 minutes per session (2005)
Teacher pseudonym	Bob
Project	Investigating the ways that teachers use technology in the teaching of writing in Stage 2
Description of the research project	Data were collected through semi-structured interviews, observation of the teacher at work and analysis of his teaching program. Further data were collected through interviews with this teacher's students and the work they produced as the culminating assessment task in this classroom.
Data collection period	Term 2 and Term 3, 90 minutes per week session (2005)
Teacher pseudonym	Kate and Sally

Project	Early career teachers in virtual writing conferences with Year 5 children
Description of the research project	Early career teachers worked in a final year language elective subject. The teachers were observed and interviewed as they conducted virtual writing conferences with students in Year 5. The teachers and students connected through email and the writing conference was conducted using the tracking tool in Microsoft Word
Data collection period	Session 2 2 hours per week during tutorials (2006)
Teacher pseudonym	Sienna
Project	"GetReel": Primary school students create television commercials
Description of the research project	The second named researcher worked in a Year Six classroom for two hours each week over a period of ten weeks with Sienna, the school's teacher/librarian. Data was collected with a focus on the process the teacher/librarian and the students engaged with as they constructed their multimodal 'texts' in response to the GetReel competition. Data included the use of researcher observations, semi-structured interviews with the teacher/librarian, group focus interviews with the students and the collection of student work samples.
Data collection period	Term 2, 2 hours per week (2004)
Teacher pseudonym	Jemma and Jasmine
Project	'The laptop project' – exploring the ways that teachers accommodate 1-1 laptops in their classrooms
Description of the research project	These data were collected as part of an action research design. Both researchers worked with these teachers to team teach in whole class, small group and individual settings. Data were collected through interviews with the teachers and observations of them at work with the children – each with a laptop computer on their desk.
Data collection period	Term 1 and Term 2, 2 hours per week (2006)
Teacher pseudonym	Kay
Project	Critical friend
Description of the research project	Kay has collaborated with both researchers throughout all periods of data collection. Kay is a co-author with the second named researcher.
Data collection period	Ongoing collaboration

Table 10.1 - Teacher participants and their projects

Findings

Each research project described in Table 10.1 provided the researchers with considerable data reflecting challenges faced by teachers as they consider the role of ICT in classroom literacy learning experiences. For the purposes of this paper, and to reconnect with each teacher post research project, subsequent interviews were conducted with the teachers. Opportunity to compare and contrast data from the research projects and the more recent teacher interviews revealed a number of emergent themes. Each theme will be explored in connection with the research projects and teacher reflections.

Teacher attitudes towards ICT

The teachers' attitudes to ICT were reflected in the ways they facilitated student use of technology in the classroom. A shift in teacher thinking was identified in the data where teachers described 'fear' as one of the challenges they faced in the past; fear that they lacked knowledge and skills to teach the students. Rhonda is a teacher who described feeling particularly intimidated by the use of ICT in classrooms at the beginning of the project she was involved with. However, in recent interviews, she reported "I do not allow the technology to overwhelm me any longer", suggesting a shift in confidence. None of the participant teachers in this paper identified fear as an ongoing challenge in using ICT to support learning.

All of the teachers perceived ICT as a time-consuming element of their planning and preparation for teaching, but indicated that it was important to be prepared for the lessons on offer by learning to manipulate the technologies available. These teachers reported:

> "I also find it a challenge to keep up with new technologies – Web 2.0 tools" (Sienna)

> "Time – trying to explore new programs [is a challenge]" (Maria)

> "[finding] time to play with what is available before implementing" (Joshua)

Jasmine indicated that more responsibility should have been taken by governing bodies in supporting teachers to learn: "the biggest issue is time ... if we were able to access a number of release days devoted to technology on a regular basis, then I'm sure teachers would become more confident in using technology". Although the demand for time spent learning about the technologies available was identified as challenging by all teachers, it is evident in the data that most of these teachers had embraced the challenge as they continued to plan and implement literacy learning experiences supported by ICT.

Further analysis of the data indicated the motivation for the teachers' investment of their time. Interviews with the teachers revealed their genuine desire to meet the needs of the students in their class in a climate where ICT expose children to information and communication opportunities different from those previously available. Indeed, if we further reflect upon participant involvement in the research projects outlined in Table 10.1, each teacher (with the exception of Jemma and Jasmine) volunteered to take place in the project. Data collected through interview with Madeleine is representative of the reports by the teachers on this subject. She had enrolled in a year long professional development course and described her expectations:

> looking forward to a brain fix and how to do Blogs/websites as the Year 4 kids have the knowledge and I have to keep up and offer the best of what is available and continue to provide selection and quality application of technology in my teaching and make their learning effective, efficient too and relevant to their life; even relevant for their future.
> (Madeleine)

Recognition of the need for "keeping up to date, not only with the technology, but the children" (Joshua) was a common theme throughout our observations and interviews with the teachers. What differed between the teachers was the ways that they used the technology to support literacy learning experiences.

Connecting ICT with literary experiences

All of the teachers reported using ICT to meet the professional requirements such as programming, assessing and evaluating. Their programs incorporated the use of ICT across a range of curriculum areas and they described using ICT to support literacy learning in a variety of ways. During interviews, most of the teachers identified the importance of integrating ICT into the literacy learning experience. This integration was observed in classrooms; Kay described her use of audio books on computers to support reading development as a "roaring success with non literate and highly literate, though reluctant readers". Further, Kay reported the use of trial and error in selecting suitable technology to support the learning: "we did try [the audio books] on an ipod shuffle, but it was more difficult for students and myself to keep track of where students were up to". Other examples of integration of ICT into literacy learning were observed in Joshua's Year 4 classroom. This teacher reported that in deconstructing texts the children could "hear how things are organised" and this then aided the construction of a podcast, which was "heavily scripted and reviewed often to ensure the correct message is heard". Year 6 children in Sienna's class also constructed texts with the support of ICT as they wrote scripts and recorded commercials about youth issues in their community. In both examples, the children were highly engaged in the process of deconstructing and constructing texts using the language and text structure appropriate for the genre and intended audience. In examples such as these, the teacher kept literacy learning as the focus while ICT served to support powerful literacy learning experiences.

Not all of the data reflected this shift in understanding of the role of ICT in *supporting* rather than *being* the learning. During data collection periods, some teachers were observed instructing the children to "do PowerPoint" because they had not made one before or for ease of teaching when every child is working at the same task. During these times, the literacy learning was overshadowed by the skills required to manipulate the technology. Such was the problem that emerged in Bob's Year 4 classroom where the children were working in mixed ability groups to create PowerPoint presentations. Bob explained that because the children had differing spelling and composition skills, he was unable to deliver his planned teaching of spelling and grammar and that his focus would shift to teaching 'multimedia skills' during this time of the literacy block instead.

The data demonstrates the differing levels of understanding and pedagogical development between teachers of different age and experience. Although this degree of difference is supported by Labbo's (2005) observation that many teachers begin in and then move outside their zone of proximal comfort, these differences were observed to cause tension for Joshua. Passionate about the importance of integrating ICT into literacy learning, he identified "teachers just teaching aspects of technology, rather than trying to integrate it in a meaningful way" as one of the issues that continue to challenge him in using ICT to support learning. Such enduring attitudes can have a strong impact on the relationships between and among staff and children.

Teacher ownership of technology integration

Our data consistently indicates relationships among individual teacher's attitudes to technology, their perceived expertise with the technology and their understanding of how the technology fits with their pedagogical understandings; all of which impact upon opportunities for student learning.

Many of the teachers we have worked with felt some pressure to include ICT within their classroom practice. For example, the project that Jemma and Jasmine were involved with was very much guided by the vision of their school principal and the demands of the community within which the school was situated. The ownership and passion for the project was not with the two teachers who were at the forefront of its implementation. As such, the project outcomes differed from those initially anticipated; Jemma and Jasmine were left feeling that their professional expertise was somewhat diminished and they were frustrated by the "imposition" on their literacy teaching. The laptop computers became something "extra" to the demise of their regular teaching program. The attitudes of the teachers, and their frustrations, influenced their promotion of the project with the students. The students saw the laptops as "computer time" rather than tools to support their literacy learning.

In contrast, those projects where the teachers held the vision and enthusiasm resulted in ownership of the project from both the teacher and the students' perspectives. Joshua, for example, volunteered to work with the iPods and used the experience to reconceptualise his teaching of the Talking and Listening strand. He found the need to create a virtual learning space to support his teaching, challenging the traditional notion of a classroom, which resulted in him and his students taking responsibility for the creation and maintenance of this space. This shared responsibility challenged the role Joshua had previously assumed with his students as they worked together on the project as co-learners.

Analysis of the language used by the teachers to describe their projects revealed much about where the control for the ICT use lay. Jasmine, who was very frustrated when involved with the laptop project, described in more recent interviews, "I am adjusting", when talking about her latest involvement with technology (in this case interactive whiteboards). Sienna too indicated a shift in her thinking, describing, "in the past I have taught technology in isolation, focusing more on developing particular IT skills or knowledge of a single application". She further describes having had "separate IT outcomes and these were the focus for our lessons". More recent discussion of her practice revealed that she now aimed for "seamless integration into all aspects of my teaching and learning". Many of the teachers (Rhonda, Jasmine, Jemma, Sienna, Madeleine) spoke consistently about the responsibility for the technology and associated knowledge for its use as lying with them as opposed to the students. This was in contrast to other teachers (Joshua, Kate, Kay) who strongly indicated the students' considerable knowledge as a valuable resource in enriching their classroom experiences. In these cases the ownership and responsibility were shared.

'Managing' ICT

Reliable, consistent access to ICT was observed to continue to challenge the ways that teachers are able to achieve integration into literacy learning experiences. Some illustrative examples follow.

In one school, an interactive whiteboard was installed in the Kindergarten classroom at the beginning of the year, at the publication of this paper – some six months later, it is still not 'functional' and simply remains unusable on the wall.

In another school, a government grant afforded the purchase of 30 laptop computers for the individual use of children in Year 5.

Unfortunately, the school did not have Internet access in the Year 5 room and, one year on, this situation remains.

Rhonda reported "troubleshooting in younger classes is a nightmare for me" and was observed to retreat from even attempting to use ICT, preferring to assign literacy learning tasks requiring computer use to support teachers and colleagues.

The element of time continued to preoccupy the planning and teaching of these teachers. Several of the teachers were observed to direct children to preselected websites for use during the literacy block. They reported that the websites were "appropriate because they fit the needs of the students or have been designed with the students in mind (Kay)", "they contain the right information" (Bob) and "it saves time" (Bob). Conversely, Kate reported encouraging the children in her class to "sift through websites to find information that can be useful". It would appear that the teachers reported on in this study managed the ICT to suit the focus of their lesson (for example, effective key word searching) and the purpose of the task (e.g. locating and identifying information).

Issues of equity

Equity in access to and use of ICT for both teachers and children was an emerging theme in the data.

Teachers reported feeling concerned about children who do not have computer and/or Internet access at home and the ways that they can compensate for this in the classroom. One teacher described it as a "balancing act" between the child who has "everything at home and another nothing". The perception in the literature is that children are more "tech savvy" than their teachers, but these participant teachers reported a different reality. While some children are highly competent in using ICT, a discrepancy exists between many students' knowledge about ICT texts and the skills that they have mastered for their creation. For the teachers, managing these different levels of expertise amongst the students is a challenge. Joshua described throughout the iPod project the challenge of establishing mutual understandings and associated metalanguage to describe the technology and connections to learning. He found that he entered the project with the understanding that "iPods were the technology of the students" but in reality found that many of them didn't have the experience and expertise he assumed, describing "a technology rich and a technology poor culture within the classroom".

Further issues of inequity of access and learning for teachers emerged from analysis of the data. Sally felt that providing computer lessons in a lab by a specialist computer teacher without the presence of the classroom teacher was a mistake that only served to "de-skill teachers", but this was contrasted by observations and interviews with Jemma, a specialist computer teacher in her school. She cited narrow vision by school leaders and the broader schooling system as limiting her development as a classroom teacher integrating ICT into literacy learning experiences.

Accessing funds to replace aging computers and associated peripherals was an element that presented as an issue for teachers. Those with new computers and adequate access to peripherals such as data projectors reported feeling well supported with hardware, resulting in the perception of an equitable classroom environment. What was interesting, however, was that the teachers who reported and were observed to be more confident with the integrated use of ICT in literacy learning reported less on the failure of the technology and more on the multitude of ways that they had experimented with ICT in literacy learning.

Discussion

In this climate of ongoing change, it is important that educators take the lead in the development of pedagogy and the integration of new literacies into the curriculum (Leu, Mallette, Karchmer & Kara-Soteriou, 2005) rather than leaving it to corporate experts (Luke, 2000) or the information technology community (Leu, 2002a). Each teacher has revealed the need to see the value of the technology in light of their own teaching philosophy and vision for their students. Where this understanding is not evident, we have found that technology has been used in ways that are disjointed, unconnected and separate from other classroom experiences.

We have found that teachers who see purpose in using technology to support their literacy teaching add considerable value and depth to classroom experiences. The wealth of 'new' texts, the different ways technology can aid text construction, the affordances of the technology in teaching specific literacy processes and the different opportunities they offer were all identified as enablers of ICT integration.

Our review of collected data has strongly revealed that research by educators, government funding for teacher professional development and commitment by teachers to embrace change is needed to ensure high quality, authentic learning experiences for contemporary school children.

References

Abas Z W, Khalid H M (2007). Achieving pedagogical richness to meet the needs of ODL learners. In P Tsang, R Kwang & R Fox (Eds). *Enhancing learning through technology*, (pp 161–170). London: World Scientific Publishing

Allington R L (2002). The six Ts of effective literacy instruction. Retrieved 2 March 2004, from www.readingrockets.org/article.php?ID=413

Anstey M, Bull G (2006). *Teaching and learning multiliteracies: Changing times, changing literacies*. Kensington Gardens: International Reading Association and Australian Literacy Educators' Association.

Comber B, Nixon H, Reid J (Eds) (2007). *Literacies in place: teaching environmental communications*. Primary English Teachers' Association. Australia.

Durrant C, Green B (2000). Literacy and new technologies in school education: Meeting the L(IT)eracy challenge? *Australian Journal of Language and Literacy*, 23(2): 89–105.

Frazel M, Souza J R (2003). *Tips and Tricks for Using Handhelds in the Classroom*. Westminster, CA: Teacher Created Resources

Harste J (2003). What do we mean by literacy now? *Voices from the Middle*, 10(3): 8–12.

Herrington J, Oliver R, Reeves TC (2003). Patterns of engagement in authentic online learning environments. *Australian Journal of Educational Technology*, 19(1): 59–71.

Hill S (2004). Hot diggity! Findings from the Children of the new millennium project. Paper presented at Early Childhood Organisation Conference EDC 6 March 2004.

Holland H (1996). Way past word processing. *Electronic Learning*, 15(6): 22-24.

Johnson D (2005). Miss Rumphius as a role model for preservice teachers. In R A Karchmer, D J Leu, M M Mallette, J Kara-Soteriou (Eds). *Innovative approaches to literacy education: Using the Internet to support new literacies*, (pp182-198). Newark: International Reading Association.

Jonassen D (2003). Using cognitive tools to represent problems. *Journal of Research in Technology in Education*, 35(3): 362–379.

Kankaanranta M (2005). International perspectives on the pedagogically innovative uses of technology. *Human Technology*, 1(2): 111–116.

Kemmis S, MacTaggart R (1988). *The Action Research Planner*, Third Edition Geelong: Deakin University Press

Kuhn M (2001). Taking computers out of the corner: Making technology work in the classroom. *Reading Online*, 4(9).

Labbo L, Reinking D, McKenna M C (1998). Technology and literacy education in the next century: Exploring the connection between work and schooling. *Peabody Journal of Education*, 73(3-4): 273–289.

Labbo L D (2005). Moving from the tried and true to the new: Digital morning message. *The Reading Teacher*, 58(8): 782–785.

Lankshear C, Knobel M (2003). *New literacies: Changing knowledge and classroom learning*. Philadelphia: Open University Press.

Leu D J (2000). Our children's future: Changing the focus of literacy and literacy instruction. *The Reading Teacher*, 53(5): 424–430.

Leu D J (2001). Internet project: Preparing students for new literacies in a global village. *The Reading Teacher*, 54(6): 568–572.

Leu D J (2002a). The new literacies: Research on reading instruction with the Internet and other digital technologies. Newark, DE: International Reading Association. Retrieved 30 August 2005, from www.web.syr.edu/~djleu/newlit.html.

Leu D J (2002b). Internet workshop: Making time for literacy [Exploring literacy on the Internet]. *The Reading Teacher*, 55(5). Retrieved 13 October 2005, from www.readingonline.org

Leu D J Jr, Mallette M M, Karchmer R A, Kara-Soteriou J (2005). Contextualising the new literacies of information and communication technologies in theory, research and practice. In R A Karchmer, D J Leu, M M Mallette, & J Kara-Soteriou (Eds) *Innovative approaches to literacy education: Using the Internet to support new literacies.* (pp1–10). Newark, DE: International Reading Association.

Lewin L (1999). 'Site reading' the World Wide Web. *Educational Leadership*, 56(5): 16–20.

Luke C (2000). Cyber-schooling and technological change: Multiliteracies for new times. In B Cope & M Kalantzis (Eds) *Multiliteracies: Literacy learning and the design of social futures* (pp69–91). London: Routledge.

Macleod A (2006). From ICLT conservative to ICLT savvy in taking on technology. *Independent Education*, 36(1): 21–25.

McCombs B L (2000). Assessing the role of educational technology in the teaching and learning process: A learner-centred perspective. White paper for the US Department of Education: Secretary's conference on Educational Technology 2000. Retrieved 18 October 2005, from www.ed.gov/rschstat/eval/tech/techconf00/mccombs_paper.html

Moreillon J (2001). What does technology have to do with it? Integrating electronic tools into a children's literature course. *Reading Online*, 5(2).

Oblinger D G (2005). Learners, learning and technology. *Educause Review*, Sept/Oct 69–75. Retrieved 23 February 2007, from www.educause.edu/educatingthenetgen/

Prensky M (2001). Digital Natives, Digital Immigrants. *On the Horizon*, 9(5), October 2001. www.marcprensky.com/writing/

Reinking D, Labbo L, McKenna M C (2000). From assimilation to accommodation: a developmental framework for integrating new technologies into literacy research and instruction. *Journal of Research on Reading*, 23(2): 110–122.

Roberts D F, Foehr U G, Ride-Out V (2005). Generation M: Media in the Lives of 8–18 Year-Olds, A Kaiser Family Foundation Study. In D G Oblinger (2005). *Learners, learning and technology. Educause Review*, Sept/Oct 69–75. 23 Retrieved February 2007, from www.educause.edu/educatingthenetgen/

Roblyer M D (2006). *Integrating Educational Technology into Teaching, 4th Edn*. Upper Saddle River, NJ: Pearson/Merrill Prentice Hall/International Society for Technology in Education.

Sangiuliano G (2005). Books on tape for kids: A language arts-based service-learning project. In R A Karchmer, D J Leu, M M Mallette & J Kara- Soteriou (Eds), *Innovative approaches to literacy education: Using the Internet to support new literacies*, (pp. 13–27). Newark, DE: International Reading Association.

Shambaugh R N (2000). What does it mean to be x literate? Literacy definitions as tools for growth. *Reading Online*, 4(2).

Snyder I (1999). Integrating computers into the literacy curriculum: more difficult then we first imagined. In J Hancock, (Ed) *Teaching Literacy Using Information Technology: A Collection of Articles from the Australian Literacy Educator's Association* (pp. 11–30). Carlton South: Australian Literacy Educators Association

Turbill J (2003). Exploring the potential of the digital language experience approach in Australian classrooms. *Reading Online*, 6(7).

Vygotsky L (1978). *Mind in society*. Cambridge MA: Harvard University Press.

11
Applying multiple literacies in Australian and Canadian contexts

Diana Masny
University of Ottawa

David R Cole
University of Tasmania

As human beings we marvel at a dance performance, a musical recording, a novel, a film. For instance, take pieces of metal that come together to form a free-standing sculpture. Metal, as in music, dance or film, is a free-flow matter (Deleuze & Guattari, 1987). As it stands there, what does metal do? It takes on expressiveness. Similarly, multiple literacies that involve reading the world, word and self take on expressiveness. Words on paper, musical notes on a staff take on sense, expressiveness.

Light, colour, sounds, lines and textures are powers that allow us to perceive worlds but each one is perceived through connections. As Colebrook states (2006, p103), we have colours because of the force of light and sensations that encounter each other just as we have the texture of a canvas through the encounters of light with depth and thickness. Similarly, literacies, through the encounters of letters and words with paper or with a computer, and encounters of notes on a musical staff or sounds that come together, are powers that allow us to perceive/read the world, word and self. It is from continuous investments with these connections that literate individuals are effected. Through a multiple literacies theory such as the one presented in this article, there is potential to release literacy from its privileged position as the printed word by not allowing it to govern all other literacies. In this way, literacies open themselves to what is not already given.

In this article, we foreground Masny's Multiple Literacies Theory (MLT). Within this perspective, literacies are processes and from investment in literacies as processes, transformations occur and *becoming other* is effected. There are, however, other perspectives on literacies that have been foregrounded, namely New Literacies Studies and Multiliteracies. First, this article is devoted to a brief overview of the New Literacies Studies. Second, the Multiple Literacies Theory developed by Masny (2001) is presented. Third, MLT is linked to Australian education in language and literacies. It includes a discussion of the differences between Multiliteracies (Cope and Kalantzis, 2000) and MLT. Fourth, a case study application of MLT in research in Australia is provided. Fifth, MLT is applied to policy, teaching and research in Canada. Sixth, Masny reconceptualises MLT. Concepts developed within MLT are paradigmatically derived from Deleuze (1990, and 1995) and Deleuze and Guattari (1987, 1994) and presented. Seventh, a case study application of MLT in research in Canada follows. The final section is open to possibilities for lines of flight to create and transform experiences, thereby becoming *other than* through reading of the world, word and self, i.e. multiple literacies.

New literacy studies (NLS)

Before presenting the Multiple Literacies Theory (MLT), we want to point out that in the research on literacy, important contributions have been advanced by many. I want to focus on the New Literacy Studies (NLS) in order to argue that the paradigmatic position held by NLS is different from the paradigm espoused by MLT. Then, I will present MLT.

The New Literacy studies (Barton, Hamilton and Ivanič, 2002; Gee, 1996; Kim, 2003; Street, 1984, 2003), propose a definition of literacy that takes into account participants' cultural models of literacy events, social interactional aspects of literacy events, text production and interpretation, ideologies, discourses and institutions (Baynham, 2002). The term 'event' within NLS is adapted from Heath (1983) and ethnography of communication. An event refers to any occasion in which engagement with a written text is integral to participants' interactions and interactive processes (Heath 1983, p93). Texts that involve the interaction between verbal and visual are to be understood as multimodal (New London Group, 1996). The terms, events and texts, have been highlighted so as to understand how they are used within NLS.

While there might be surface similarities, in terms of their approaches to the study of literacies (in the plural) from an ideological perspective that sees them as situated historically and socially, they are distinctive in a number of important ways. As you will see shortly, these distinctions are not so much superficial differences between the NLS's ideological model and MLT, rather they arise in deeper paradigmatic questions that underlie these two perspectives – this point will be raised again in MLT in the Australian context.

Conceptualising multiple literacies theory (MLT) 1997–2002

MLT was devised with a more critical perspective for social justice (Masny and Ghahremani-Ghajar, 1999). In this version, the concept of literacies refers to literacies as a social construct. As such, literacies are context-specific. They are operationalised or actualised *in situ*. They take on meaning according to the way a sociocultural group appropriates them. Literacies of a social group are taken up as visual, oral and written. They constitute texts, in a broad sense, that interweave with religion, gender, race, ideology and power.

An individual engages literacies as s/he reads the world, reads the word and reads her/himself. Accordingly, when an individual talks, reads, writes, and values, construction of meaning takes place within a particular context. This act of meaning construction that qualifies as literate is not only culturally driven but also is shaped by sociopolitical and sociohistorical productions of a society and its institutions.

Figure 11.1 presents several literacies which are described below. They are community-based, school-based, personal and critical literacies (Masny, 2005).

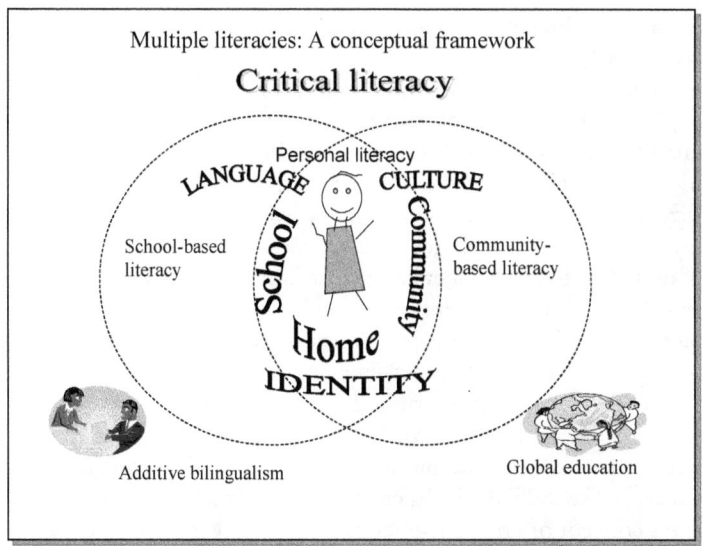

Figure 11.1 Multiple literacies: a conceptual framework

Multiple literacies

In this conceptual framework, the individual is reading the world, the word and self in the context of the home, school and community (local, national and international). This entails on the part of the individual a personal as well as a critical reading.

1. Personal literacy. This framework for multiple literacies corresponds to a worldview in which the individual is immersed in different societal settings (school, home and community) shaped by social, political and historical contexts within that society. Personal literacy focuses on reading oneself as one reads the world and the word. It is within that perspective that personal literacy contributes to the shaping of one's worldview. It is a way of 'being', based on construction of meaning that is always in movement, always in transition. When personal literacy contributes to a way of becoming, it involves fluidness and ruptures within and across differing literacies. S/he who reads the world and the word is in a process of becoming, that is, the person creates and gives meaning to that process of becoming in relation to texts. Text is assigned a broad

meaning to include visual oral, written and possibly tactile forms (Masny, 2001).
2. Critical literacy. No reading of the world, the word or oneself could take place in any significant manner without a critical reading or reading that calls on reflections (of texts). For many researchers, the work of Freire (Freire & Macedo, 1987) comes to mind when referring to reading the world and the word. His work has inspired many researchers. As well, there have been conceptual frameworks that are linked to critical literacy such as critical theory and critical feminist theory. The concept of critical literacy espoused by Freire is paradigm specific. The conceptual framework is situated within modernity. His theory of critical literacy is a theory of practice that serves to liberate and transform individuals by attending to a sense of betterment of the individual. Central to Freire's notion of critical literacy is that socio-economic structures are poised to mainstream OR marginalise individuals. In creating links with critical theory, Friere's concept of critical literacy creates a context for conscious examination of power relationship based on historical, political and social conditions at a particular time and space (within a particular community).
3. Community literacy. Community-based literacy refers to an individual's reading of literate practices of a community.
4. School-based literacy. School-based literacy refers to the process of interpretation and communication in reading the world, the word and self in the context of school. It also includes social adaptation to the school milieu, its rites and rituals. School-based literacy emphasises conceptual readings that are critical to school success. Such literacies are mathematics, science, social sciences, technologies and multimedia.

MLT in the Australian context

In Australia since the 1990s, the social literacy movement of Multiliteracies has been steadily gaining increased leverage and power (Unsworth, 2001). Whilst MLT does share many similarities with multiliteracies as a set of organising principles for literacy provision, it also has major differences that we shall explore here. Unsworth's (2001) and the New London Group's (1996) models of multiliteracies have been consistent enough to drive the implementation of multiliteracies in Australia, and they act as comparative devices to MLT for this section:

1. Multiliteracies are philosophically based in phenomenology (Cope & Kalantzis, 2000), whilst MLT is based in transcendental materialism (Deleuze & Guattari, 1987). Whilst this philosophical difference between the two approaches may seem to be trivial at the coal-face of literacy work, it has profound effects for both systems. The multiliteracies camp argues that the social agenda for literacy should be in experience. MLT would counter that the social agenda of literacy is in the many aspects of life that flow through the subject and constitute memories, desire and the mind. As such, experience is extremely difficult to render as a stable category when examining exactly which aspects of life determine literacy learning according to MLT. The philosophy of multiliteracies maintains the stable category of experience, especially when contrasting its construction of literacy with respect to previous iterations of literacy that relied heavily on print literacy practices. It says that the new literacy learning experiences are dominated by the media, which should be replicated in our design of literacy curricula.
2. Technology is of fundamental importance in multiliteracies, whereas it is of equal importance with every other contemporary literacy practice in MLT. The use of multiliteracies encourages literacy teachers to engage with technology in every aspect of the literacy learning program, as it prepares students for the technological and global workplace (Cope & Kalantzis, 1995). MLT will use technology wherever necessary, but does not allow its use to be a dominant or overriding narrative with respect to contemporary literacy.
3. Power is distributed differently in the MLT and multiliteracies models of literate behaviour. In MLT the emphasis is very much on local interactions causing changes and micro-systems that directed power from the bottom-up. In multiliteracies, the focus on intelligent design spreads as a system property that guides all participants to work towards the globalisation of literate behaviours and ultimately the power of corporations.
4. Multiliteracies encourage communities of learners, whereas MLT promotes action in learning. This action may come together in

terms of a specified community, yet the actions that MLT produces are disparate and complex, and not defined by any preconceived agenda. The meaning that one may take from MLT action learning is invariably communal (Goodchild, 1996); however, these meanings are not fixed in a standard democratic or civil direction, as is the case with multiliteracies.
5. Creativity takes on a fundamentally different orientation in MLT and multiliteracies. MLT relies on the random collisions of effects (Parisi, 2004), whereas multiliteracies prioritise organised and structured projects. Multiliteracies use interdisciplinary curriculum methods to encourage students to think holistically and to link knowledge areas. MLT works through local knowledge to produce moments of inspiration and art (Deleuze, 1995).
6. Otherness, strangeness and alienation are included parts of the MLT system, as they may be explored through personal literacy (Fiumara, 2001) and affect; whilst multiliteracies will tend to shut out such considerations through communities of practice working towards pre-defined social goals.

The combined difference of MLT as opposed to multiliteracies as a basis for Australian literacy is that it is a starting point that works multiplicity fully into the system. This means that it has direct consequences for immigrants, indigenous populations or any marginalised community. It transforms the ways in which the mainstream works, as it tends to bring the random forces that are in play in the system into the centre. For example, the continued controversies that surround boys and literacy would be resolved through MLT by constructing units of work that inculcate boys' desire into the machinery of the literate practices. This does not mean excluding girls' desire from study, but works to preserve male affect in the classroom to help the boys build their literacy. This is against a backdrop of girls often being more articulate and expressive in their language usage when it comes to emotion and empathy than their young male counterparts (Graham, 2007).

Case studies using MLT: Australia

Tasmanian self-recorded literacy videos

During 2006, students in northern Tasmania from grades 7–9 (age 11–14) were asked to take part in literacy research. The four schools that accepted the invitation to join in with the research were public institutions from an Australian country town environment. The students were asked to reflect on their literacy learning and make videos articulating their understanding of their literacy progress (n=45). They have used cameras attached to computers in a variety of environments, ranging from a computer at the front of the class, to a computer in a quiet room next to the library. The preliminary results from this research may be analysed using the Deleuze & Guattari empirical framework (Deleuze, 1995), which is an analysis of the sensible and non-sensible aspects of research, the integrated use of experimentation above and beyond the fixed terms of pre-defined categories. This analysis represents a playful and multilayered representation of the self-recorded literacy videos of the students. It is related to MLT through the construction of cam-capture literacy (Cole, 2007) and the following categories are unstable and interlinked cam-capture middle school zones:

1. Boredom. The videos have elicited the deeply felt emotion of boredom – it permeates the whole of the literacy practices in all of the schools as the students see them. Boredom is not a superficial surface effect of education, but exists on every level of their life at school. It could be said that it is vital to them as an organising and originating principle for the type of literacy that they do at school.
2. Time. The pace of the videos differs dramatically from student to student. Some rush through their pre-prepared speech at such a rate of knots that their words are barely audible. Others speak so slowly and deliberately that the videos seem to be recorded at half-speed. Few students are able to talk naturally and directly at the camera.
3. Face. Many of the students had prepared their images in advance before the video shoot. The girls had put on make-up, boys brushed their hair. The videos only frame the face and shoulders of the students, so they have concentrated on these parts of their bodies to represent themselves. Students preferred to be framed in profile by tilting their heads to one side of the camera as they thought that this looks cooler.

4. Inarticulation. This research has proved that teenagers have great difficulty in articulating their literacy learning practices. If given direct questions to answer such as: What helps me to get better at literacy? They were left speechless. If they were asked: What am I good at in literacy? They would say reading or writing. Some would follow-up their comments with – I'm bad at spelling!! Very few had the ability to critically analyse their abilities in literacy in any depth.
5. Teacher intervention. Several teachers, who thought that the students were not taking the research seriously enough, sat by the computers and quizzed their best literacy students about what they had just been studying in literacy. These videos resemble reading comprehension sequences, with the students mechanically responding to prompts. The students register noticeable relief and satisfaction if they think that the teacher is pleased with their performance.
6. Chaos. There are videos taken by students during recess. These involve tapes of dancing; making shapes on camera with their bodies; moving the camera to look around the room quickly or in rhythmic bursts; laughing at other students in the room whilst filming them; and random filming with a disconnected narrative from a student off-camera.
7. Self-consciousness. Whether speaking about how repetitive they thought their literacy lessons were, or how they could get better at writing, the students all displayed self-consciousness. This means that they were worried about how the video would come out, and aware that somebody was going to view it – namely the researcher!

MLT doesn't give us a magic wand to make these students all suddenly value their literacy lessons! It does give us a perspective whereby these ideas may be listened to and understood. Furthermore, MLT is an organising principle that shows us ways of using these student reactions to literacy practices as starting points for learning (Doecke & McClenaghan, 2004). For example, the exploration of boredom as the bedrock of school literacy should act as a springboard *to act other*wise and engage ways to articulate the tenets of boredom in every aspect of life.

MLT in the Canadian context

1. Policy. Masny elaborated a conceptual framework of multiple literacies that was adapted as a literacies model for the actualisation of French so that through its educational system, Alberta's French language community could thrive. The rationale for adopting a curriculum that took up multiple literacies was that, at the time, the curriculum promoted mostly school-based literacy and provided little opportunities for legitimating other literacies (e.g. personal and community literacies). Examples are the kindergarten programs both in immersion (1999b) and in French First Language (1999a) developed by the Alberta Ministry of Education, and the kindergarten immersion program in the social sciences developed by the Manitoba Ministry of Education (2003). In addition, multiple literacies also became a foundational element for Affirming Francophone Education in Alberta (2001).
2. Teaching practice. In 2003, the Canadian Council of Ministers of Education developed a Pan-Canadian project for French language schools. The training kit assists teachers from Kindergarten to Grade 2 in demonstrating the importance of being proficient in French in order to develop multiple literacies in French: personal, critical, school and community. In a French-minority language setting in Canada, only in a minority of homes will you find both parents speaking French with their children. Most times, both languages (French and English) are spoken. Sometimes, no French is spoken at all. Yet, parents who attended a French-language elementary school are considered rights holders of Section 23 of the Canadian Charter of Human Rights and Freedoms. As such, they have the right to send their children to French language schools. More recently (2006), the Canadian Federation for adult literacy in French has developed an intervention program for family literacy. The foundation for this program is based on developing multiple literacies (personal, school and community).
3. Research. Most recently a four-day workshop funded by the Social Sciences and Humanities Research Council of Canada and the Official Languages Program focused on presenting theoretical and applied research conducted in French Canada using Masny's Multiple Literacies framework in relation to the arts (music), science, mathematics, children's literature, early childhood, family literacy,

and health, in the context of the home, school, and community. The purpose of the workshop was to establish a community dialogue between Canadian university and community researchers, and government (federal, provincial, school boards) and community agencies (national and regional) on the role of Multiple Literacies in policy making, program and curriculum development in governmental and non governmental institutions. The proceedings will be published in 2008.

Conceptualising MLT 2002–

The framework is a constant becoming – indeterminate and not fixed. The MLT framework underwent transformation to one mainly influenced by Deleuze (1990, 1995) and Deleuze and Guattari (1987, 1994), in particular as multiple literacies tie into such concepts as desire, subjectivity, difference, investment, reading and deterritorialisation. Each concept will be briefly described in the next section.

Accordingly, Masny's MLT refers to literacies as texts that take on multiple meanings conveyed through words, gestures, attitudes, ways of speaking, writing, valuing and are taken up as visual, oral, written, and tactile. They constitute texts, in a broad sense (for example, a musical score, a sculpture, a mathematical equation) that fuse with religion, gender, race, culture, and power, and that produce speakers, writers, artists, communities. It is how literacies are coded. These contexts are not static. They are fluid and transform literacies that produce speakers, writers, artists, communities. The meaning of literacy is actualised according to a particular context in time and in space in which it operates. In short, through reading the world, the word and self as texts, literacies constitute ways of *becoming* with the world. The framework allows for multiple literacies to become *other than* and consider moving beyond, extending, transforming and creating different and differing perspectives of literacies (Dufresne & Masny, 2005). It is interested in the flow of experiences of life and events from which individuals are formed as literate.

In MLT, by placing the emphasis on how, the focus is on the nature of literacies as processes. Current theories on literacies examine literacies as an endpoint, a product. While MLT acknowledges that books, Internet, equations, and buildings are objects, sense emerges when relating experiences of life to reading the world, word and self as texts. Accordingly, an important aspect of MLT is focusing on how literacies intersect in *becoming*. This is what MLT produces: becoming, that is, from continuous investments in literacies literate individuals are formed.

Conceptual framework Conceptual glossary

Deleuzean epistemology and

1. **... the subject.** Most research in education and in literacy learning operates within modernity and on the assumption of the autonomous thinking subject. The grounding of language, thought and representation originates with a rational human being who is often referred to as the centered subject in a world that can be subjectively constructed. Deleuze (1987) moves away from the foundation of the subject who thinks and represents. Rather, it is the subject who is the product of events in life. As a result, such reversal about the subject forces a change in discourse structure and conceptualisation about the subject. In short, "the subject becomes an effect of events in life" (Masny, 2006, p2). The subject is not in subject position actively controlling. The mind, one mode of becoming, is a site that connects and transforms the individual, thereby becoming *other than*.
2. **... investment and events.** Investment is another term that is associated to other paradigms as well. In MLT, investment refers to connections of events stemming from experiences of life. Within Multiple Literacies Theory (MLT), events refer to "creations...selected and assessed according to their power to act and intervene rather than to be interpreted" (Colebrook, 2002a, pxliv). An event, according to Deleuze (1990), refers to life that produces lines of flight, moments that create ruptures and differences that allow creativity to take off along various planes, similar to a rhizome. It is from the continuous investment in literacies that individuals are formed as literate.
3. **... reading.** Reading is about sense. Sense is not about interpretation; sense is an event that emerges (Colebrook, 2002). Sense is virtual. It is activated when words, notes and ad icons are actualised *in situ* and in interested ways. Take an example of the

smell of coffee and it is four o'clock. The coming together of the smell of coffee and 4 o'clock disrupts (reading intensively) and brings on the thought of vacation (reading immanently). Sense expresses not what something is but its power to become.

4. ... **becoming and difference.** How do literacies work in becoming? Becoming implies indeterminacy, you might say that becoming is a product continuously producing while literacies are processes that form and shape becoming. The concept of becoming is central to MLT. Becoming is the effect of experience that connects and intersects. Transformations are continuous. What it once was is no longer. It is different. It is through transformation that becoming happens.

5. ... **desire.** Desire is an assemblage of experiences that connect and are constructed. Take for example, the smell of coffee at 4 o'clock. It could be the thought of a coffee break. It could be the thought of another vacation. For Deleuze (1987) desire is an effect of experiences in life that come together. The actual coming together, an assemblage of experiences creates a virtual experience which then could be actualised such as the coffee break or the vacation. The clock has both an actual dimension and a virtual one.

Case studies using MLT: Canada

Acquiring literacies involve different writing systems and create an environment for worldviews to collide because of the sociocultural, political and historical situatedness of learning literacies. Worldviews collide when different values and beliefs about language – about literacies – are introduced as a result of encounters with other literacies. Learning literacies does not take place in a progressive linear fashion. In a Deleuzian way, it happens in response to problems and events that occur in life experiences. Literacies are not merely about language codes to be learned. Learning literacies is about desire, about transformation, becoming *other than* through continuous investment in reading the world, the word and self as texts in multiple environments (e.g. home, school, community).

~~Methodology~~

The multiple literacies framework is the lens used to examine how competing writing systems in learning a second literacy transform children and become *other than*. Furthermore, putting a line through methodology indicates that the concept and the term are being deterritorialised and reterritorialised as a rhizomatic process that does not engage in methodological considerations in a conventional way. It resists temptations to interpret and ascribe meaning; it avoids conclusions.

The case study involves a 7-year-old girl, Cristelle, in Grade 2 attending a French language school in west Ottawa[1]. Her family lives in a mainly English-speaking middle class community with a predominance of technology companies. Cristelle's father is unilingual English while her mother is bilingual, French and English. At home, French is used mostly around school work. Most of the time, the family speaks English. Cristelle was filmed during a French period. An interview followed based on the videotaping that was done earlier. Next, videotaping took place at home during meal time or play time and during reading and writing activities. An interview followed with the family.

Vignettes

Do not look to these vignettes as data and seek to find concrete proof of transformation. Data in the more traditional way is about empirical data. Deleuze and Guattari (1994) have moved away from empiricism because it supposes a foundation grounded on human beings who seek to fix categories and themes. They call upon transcendental empiricism. It transcends experience (immanence). It deals with perceptions and the thought of experience creating connections and becoming *other than*.

The analyses presented at the end of each vignette are informed by the MLT framework 2002. Square brackets indicate that the utterances are translated from French.

Vignette 1

M   Euh, usually after school we'll start off with French, to do the homework, euh I notice that we switch, I go back and forth and like I'm trying to keep it all in one language. But eum, when I

---

[1] This study was funded through a grant from the Social Sciences and Humanities Research Council of Canada (SSHRC) and the Official Languages Dissemination Program.

	go pick her up at the daycare she doesn't want to speak French anymore. So I try and continue on in French. So right after school, going into homework exercise. (…) Eum, I when I remember I try to speak to her in French, if she answers me in English, like today we were at the grocery store, I just kept talking her in French, she'll speak to me English, sometimes 'cause I've noticed she'll say a sentence like: «aujourd'hui [today] we were at the», like she writes it all up, so she does half and half, and I want her to, like she'd start a sentence.
Cr	Who cares?
M	And she switches to English. I'll say: «continue en français [continue in French].» 'Cause I don't want her to give up. I want her to to continue so, if if I remember, I do, mostly right after school [***] morning [***].
R	… would you say for Cristelle, when it comes to both languages, she uses more of one than the other.
M	Ya, definitely English.
	(Home 13 March 06)

In the preceeding vignette, Cristelle's comment is somewhat revealing. Is it an instance of wanting to unhinge the un/familiar, or perhaps deterritorialise what has been territorialised? Mother's comments reveal tensions between wanting to have a sound base in French and yet recognising that one language, English, is used more often. From these language and literacy events in a family/community context, the parents and Cristelle are formed as literate and in this process transformed and becoming *other than*.

Vignette 2

Since this study focuses on perceptions of writing systems, Cristelle shares her views regarding writing.

R	[what do you think about your story?]
Cr	[that it's a bit funny, and the drawing is funny]
R	[it's your drawing that's funny. Yes, but your story, how do you find it?]
Cr	[not so funny, because there aren't many things that are funny]

R	[what would need to be done for your story to be funny?]
Cr	[funny drawings]
R	[you would want funny drawings all over?]
Cr	[yes!! (with great glee)]
R	[but then there isn't any writing. Is that what you want?]
Cr	[yes]
R	[you don't want to write?]
Cr	[I don't want to write]
	(Class French activity 12 December 05)

What reading of self is taking place? How is writing and drawing regulated in the classroom? It would seem that deterritorialisation of drawing has been reterritorialised as writing. The boundaries for Cristelle are no longer blurred.

Vignette 3

The reading of self seems to resonate with the perceptions that her mother has regarding Cristelle's writing.
[laugh]

P	«Why does salad exist?»
Cr	«Why does salad exist?»
M	[why does salad exist?]
Cr	[Mama is a birdhead.]
M	[Mother is a birdhead. It was for interrogative sentences and she wrote, why salad exists and then when I corrected, she didn't like it. She said, you want me to redo my homework. Because she is frustrated. I am ready to help her.]
R	[Is she frustrated because she has errors or?]
M	[She is frustrated, she wants to do the sentence in French and she uses oral English borrowings to do it.]
M	So, I would say, I put you know: « d'où vient la salade »[where does salad come from], and she goes: «no, you have to write où», où avec le 'u' avec. [Then I say it doesn't work that way. So then gets frustrated]
M	J'ai dit : « non ça fonctionne pas comme ça »[I said it doesn't work that way], so then she gets frustrated. I know it's it's partially me, it's partially her, but I find that she gives up really

easily when when she does writing exercises. [And at the moment it doesn't really interest her.]
(Home 13 March 06)

Are events and experiences resisting the normative flow and colliding? Are such events wanting to go beyond constituted forms? Thinking is only thinking when it is creative. "Life's power is best expressed not in the normative but in the perverse, singular and aberrant" (Colebrook, 2006, p20). Is it from these events that Cristelle becomes and multiple literacies are the processes through which becoming happens?

Vignette 4

When an individual learns to read/write, the boundaries between what is acceptable and appropriate seem blurred. In the following vignette, Cristelle learns to write. Certain aspects of learning to read/write are connected with previous learning experiences. Other aspects are connected with associations that do not necessarily relate to the writing system or the conventional norm.

R   [last time you had a discussion with Danielle the research assistant and you said you like funny things. What do you mean?]
Cr   [I like to write like a see a big space]
R   [would you show me how you wrote this?] video clip

[h	m	C
e	i	a
l	s	l
l	t	l
o	e	o
	r	u]

Cr   [I had one word here and then another there and I continued.]
R   [what were you trying to say]
Cr   [hello, my name is Callou]
R   [and you chose to do it in this way]
Cr   [because I told Anne, her classmate, to look and Anne said, Cristelle, this not the way to write.]
R   [and you chose to write this way.]
Cr   [yes and then after I erased it.]

R [why did you want to write this way?]
Cr [because I like to be funny.]
R [what made you change your mind like this and after you erased]
Cr [because Mrs Soneau (the teacher) was coming over to see me.]
R [when she comes to see you, what do you do?]
Cr [she comes to correct]
R [she comes to correct and ...]
Cr [she looks at my paper]
R [and what should you be doing?]
Cr [write a story, I mean you need to put the words together, stuck together]
R [and so this is what you have to do when she comes. And you don't like to do that. What do you like to do?]
Cr [the same thing as that (pointing to the video clip)]
R [do you often do stories like this?]
Cr [no].
(Class – French activity 12 December 05)

Is this also an instance of reading the world, word and self, in terms of flow of experiences? What more could Cristelle do given an opportunity? What creativity could unfold? Deleuze states that to create is to resist (1994, p110). Cristelle is creating through the responses of resistance (directionality in writing). Can such events become lines of flight? Colebrook (2002, pxliv) says that events, according to Deleuze, "are seen as creations that need to be selected and assessed according to their power to act and intervene". As worldviews collide, it is out of multiple literacies that the learner is effected, that some literacy creations/experiences are foregrounded while others are eclipsed.

Where to ...?

There are several questions with regard to literacy practices that permeate the research in Canada and Australia. In the Canadian study which focuses on how writing systems operate, the mother has her views and so does Cristelle and these views seem to be on a collision track. The mother's worldviews in relation to writing could be aligned with normativity. The thought of colliding with Cristelle's worldviews creates openings or the 'inbetweenness' that the mother speaks of (that is, the necessity of learning one language first well, and then the realisation that while French is tremendously important, much of what goes on in the house takes place in English). On the other hand, the resistance from Cristelle to writing is apparent. Cristelle's vignettes provide the thought of worldviews colliding with normativity. These are experiences that transform and becoming other in untimely and unpredictable ways. Writing needs to be fun and amusing, and to mesh with her worldviews. While these experiences are connecting with each other, at times, there is resistance. Cristelle's resistance is also about creating (hello mister Callou) (for more on resistance, see Dufresne, 2006).

In the Australian case study, like Cristelle, the students do not seem interested in literacy practices, or at least not school-based ones. Can boredom be a form of resistance, boredom as a response to normativity? Worldviews, that of the students, are colliding with the worldview related to school-based literacy. The video became many tools – some connected to making videos about their understanding of literacy, the others took them to an untimely place; tapes of dancing, making shapes with their bodies and using the camera to imitate rhythmic bursts. Was this an instance of seeking stability in their world? Would literacy practices legitimated in school constitute destabilisation? Was this in response to a problem in the making? They connected these sessions with their reading of the world and self. They became texts through the body shapes and rhythm. From investment in these forms of literacy, they are formed and transformed.
In both case studies, there are links to creativity. Thinking is only thinking when it is creative and going beyond already constituted forms. How do such investments create possibilities for becoming since investment in languages and literacies is an investment in difference, in becoming *other than*? Is it the thought of the blurred boundaries that are challenging views on acquiring multiple languages and multiple literacies?

The multiple literacies theory retained in this article becomes a way to examine how out of complexity and multiplicity, in untimely ways, differences are continuously transforming in becoming *other than*. In the words of Deleuze and Guattari (1994, p169): "We are not in the world. We become with the world". In the context of this article, we become with reading the world, the word and self – multiple literacies.

References

Barton D, Hamilton M, Ivanič R (Eds) (2002). *Situated Literacies*. London: Routledge.

Baynham M (2002).Taking the social turn: The New Literacy Studies and SLA. *Ways of Knowing Journal*, 2: 43–68.

Canadian Council of Ministers of Education (2003). Pan-Canadian French as a First Language Project: La trousse de francisation [French actualization kit for teachers from Kindergarten to Grade 2]. Toronto www.cmec.ca/else/francisation/cd-rom/inc/info/litteraties.htm

Canadian Federation for Adult Literacy in French (2006). *Foundations for the intervention in Family literacy: the case for developing multiple literacies*. Ottawa http://72.14.205.104/search?q=cache:q4UUIeGEzPAJ:cnpf.ca/docume nts/margo_fauchon_presentation.pdf+FCAF+litt%C3%A9raties&hl=e n&ct=clnk&cd=12.

Cole D R (2007). Cam-Capture: An Eye on Teaching and Learning. In J Sigafoos and V Green (Eds), *Technology & Teaching: A Casebook for Educators*, (pp55–68). New York: Nova Science Publishers, Inc.

Colebrook C (2002). *Deleuze*. New York: Routledge.

Colebrook C (2006). *Deleuze: A Guide for the Perplexed*. London: Continuum.

Cope B, Kalantzis M (2000). *Multiliteracies: Literacy learning and the design of social futures*. South Yarra: Macmillan Publishers.

Cope B, Kalantzis M (1995). *Productive Diversity: Organisational Life in the Age of Civic Pluralism and Total Globalisation*. Sydney: Harper Collins.

Deleuze G (1990). *The Logic of Sense*. (M Lister, Trans. with C Stivale). New York: Columbia University Press.

Deleuze G (1995). *Negotiations 1972–1990* (M Joughin, Trans.). New York: Columbia University Press.

Deleuze G, Guattari F (1987). *A Thousand Plateaus: Capitalism & Schizophrenia Part II* (B Massumi, Trans.). London: Athlone Press.

Deleuze G, Guattari F (1994). *What is philosophy?* (H Tomlinson & G Burchell, Trans.). New York: Columbia University Press.

Doecke B, McClenaghan D (2004). Reconceptualising experience – growth pedagogy and youth culture. In W Sawyer & E Gold (Eds), *Reviewing English in the 21st century,* (pp51–60). Sydney: Phoenix Education.

Dufresne D (2006). Exploring the processes in becoming biliterate. *International Journal of Learning,* 12(8): 347–354.

Dufresne T & Masny D (2005). Different and differing views on conceptualizing writing system research and education. In V Cook et B Bassetti (Eds), *Second Language Writing Systems.* Clevedon, Buffalo: Multilingual Matters.

Fiumara G C (2001). *The mind's affective life; a psychoanalytic and philosophical inquiry.* Hove: Brunner-Routledge.

Freire P, Macedo D (1987). *Literacy.* Westport, Conn: Bergin &Garvey.

Gee J P (1996). *Social linguistics and literacies: ideology in discourses,* 2nd Edn. London: Taylor & Francis.

Graham L (2007). Done in by discourse ... or the problem/s with labelling. In M Keefe & S Carrington (Eds), *Schools and Diversity,* 2nd Edition, (pp46–65). Frenchs Forest, NSW: Pearson Education Australia.

Goodchild P (1996). *Deleuze and Guattari: An Introduction to the Politics of Desire.* London: Sage Publications.

Heath S B (1983). *Ways with words: language, life, and work in communities and classrooms.* Cambridge, New York: Cambridge University Press.

Kim J (2003). Challenges to NLS – Response to "What's 'new' in New Literacy Studies" [Electronic version]. *Current Issues in Comparative Education,* 5. www.tc.columbia.edu/cice/articles/jk152.htm

Kress G, van Leuwen T (2001). *Multimodal Discourse: The Modes and Meia of Contemporary Communication.* London: Hodder Arnold Publication.

Masny D, Ghahremani-Ghajar S S (1999). Weaving multiple literacies: Somali children and their teachers in the context of school culture. *Language, Culture and Curriculum,* 12(1): 72–93.

Masny D (2001). Pour une pédagogie axée sur les littératies [Toward a pedagogy based on literacies]. In D Masny (ed), *La culture de l'écrit : les défis à l'école et au foyer,* (pp15–26). Montréal: les éditions Logiques.

Masny D (2005). Multiple literacies: An alternative OR beyond Friere. In J Anderson, T Rogers, M Kendrick & S Smythe (eds), *Portraits of literacy across families, communities, and schools: Intersections and tensions* (p71–84). Mahwah, NJ: Lawrence Erlbaum Associates.

Masny D (2006). Learning and Creative processes: a Poststructural Perspective on Language and Multiple Literacies. *International Journal of Learning,* 12(5): 147–155.

Ministry of Education (Alberta). (1999a). *Kindergarten French First Language programme* www.education.gov.ab.ca/french/maternelle/francophone/fr_mat.pdf

Ministry of Education (Alberta). (1999b). *Kindergarten immersion programme.* Edmonton http://ednet.edc.gov.ab.ca/french/Maternelle/immersion/intro.pdf

Ministry of Education (Alberta) (2001) *Affirming Francophone Education: Foundations and Direction.* Edmonton. www.education.gov.ab.ca/french/m_12/franco/affirmer/CadreENG.pdf

Ministry of Education (Manitoba) (2003). *Immersion Kindergarten Social Sciences curriculum.* Manitoba. www.edu.gov.mb.ca/frpub/ped/sh/dmo-imm_1re/introduction.pdf

New London Group (1996). A Pedagogy of Multiliteracies: Designing Social Futures. *Harvard Educational Review,* 66(1): 60–92.

Parisi L (2004). *Abstract Sex: Philosophy, Bio-technology and the mutations of desire.* London: Continuum Books.

Street B (1984). *Literacy in theory and practice.* Cambridge: Cambridge University Press.

Street B (2003). What's new in the New Literacy Studies? Critical approaches to literacy in theory and practice. *Current Issues in Comparative Education,* 5(2): 77–91. www.tc.columbia.edu/cice/Archives/5.2/52street.pdf

Unsworth L (2001). *Teaching multiliteracies across the curriculum: Changing contexts of text and image in classroom practice.* Buckingham: Open University Press.

12
icurricula, ipedagogies and outmoded ideologies: literacy teaching and learning in the digital era

Jackie Marsh
University of Sheffield, UK

In this paper, I draw on a number of research projects conducted in England in a consideration of the possibilities for and challenges to the development of appropriate literacy curricula and pedagogy in the digital era. Following intensive interest over the last decade in the changing nature of literacy due to technological advances, there are national and local initiatives to transform the literacy curricula offered by early years settings and primary schools in order to respond appropriately to the contemporary communicative landscape. These developments have led to a number of innovative and exciting projects that have impacted upon children's motivation, engagement and attainment, in addition to re-energising a generation of teachers who have experienced unprecedented levels of change in educational policy. However, such developments are not without challenges and this paper, in addition to highlighting key achievements, outlines the barriers faced by early years educators and teachers as they strive to push forward the digital literacy agenda in the face of neoliberal educational reform, recurrent moral panics and the increasingly divergent movement of the tectonic plates of home and school. I consider the ways in which the recent developments in England resonate (or not) with similar patterns of curricula and pedagogical change in an international context.

Changing landscapes of communication

In 2003, Gunther Kress outlined the way in which the subject English was being transformed in a new media age due to two shifts: one in the primary mode of communication (from word to image) and the other a shift in dominant media (from page to screen). He stressed that the transformations precipitated by these moves would be profound:

> It is already clear that the effects of the two changes taken together will have the widest imaginable political, economic, social, cultural, conceptual/cognitive and epistemological consequences. (Kress, 2003, p1)

The implications of this paradigmatic shift have been widely discussed (Carrington, 2005; Luke and Luke, 2001: Lankshear and Knobel, 2006; Merchant, 2007a) and it is clear that we have reached a point at which traditional approaches to the teaching and learning of literacy need to be radically revised if pupils are to develop the skills, knowledge and understanding necessary for full engagement in the digital world. However, even when policies have been developed that give teachers opportunities to broaden literacy curricula and pedagogy, often practice remains locked into traditional, print-based models. The reasons for this are complex and in this paper I wish to examine current practice in early years settings and primary schools in England in order to examine in greater depth some of the barriers to change.

Part of the difficulty lies in the fact that distinctions are still being made between 'traditional' literacy, focused on print on paper and the alphabetical principle, and 'new literacies', which incorporate a range of modes and include a variety of media. Whilst I will draw on the distinction myself within this paper in order to analyse the changes currently taking place, a more fruitful way forward would be to focus instead on the notion of communication (Street, 1998) and refer to communicative texts, practices and events as they are instantiated across modes and media. In this conceptual framework 'literacy' would signify engagement with lettered representation (Kress, 2003) on both paper, screen and the wider environment and the interaction between literacy and other modes such as sound, image and gesture would be accepted as normal practice. The production and analysis of multimodal, multimedia texts would be embedded within curricula frameworks and emphasis placed on developing learners' skills, understanding and knowledge with regard to communication across all modes and media. In this model, there would be little need then to maintain the distinction between 'traditional' and 'new' literacies. Whether or not this took place within a subject titled 'English' is a moot point, but we do need to challenge the current policy fixation with literacy as the defining term for this subject, a 'literacy fetishism' (Green, 2006, p17) driven by neoliberal concerns, which means that those engaged in literacy education constantly struggle with terminology in order to make this meaningful in a digital era. It may seem somewhat contradictory, therefore, to use phrases such as 'new literacies' or 'digital literacy' in this paper, but as they currently signal changing epistemological and ontological engagements with literacy as a social practice (Lankshear and Knobel, 2006) and challenge an over-emphasis on print on paper, their use will be maintained.

In England, national policy has shifted to the point that there is now acknowledgement that something has to change due to developments with regard to digital literacy. The Qualifications and Curriculum Authority (QCA) undertook a consultation in 2004/5, 'English 21', which resulted in the publication of the report *Taking English Forward* (QCA, 2005). The introduction to the report states that developments need to take place in order to respond to social and technological progress:

> The English 21 responses show that there are challenges for the future, to extend the current curriculum and to move ahead. Changes in society and technology are altering the nature of speaking, listening, reading and writing. The subject English needs to develop in the light of these changes. (QCA, 2005, p3)

In 2006, the Primary National Strategy was revised and the literacy framework introduced work on multimodality and outlined the need for children to respond to and create texts on screen (DfES, 2006). This was a significant development in the light of previous primary and early years curricula frameworks that had ignored the impact of media on subject English (Marsh, 2004). Teachers, literacy consultants and advisers have been responding to these invitations for change in innovative ways over the last few years and in this paper, I will highlight some of this work and identify the key achievements before moving on to analyse the challenges faced in taking forward this agenda.

In this paper, I draw from three projects that have all involved teachers working in collaborative networks. The first of the projects, 'Digital Beginnings' involved nine early years settings in England undertaking projects in which they introduced aspects of popular culture, media and new technologies into the curriculum (Marsh et al., 2005). The second project (Marsh, 2007), 'Blogging as a critical literacy practice' was undertaken in one primary school in the north of England as part of a United Kingdom Literacy Association (UKLA)-funded two-year research project on critical literacies, which involved a network of teachers across the UK. The third project I will discuss was conceived and led by the British Film Institute and involved teachers and advisers across more than 50 Local Authorities (LAs) in England being trained in the development of moving image media education. The final evaluation report for this two-year project, focusing on the work of 35 LAs, is currently being completed (Marsh and Bearne, in press), but the emergent findings are drawn upon in this paper in order to inform the analysis of the key successes and challenges educators face in attempting to respond to the changes demanded by the needs of the digital age. Due to space limitations, I will not outline the methodologies used across all of the projects, but will indicate that all of them involved teachers who were engaged in action research projects in which they developed new initiatives that were then evaluated using a range of methods, including observations of and interviews with children, analysis of children's work and assessments using national frameworks. This is a model that is well-established as a means of developing literacy curricula and pedagogies that challenge traditional approaches (Nixon and Comber, 2005; PNS/UKLA, 2004).

Key achievements

In all of the projects featured in this paper, there have been a number of highly favourable outcomes in terms of pupil engagement and achievement. The focus on integrating media and new technologies into the literacy curriculum has had a discernible impact. For example, in the 'Digital Beginnings' project (Marsh et al., 2005), nine early years settings introduced aspects of popular culture, media and new technologies into the communication, language and literacy curriculum. Activities included making electronic and digital books, watching and analysing moving image stories and creating presentations using electronic software. One of the aims of the study was to examine the impact of these action research projects on the motivation and engagement of children in curriculum activities related to communication, language and literacy. In order to identify this, practitioners undertook three observations of 14 children prior to the project and three observations of the same children during the project, using *The Leuven Involvement Scale for Young Children* (Laevers, 1994). Outcomes indicated that children's levels of engagement in activities were higher when the curriculum incorporated their interests in popular culture, media and new technologies (Marsh et al., 2005).

In addition to motivation, levels of attainment in writing rose in those LAs that collated quantitative data throughout the BFI project (Marsh and Bearne, in press). This relationship between the development of digital literacy practices and the impact on attainment, in relation to print-based practices, is a pattern established in previous studies (PNS/UKLA, 2004). What is now needed is a fundamental change to the assessment of literacy so that it moves beyond an emphasis on the word and on the printed page. Whilst these analyses of the impact of engagement in digital literacy practices on children's motivation and engagement are necessary for convincing policy-makers and others of the need to broaden their conceptualisations of literacy, they are in danger of perpetuating the privileging of print-based practices and maintaining the emphasis on assessing outmoded forms of knowledge. There is a need to assess the impact of these curricula and pedagogical changes on a broader range of skills, understanding and knowledge appropriate for the demands of the digital age and work in this area, based in primary classroom, is beginning to emerge (Bearne et al., 2007; Walsh et al., 2006). Table 12.1 outlines some of those competences/outcomes which were developed across the various projects, although the table is not intended to offer an exhaustive list.

There was a range of other successful outcomes in the projects which I do not have space to document here, including enhanced teacher motivation and increased subject knowledge of teachers. Nevertheless, whilst the projects were successful in moving forward the agenda with regard to the teaching and learning of literacy in a digital age, a number of barriers were faced, which I move on to analyse in the next section.

Key competencies	Examples from projects
Understanding of the affordances of various modes and the ability to choose appropriate modes for specific purposes	Children produced a wide range of multimodal texts that required understanding of the affordances of modes and how modes could work best together to achieve goals. These included: texts that were solely written or oral or consisting of only still images or moving images; texts combining one or more of these modes; animated films; live action films; podcasts; animated powerpoint presentations; photostories.
Understanding of various media and the ability to choose appropriately for specific purposes	Children used a wide range of media in the production of texts and made critical judgements about which media to use.
Skills in the various modes that enabled them to decode, understand and interpret, engage with and respond to and create and shape texts	Children developed a wide range of skills including: knowledge of the alphabetic principle and abilities in reading and writing print; ability to read both still and moving images; understanding of the features of various genres; understanding of the principles of transduction in the production of multimodal texts; ability to navigate texts across media, follow hyperlinks, read radially etc.
Ability to analyse critically a range of texts and make judgements about value, purpose, audience, ideologies	In the development of multimodal texts, children were reviewing a wide range of online and offline texts in order to inform their work. They also regularly reviewed their own and peer's work.
Ability to relate texts to their social, cultural, historical contexts and literary traditions	Children were able to relate multimodal texts to their social, cultural and historical contexts and were adept at recognising intertextuality.
Ability to select and use appropriately other texts for use in the design process	In the blogging project, children produced texts that remixed media content. Children made animated and live action films, and powerpoint presentations, that incorporated music.
Ability to collaborate in text production, analysis and response	Children were successful in collaborating both with known and unknown others in the production and analysis of texts. Social networking software, for example, enabled them to comment on others' work and develop an understanding of the value of networks.

Table 12.1: Skills, knowledge and understanding developed across the projects

Barriers

There has been extensive work that has reviewed the lack of integration of ICT across the curriculum, an issue which is related but has different concerns to that of the development of new literacies. Nevertheless, this literature can be drawn upon in a review of the lack of curricula and pedagogical progress in relation to new literacies. As Hennessey, Ruthven and Brindley (2005) suggest, in any systematic study of schools' use of ICT in England, "appropriate and effective classroom use of ICT is found to be rare" (2005, p162). There are numerous reasons for this. Ertmer (1999) identifies first- and second-order barriers to more extensive use of ICT in classrooms. First-order barriers are those external to teachers and include factors such as lack of access to resources and training. Second-order barriers are internal and include teacher beliefs and attitudes, some of which may prevent innovative developments from taking place. In a recent review of research in this area, Foon Hew and Brush (2007) reiterate Ertmer's conceptualisation of first-and second-order strategies and suggest that the first-order barriers to integration of technology into teaching are: resources; institution; subject culture; and assessment. Second-order barriers were found to be: attitudes and beliefs; knowledge and skills. Whilst this is helpful in suggesting that the obstructions to progress work at both structural and agentic levels, the factoring together of quite disparate elements in the 'first-order' category means that the roots of the issues are not identified and as a result some barriers are not considered at all. Instead of presenting an external/internal dichotomy, I propose that the barriers to curriculum and pedagogical change in relation to digital literacy are examined in terms of their social and cultural, historical, economic and political roots. This enables a review of structural and agentic issues across key areas and emphasises the dynamic between factors that are internal and external to educators themselves.

Social and cultural

The social and cultural milieu in which educators operate has a significant impact on their work. As technological developments intensify the pace of change in society at large, there is a corresponding proliferation of moral panics in relation to children's use of these technologies. In the UK last year, a letter was sent to a national broadsheet, signed by over 100 early years specialists, academics and practitioners, which outlined a series of concerns about contemporary childhoods. The letter included the following paragraph:

> Since children's brains are still developing, they cannot adjust – as full-grown adults can – to the effects of ever more rapid technological and cultural change. They still need what developing human beings have always needed, including real food (as opposed to processed 'junk'), real play (as opposed to sedentary, screen-based entertainment), first-hand experience of the world they live in and regular interaction with the real-life significant adults in their lives (Abbs et al, 2006).

This is misleading on a number of accounts. There is a false juxtaposition here that sets up engagement with technologies and 'real' play as oppositional. In addition, it should be noted that screen-based entertainment is not exclusively sedentary (Marsh et al., 2005). Further, in March 2006, David Willets, the Conservative Shadow Education Secretary, set up a formal inquiry into 'Lost Childhoods' in England, following a UNICEF (2006) report that indicated that the UK ranked bottom in a well-being assessment of children in 21 industrialised countries. Rather than questioning the methodology utilised in the UNICEF study, this knee-jerk reaction typified a range of responses to the current climate, which included the emergence of a book titled *Toxic Childhood* (Palmer, 2006).

These reactions were symptomatic of the frequent, negative reactions some adults express towards changing childhoods. There is no doubt that contemporary childhoods are being transformed, with social and cultural changes taking place that have significant implications for the teaching and learning of literacy. I will review only a few here in order to highlight the barriers identified by teachers in the studies focused upon in this paper. The first of these is the way in which public spaces are changing for children and young people. Many children and young people are involved in social networking sites such as *Bebo* and *MySpace* (Dowdall, in press) and this is potentially confusing and alienating for teachers who grew up with very different experiences of engagement with known and unknown audiences. Teachers are anxious about safety aspects of the Internet (Demos, 2007) and yet in a recent US study conducted by the National School Boards Association (NBSA, 2007), only 0.08 per cent of young people reported meeting people they had met over the Internet without their parents' permission. This is not to minimise the concerns expressed by teachers, but suggests that instead of becoming over-protective in online spaces, we need to engage with young learners as they develop further their critical capacities and begin to make judgements about, for example, which aspects of their identities they share with which audience(s) at any one time. In addition, as Web 2.0 dissolves further the boundaries between production and consumption and celebrates a 'mash-up' or 'remix' culture (Lankshear and Knobel, 2006) in which 'produsage' (Bruns, 2006) abounds, anxieties around copyright and the line between collaboration and collusion proliferate. Peter Winter, the teacher involved in the blogging project, for example, had a number of concerns about this as the children began to mine the web for material to place on their blogs, but instead of becoming paralysed by fears surrounding this issue, he encouraged the children to consider the nature of their sources and acknowledge them where appropriate, or link directly to their web source. There are no simple solutions to an area that confounds many copyright lawyers and as this field develops, teachers need to be part of the dialogue about the nature of intellectual property in the digital age.

A further social and cultural barrier to change identified by teachers in the studies focused upon here was the presence of concerns about a digital divide. Teachers expressed worries that increasing the use of technologies in classrooms might exacerbate the differential expertise of children due to their access to and use of hardware and software outside of school. However, at times teachers assumed that all working-class children would have more limited access to technology than middle-class children. Whilst there are some social class differences in children's access to and use of technologies outside of school (Livingstone and Bovill, 1999; Marsh et al., 2005), there are also indications that socio-economic status does not relate simply to access and use (Selwyn and Facer, 2007; Valentine, Marsh and Pattie, 2005). In the future, the digital divide might focus more squarely on the differences between those who have an understanding of how technologies and related resources (such as social networking sites) can enable them to achieve their aims than those who do not (Lankshear and Knobel, 2006).

Finally, in relation to the social and cultural dimension, an additional challenge to be faced, and one which featured in all of the studies, is the growing divide between home and school literacy practices. Butler and Robson (2001), in an analysis of the way in which social class operates in neighbourhood change in London, described different social class groups as tectonic in nature in the way in which the various groups they studied rarely integrated in social and cultural institutions. They suggested that, "Social groups or 'plates' overlap or run parallel to one another without much in the way of integrated experience" (Butler and Robson, 2001, p2157). I think that this metaphor can be meaningfully applied to the way in which school and home contexts operate in the digital age. Whilst not ignoring the way in which children and young people transfer practices and knowledge across the various spaces they inhabit (Bulfin and North, 2007), the tectonic plates of home and school appear to be moving in very different directions in relation to digital literacy practices. This can be characterised across numerous digital literacy practices, but here I will focus on one in order to illustrate the extent of the difficulties faced by educators, that is the use of social networking sites, one example of which is online virtual worlds. Virtual worlds have become increasingly popular with primary-aged children over the last two years and sites that are frequently mentioned by children and parents include *Club Penguin*, *Webkinz*, *Neopets* and *Barbie Girls*. The worlds differ in terms of their affordances, but sites such as *Club Penguin* and *Barbie Girls* enable children to create and dress-up an avatar, decorate their avatar's home, buy and look after pets and play games in order to earn money to purchase items for their avatars and homes. Both of these virtual worlds also enable interactive chat that is tightly controlled and monitored in order to allay parental concerns regarding internet safety. This seems to be a successful strategy, as there are numerous sites across the web in which parents state that they feel comfortable with the safety measures in place, as this typical post attests:

> i let my kids use club penguin and i think it is perfectly safe
>
> i read through all the parents bit and privacy and safety and it is completly safe
>
> it also teaches your kids the rules of chatting online and i would reccomend it to every one else
>
> Posted by: sophie 20 February 2007 at 01:22 PM[1]

This parent's desire for her children to learn the practices associated with social networking is one shared by many others. In a recent report, the National School Boards Association (NSBA, 2007) in the USA surveyed 1039 parents and stated that the majority of parents held positive views regarding the educational potential of social networking sites. Similarly, in the 'Digital Beginnings' study, parental attitudes demonstrated positive attitudes towards the role of new technologies in their children's lives (Marsh et al., 2005).

Although these virtual worlds are ostensibly aimed at 8–14 year-olds, inevitably there are reports of five-and six-year-olds using them. These sites offer children opportunities for engaging in online social networking with others and the literacy skills, knowledge and understanding they can foster include:

- reading skills and strategies including: word recognition (e.g. the vocabulary choices in 'safe chat' mode; instructions; in-world environmental text), comprehension, scanning text in order to retrieve appropriate information, familiarity with how different texts are structured and organised, understanding of authors' viewpoint, purposes and overall effect of the text on the reader;
- writing skills and strategies including: spelling, punctuation, syntax, writing using and adapting a range of forms appropriate for purpose and audience, using language for particular effect;
- writing for known and unknown audiences;
- using text to negotiate, collaborate and evaluate.

---

[1] Posted on 'Business Week' blog at:
http://www.businessweek.com/careers/workingparents/blog/archives/2006/09/while_moms_away.html

In addition, children develop skills across the visual, gestural and aural modes. There are aspects of these sites that deserve further investigation, such as the restrictive representations of femininity in *Barbie Girls* and the promotion of commodity purchasing as a key activity in both *Barbie Girl* and *Club Penguin*. In addition, just as forms of capital (Bourdieu, 1990) operate in virtual worlds inhabited by adults, such as *Second Life*, the child-orientated worlds are also shaped by the flows of social, economic and cultural capital. Nevertheless, it is clear that these sites are becoming increasingly popular with the 5–11-year-old age group and will no doubt become even more pervasive in the years ahead.

However, despite the burgeoning popularity of virtual worlds and other Web 2.0 sites for this age group, primary schools in general have yet to recognise their potential. Indeed, firewalls implemented by many LAs prevent teachers from exploring these worlds and other social networking sites in school. In the blogging project, for example, the children were originally able to link to their school-made films posted on YouTube but then the LA blocked this site from the authority network and another host had to be found. Even in cases in which LAs have enabled schools to be more adventurous, there is no guarantee that these sites will be used in schools in ways that replicate home uses. Merchant (2007b), for example, reports on a network of primary schools in England that created a virtual world for children using Active Worlds, but then recounts how traditional practices were embedded within the design of the worlds and the use made of them by teachers. This is a phenomenon replicated across most of children's out-of-school digital literacy practices. In the 'Digital Beginnings' project (Marsh et al., 2005), it was found that the digital literacy experiences young children had in homes and early years settings were very different in nature. Parents of 1852 children aged zero to six were surveyed about children's use of media and new technologies in the home, in addition to 524 practitioners in 104 early years settings the children attended, who were asked to report on the use of media and new technologies in the settings. The differences in uses of some of the 'newer' technologies might be explained by the lapse in time that often occurs between a new technology emerging and its adoption in schools, but we found a worrying disparity in the use of 'old' technologies. For example, 53 per cent of the children had access to a computer at home in the week prior to the survey, but only 46 per cent of practitioners reported having planned the use of computers in the settings in the same week – and as the survey included practitioners based at the same early years settings, the percentage of settings using computers was, consequently, much lower than that. Therefore, as digital literacy practices become more ubiquitous in the lives of young children, many schools and early years settings in England offer an increasingly out-moded educational experience.

In this section, I have reviewed a number of the social and cultural changes taking place that constitute barriers to further development of a literacy curriculum that reflects changes in digital practices in the world external to schools. In the next section, I will move on to analyse the historical factors that might preclude curricula and pedagogical development.

Historical

There are a number of historically-constituted barriers to change, not least the way in which educational institutions operate on 19th- and 20th-century models in terms of subject divisions. In relation to the development of the subject of English, we are in a period characterised by immense change and uncertainty (Kress, 2003; 2006). There are numerous phrases used which relate to the more extensive engagement with multimodal multimedia texts which is occurring, such as 'media literacy' (Ofcom, 2006), 'digital literacy' (Merchant, 2007a), 'new literacies' (Lankshear and Knobel, 2006), 'multimodal literacy', 'visual literacy' and 'information literacy', to name but a few. Many of these developments share common features and foci, with an emphasis on the analysis and production of multimodal texts across a range of media. One might argue that this proliferation of literacies presents few problems as they all point to slightly different issues and have distinct histories, but in reality this multiplicity is leading to theoretical and conceptual confusions in addition to contributing to political nervousness regarding further developments. We appear to be at a key juncture in curriculum development and need to consider the implications for the subject English (Green, 2006; Kress, 2006). A focus on the development of the subject so that it encompasses the analysis and production of multimodal, multimedia texts and involves integration of activities that currently occur in areas of the curriculum such as media studies, ICT or 'information literacy' is timely. Whether or not this subject continues to be titled 'English' or 'Communication, language and literacy' or even 'Communication Studies' appears at the moment to be the least of the challenges faced, given the lack of common understanding about what the subject should look like in theory and practice. In the face of this turmoil, the work of Kress (2006) has been significant to furthering understanding of how the subject should be shaped in the 21st century and he emphasises the need for it to focus, above all else, on meaning:

> In a society dominated by the demands of the market, by consumption therefore, by its constant and insistent demands for choice – no matter how spurious that choice may be – there is an absolute demand that the curriculum overall should include a subject that has *meaning* as its central question, has as its central concern principles for making choices (Kress, 2006, p3).

A further historical difficulty is a lack of a tradition of research and development in relation to new literacies, particular within early years and primary literacy learning and teaching. Historically, research in the area of early literacy development has focused on the acquisition of the alphabetic principle and this has led to a lack of knowledge about the stages of learning in relation to other modes. In the BFI project, for example, there was evidence of repetition of work on moving image texts across different age groups and limited understanding in relation to what progression in terms of analysis of multimodal texts might mean. Teachers expressed anxieties about the lack of a framework for supporting continuity and progression in this area. Whilst there are some models of progression in relation to media texts or moving image texts (see, for example, BFI/DfES, 2003), these need to be integrated into the literacy curriculum in order for schools to make substantial progress. This is not to suggest that models developed should be linear or lead to narrow conceptualisations of what children are able to do at any given age, but there is a need to develop research projects that enable teachers to understand continuity and progression in relation to the analysis and production of multimodal texts.

There are other ways in which the present is informed by the past and in turns shapes future developments in teaching and learning in this area. Bourdieu's concept of habitus (Bourdieu, 1990) can be drawn upon in order to understand why teachers' own attitudes, beliefs and practices can stand in the way of curricula and pedagogical change (Marsh, 2006). In the projects reported on in this paper, teachers' subject knowledge was limited in key areas and this in turn framed their improvisational capacities in relation to habitus. In addition to individual habitus, a number of researchers have utilised the concept of institutional habitus in an exploration of student choice of higher education institute (Reay, David and Ball, 2001). Reay and colleagues define institutional habitus as "the impact of a cultural group or social class on an individual's behaviour as it is mediated through an organisation" (Reay, David and Ball, 2001, np). In those LAs that effected the most productive changes in curricula and pedagogy in the BFI project, LA advisers focused on working at an institutional level with schools in order to address barriers to change. In some cases, this involved more than a focus on curricula and pedagogy, it also included work on schools' relationships with their wider communities. As Thomas (2002) notes, "institutional habitus should be understood as more than the culture of the educational institution; it refers to relational issues and priorities, which are deeply embedded, and subconsciously informing practice" (p431). However, schools are constrained not only by their institutional histories, but also by financial considerations. In the next section, I move from an analysis of historical barriers to curricula and pedagogical change to focus on economic restrictions.

Economic

Across all of the studies, teachers and advisers identified a lack of resources as a key limiting factor in their abilities to move the digital literacy agenda forward. For example, in the BFI project, teachers were unable to access a wide range of short films that could be utilised within the constraints of timetabling. This sometimes led to an over-emphasis on the use of extracts from moving image texts. Whilst the children's literature publishing industry appears to be growing from strength to strength in terms of book sales, the production of short films for young children is very limited and, with changes in Ofcom's[2] regulations regarding financing of films and television programmes in the UK currently taking effect, this imbalance is unlikely to change in the short term. Other resource issues teachers mentioned as barriers were: a lack of time in the curriculum overall to extend the literacy curriculum in the way that they would wish to, a lack of teaching assistants to support individual and group work and limited or no technical assistance with the hardware and software used. Whilst some of these economic factors linked to local and national educational policy, others were embedded within institutional habitus, with some schools choosing to prioritise traditional literacy practices in terms of acquisition of resources. These decision-making processes take place within specific political contexts, of course, and so I turn to this as the final area of analysis.

Political

Whilst there have been recent moves to include multimodality in the literacy curriculum in the UK, the policy context remains resistant to more radical revision. Indeed, in the same year that the curriculum opened the door to the analysis and production of multimodal texts, the Rose Review of early reading took place (DfES, 2006b), with its revisionist agenda regarding the teaching and learning of phonics. This is a clear example of the policy phenomenon Luke and Luke (2001) note, which is:

> A rhetorical displacement of the emergent problems raised by new communications technologies, cultures and economies for print based educational systems onto a new emphasis on early inoculation models of basic skills in print literacy (Luke and Luke, 2001, p95).

Alongside the narrowing of the political focus in relation to literacy, there has been a corresponding withdrawal from the systematic funding of teachers' professional development as budgets are devolved to individual schools, which has led to lack of consistency in provision and take-up. Teachers are not receiving the support they need in order to develop their subject knowledge and pedagogical content knowledge in relation to new literacy practices.

---

[2] Ofcom is the independent regulator for the UK communications industries.

When the barriers to curricula and pedagogical development are analysed in this way, rather than focusing on factors external and internal to teachers as two separate entities, it becomes clear that they work dialectically and that the strand that has normally been excluded from analyses of barriers to progress is the social and cultural dimension. In order to illustrate this, I have mapped the factors identified in the most recent review of barriers to integration of ICT (Foon Hew and Brush, 2007) against the areas discussed above. Inevitably, some of the factors cross boundaries, but I have placed them in the following table in terms of their primary orientation.

Barriers to curricula and pedagogical change identified in this paper	Barriers to curricula and pedagogical change identified in Foon Hew and Brush, 2007
Social and cultural	-
Historical	Attitudes and beliefs Knowledge and skills Institution Subject culture
Economic	Resources
Political	Assessment

Table 12.2: Comparative analysis of barriers

Whilst individual teachers' attitudes and beliefs are shaped by the wider social and cultural context in which they work, and so this factor could arguably be placed in the first box, Table 12.2 indicates that there has been a lack of attention in research on barriers to social and cultural issues. Strategies need to be developed that will enable educators to address some of the challenges faced in this area, alongside approaches that have been outlined to address the other areas, such as the provision of sufficient resourcing and professional development and changes to assessment regimes (Foon Hew and Brush, 2007). The additional strategies need to counter social and cultural barriers could include, for instance, facilitating educators' sustained critical analysis of media discourses around issues such as 'toxic childhoods' or engaging with teachers in collaborative research projects which explore the way in which the public/private divide is changing for children in contemporary society and analyse the implications for their classrooms.

Conclusion

This analysis has focused upon developments in England. However, in the political context in which neoliberal policies roll out similar educational reforms across international boundaries, a number of the same issues can be identified elsewhere. In Australia, for example, the recent review of literacy teaching (DEST, 2005) echoed the narrow focus on print-based texts embedded in the Rose Review in England (DfES, 2006b). In addition, because there is a longer history in Australia than the UK of engaging in work on digital literacy and critical literacy, some sociocultural barriers to progress are arguably more pronounced as moral panics grow proportionately, as can be seen in the recent media criticism of critical literacies (see, for example, Slattery, 2005). In the USA, barriers to change are compounded by the fact that there is a lack of historical attention to areas such as critical literacy and media studies in schools and therefore educators have greater challenges to face in terms of moving textual analysis away from an 'inoculation' model. In the developing world, very different patterns of access and use of ICT leads to other concerns and interests in relation to digital literacy (Mutonyi and Norton, 2007). However, consistent across these spaces is the need for educators to become more familiar with how literacy curricula and pedagogy are shaped by both global and local concerns. In the years ahead, therefore, it will be important to develop more extensive international collaborations and conversations in order to address some of the barriers outlined above.

Whilst the studies reported upon in this paper can offer only partial glimpses into some of the possibilities and challenges faced by primary and early years educators in England as they respond to a rapidly changing world, they do signal a need for steady reflection on the current state of affairs and careful consideration of the steps needed in the years ahead. In addition, they emphasise the value of engaging with teacher-researchers in collaborative communities of reflective practice as we take these tentative steps into the future. That task in itself brings its own challenges, but is a necessary one if theory, policy and practice are to relate effectively.

References

Abbs P et al (2006). Modern life leads to more depression among children. Letter to the *Daily Telegraph*, 12 September, 2006. Retrieved 10 August 2007, from: www.telegraph.co.uk/news/main.jhtml?xml=/news/2006/09/12/njunk 112.xml

Bearne E, Clark C, Johnson A, Manford P, Mottram M, Wolstencroft H. With Anderson R, Gamble N and Overall L (2007). *Reading on screen*. Leicester: UKLA.

BFI/ DfES (2003). *Look again: A teaching guide to using film and television with three- to eleven-year-olds*. London: BFI.

Bourdieu P (1990). *The logic of practice*. (R Nice, Trans.) Cambridge: Polity Press (original work published in 1980).

Bruns A (2006). Towards produsage: Futures for user-led content production. In F Sudweeks, H Hrachovec & C Ess (Eds), *Proceedings: Cultural Attitudes towards Communication and Technology 2006*, (pp275–84). Perth: Murdoch University. Retrieved 22 August 2007, from: http://snurb.info/files/12132812018_towards_produsage_0.pdf

Bulfin S, North S (2007). Negotiating Digital Literacy Practices Across School and Home: Case Studies of Young People in Australia. *Language and Education*, 23(3): 247–263.

Butler T, Robson G (2001). Social capital, gentrification and neighbourhood change in London: A comparison of three south London neighbourhoods. *Urban Studies*, 38(12): 2145–2162.

Carrington V (2005). New textual landscapes, information and early literacy. In J Marsh (ed), *Popular Culture, New Media and Digital Literacy in Early Childhood*. London: RoutledgeFalmer.

Demos (2007). *Their Space – Education for a Digital Generation*. Retrieved 20 August 2007, from: www.demos.co.uk/files/Their%20space%20-%20web.pdf

DEST (2005). *National Inquiry into the Teaching of Literacy: Report and Recommendations*. Canberra: DEST. Accessed August 2007, at: www.dest.gov.au/nitl/report.htm

DfES (2006a). *Primary Framework for Literacy and Mathematics*. London: HMSO.

DfES (2006b). *Rose review of the teaching of early reading: Final report*. London: HMSO.

Dowdall C (in press). The texts of me and the texts of us: improvisation and polished performance in social networking sites. In M Robinson, R Willett & J Marsh (Eds), *Play, Creativities and Digital Cultures*. New York: Routledge.

Ertmer P A (1999). Addressing first- and second-order barriers to change: Strategies for technology integration. *Educational Technology, Research and Development*, 47(4): 47–61.

Foon Hew K, Brush T (2007) Integrating technology into K-12 teaching and learning: current knowledge gaps and recommendations for future research, *Educational Technology Research and Development*, 55(3): 223–252

Green B (2006). English, literacy, rhetoric: Changing the project? *English in Education*, 40(1): 7–19.

Hennessy S, Ruthven K, Brindley S (2005). Teacher perspectives on integrating ICT into subject teaching: commitment, constraints, caution, and change. *Journal of Curriculum Studies*, 27(2): 155–192.

Kress G (2006). Editorial. *English in Education*, 40(1): 1–4.

Kress G (2003). *Literacy in a new media age*. London: Routledge.

Lankshear C, Knobel M (2006). *New literacies: Everyday practices and classroom learning*, 2nd Edn. Maidenhead, Berkshire: Open University Press.

Laevers F (1994). *The Leuven Involvement Scale for young children*, LISYC Manual and video tape, Experimental Educational Series No. 1. Leuven, Belgium: Centre of Experimental Studies.

Livingstone S, Bovill M (1999). *Young people, new media: Report of the research project: Children, young people and the changing media environment.* London: London School of Economics and Political Science.

Luke A, Luke C (2001). Adolescence lost/childhood regained: On early intervention and the emergence of the techno-subject. *Journal of Early Childhood Literacy*, 1(1): 91–120.

Marsh J (2007). New literacies and old pedagogies: Recontextualizing rules and practices. *International Journal of Inclusive Education*, 11(3): 267–281.

Marsh J (2006). Popular Culture and Literacy: A Bourdieuan Analysis. *Reading Research Quarterly*, 46(2): 160–174.

Marsh J (2004). The Primary Canon: A Critical Review. British Journal of Educational Studies, 52(3): 249–262.

Marsh J, Bearne E (in press). *BFI Training Scheme for Lead Practitioners on Moving Image Education: Final Evaluation Report.* UKLA/University of Sheffield.

Marsh J, Brooks G, Hughes J, Ritchie L, Roberts S (2005). Digital beginnings: Young children's use of popular culture, media and new technologies. Sheffield, UK: University of Sheffield. Retrieved 11 June 2006, at www.digitalbeginings.shef.ac.uk/

Merchant G (2007a). Writing the future in the digital age. *Literacy*, 41(3):118 –128.

Merchant G (2007b). Daleks and other avatars. Paper presented at the UKLA Conference, University of Swansea, July 2007.

Mutonyi H, Norton B (2007). ICT on the margins: Lessons for Ugandan education. *Language and Education*, 21(3): 264–270.

Nixon H, Comber B (2005). Behind the scenes: Making movies in early years classrooms. In J Marsh (Ed), *Popular culture: New media and digital technology in early childhood* (pp219–236). London: RoutledgeFalmer.

NSBA (2007). *Creating and connecting: Research and guidelines on social – and educational – networking.* Retrieved 20 August 2007, from: www.nsba.org/site/docs/41400/41340.pdf

Ofcom (2006). Media Literacy Audit: Report on media literacy amongst children, London: Ofcom. Retrieved 20 August 2007, from: www.Ofcom.org.uk/advice/media_literacy/medlitpub/medlitpubrss/children/children.pdf.

Palmer S (2006). *Toxic Childhood*. London: Orion Press.

Primary National Strategy (PNS)/United Kingdom Literacy Association (UKLA) (2004). *Raising boys' achievement in writing*. London: HMSO.

Reay D, David M, Ball S (2001). Making a Difference? Institutional habituses and higher education choice, *Sociological ResearchOnline*, 5(4). Accessed August 2007 at: www.socresonline.org.uk/5/4/reay.html

Selwyn N, Facer K (2007). *Beyond the digital divide: Rethinking digital inclusion for the 21st century*. Bristol: Futurelab. Accessed August 2007: www.futurelab.org.uk/resources/publications_reports_articles/opening_education_reports/Opening_Education_Report548

Slattery L (2005). Put literacy before 'radical' vanity. *The Australian*, 30 July 2005. Retrieved 20 August 2007, from: www.theaustralian.news.com.au/story/0,20867,16089271-7583,00.html

Street B (1998). New literacies in theory and practice: what are the implications for language in education? *Linguistics and Education*, 10(1): 1–24.

Thomas L (2002). Student retention in higher education: the role of institutional habitus. *Journal of Education Policy*, 17(4): 423–442.

Toffler A (1971). *Future Shock*. London: Pan

QCA (2005). *Taking English Forward*. London: HMSO.

UNICEF (2006). Child poverty in perspective: An overview of child well-being in rich countries. Florence, Italy: Unicef. Accessed August 2007 at: www.unicef.org.uk/press/news_detail_full_story.asp?news_id=890

Valentine G, Marsh J, Pattie C (2005). *Children and Young People's Home Use of ICT for Educational Purposes: The Impact on Attainment at Key Stages 1–4*. London: HMSO.

Walsh M et al (2006). *Literacy for e-learning and multimodal classroom contexts*. Sydney: CEO/ACU.

13
Eyes in the back of our heads: reading futures for literacy teaching

Jo-Anne Reid
Faculty of Education, Charles Sturt University

In this presentation, I want to challenge you – on the last day of this conference called Future Directions in Literacy – to think back over the past few days and to review and consider what you have heard. I ask you to reflect on the key messages you have taken from the presentations you have listened to, the interactive sessions you have participated in, and the discussions you have had with your friends and colleagues who have shared this experience. I want to provoke you a little, to think, to consider what it all means, this talk about literacy directions into the future, and the challenges that Leonie Rowan, Barbara Comber, Peter Freebody and Jackie Marsh have thrown to you in this slot each morning in what has indeed been an international conversation about literacy and literacy teaching.

I base my argument on a claim that the work we do as teaching professionals is work that is captured in the textual practices of our profession. In particular, I believe that the work we do in planning and programming what we want to happen in our classrooms – each day, each week, each term and over the whole year that we spend with a particular group of children in our care – is key to who we are as teachers. Our programs are the realisation – the traces – in print, or diagram or scribbled notes, of our intended practice – the best that we can aspire to. They are the means by which we represent ourselves to ourselves – either as the sorts of professional subjects who take up prescribed curriculum and adapt it to the needs of the particular children in our classes, or the type of teachers who teach to a syllabus that was not designed for any single one of them. We use them to think through what we want to do with literacy with our students, and how we might do them in particular ways. The nature of the things we plan to do and the ways we plan to do them, changes from year to year, group to group, day to day, but it is usually informed by current theories about what is good literacy practice at any particular time. And this is the argument I make here: that what we currently understand as literacy teaching is different from what teachers understood as literacy ten or a hundred years ago, but that it is not totally different, and that in some ways it is not very much different at all from what we have been doing in the past. And so, given that, how do we see our future directions? In particular, as I started by saying, how do we work with the ideas presented by key literacy researchers to divine the directions that will be best for the children we teach?

These are key words for me in this presentation: 'seeing the future', 'divining the directions that are best to take' for teaching children the things they need at the present time to be literate social subjects. By this I mean that we are teaching them to be able to function effectively in the multimodal literacies that characterise our daily formal, social and business interactions. A literate social subject is a person literate in a range of these media and able to use them for pleasure and creative expression. Even more importantly, as we face an uncertain future in relation to climate change and economic instability, we want our students to be literate in terms of being able to access the knowledge, thinking and artistry of our fellow human beings through our use of these media. Just like me, you may find that words like 'seeing the future' bring to mind the distinctly unscholarly activity of *fortune telling* – and indeed my plan for today's talk is built upon the discourse structures that this particular form of 'telling the future' provides. I want to use the thinking of the Tarot – not as a mystic or arcane ritual, but rather as a scaffold for thinking, and a technology for planning future directions in literacy. I want to use it to highlight the things that teachers of literacy might well consider for our practice as literacy professionals in primary and secondary schools.

The history of the Tarot card is not agreed upon by everyone, but it seems that use of this deck of 78 playing cards was first recorded in the north of Italy in the 15th century where it was used to play a game similar to that we now know as Bridge. The designs on the sets of cards that were taken to other European countries inspired people there to add social narratives to these images, and allowed the element of chance (inherent in all understandings of playing cards), to transform the Tarot into something else than just a game. In the hands of mystics and storytellers, it became used as a system of telling fortunes. This was done by means of the drawing of cards, 'by chance' in response to particular sets of scaffolding questions that were deemed to suit the needs of those who seek assistance in making decisions in their lives.

The Tarot pack can be laid out in any one of a range of ritual structures in order for a fortune teller to 'read' the story in the cards – the only requirement is that the layout is seen as a guide only. Where a clear meaning is not apparent either to the fortune-teller or to the 'Querent', the person whose quest it is to find an answer and a guide for the directions they will take for the future, other cards may be used as needed, to amplify and extend the story that unfolds. For my purposes here today I will use the heuristic structure that Tarot readers call the 'Celtic Cross'. The nature of the cards themselves, and their particular symbolic meanings, is neither necessary nor important for my purposes here – as I am not here to engage in telling the future, of course.

I am using the Tarot simply as a technology, to make the argument that this structure for thinking is a useful heuristic for giving careful consideration to important questions like literacy education – simply because it provides a structure that requires us to look back *as well as forward* – to our history as well as our future. And this is what I want to argue – that we will not change directions in literacy teaching unless we move forward with a clear sense of what we are changing from, and how, and why we need to change. I could have used the Aristotelian Table of Invention, for instance, to lay out the boundaries of this question, but here, today, because I want you to remember, I am telling our future direction in literacy in this way.

Here (below) is the layout of the Tarot reading we are about to make, as we seek an answer to what it is we should be doing as we go about the teaching of literacy for the rest of this term, or this year. We only ask the Tarot to foretell the future to give us this sort of structure – to support us in our decision to act in a particular way. If we already know that we are on the right path, of course, and we already know all there is to be known about what is the best literacy instruction for the children in our care, we probably wouldn't need to read this Tarot – and we certainly wouldn't need to come to a conference such as this.

Here is what the Tarot asks us – to lay out, on the table, the situation under consideration as it relates to ourselves as Querent, in search of this answer. The very first card that is laid down represents 'the present' – the situation at hand, and where we must always begin. The reading as a whole is made in terms of this card in relation to all the others, setting out the conditions for 'foretelling' or understanding future practice – what will, or may, happen. In this way, the Tarot layout can be seen as a scaffold for planning – for programming the work that will happen on our classrooms, and for understanding the directions that we will take in the next few years as a profession. This of course means that it can help us plan the sorts of conversations we will need to have and the support we may need to provide to our colleagues and student teachers over this time as well. It can help us – in short – predict the future directions in literacy that will be the most productive in achieving fair, just and equitable access to all. That is the question we bring to this particular Tarot reading (adapted from Angel Paths Tarot, www.angelpaths.com), and of course it is the 'big' question we bring to the act of programming each time we set out to plan a program of work for a group of learners.

Card 1: The present.

Bill Green argues that thinking historically about English teaching is "easier said than done", as it always means "reassessing our present, as an always-already problematic form of presence, and it also means thinking about and speculating on the future, as a space of difference and danger, promise and impossibility" (Green, 2003, p139).

This first step in our Tarot reading for the future asks us to be mindful of where we are, who we are working with, what are their, our own, needs and strengths. It asks us to open our thinking to the associated considerations that immediately complicate this present and make it far less simple and understandable. Starting here in the present means looking closely at our 'situation of practice' in all its complexities. As I understand it, the project of histories of the present is to make the present a "strange rather than a familiar landscape" and unsettle the things we take for granted (Green & Reid, 2002, p37).

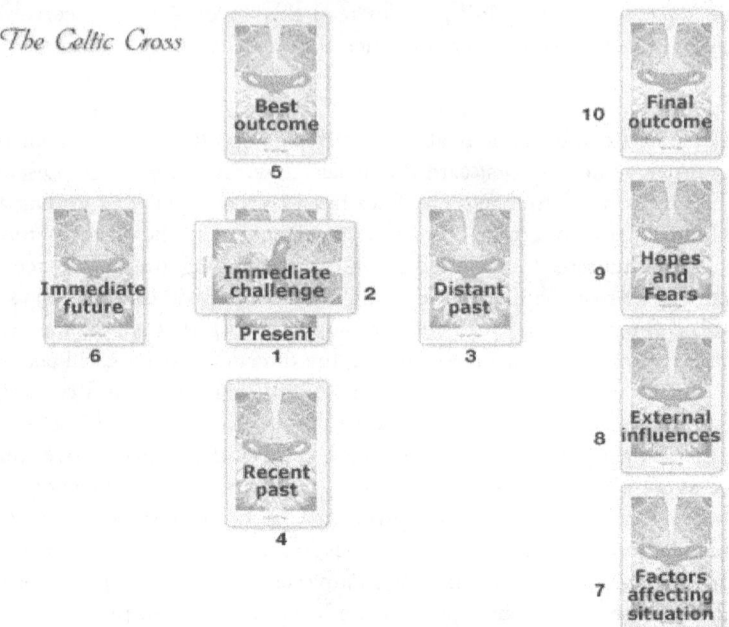

For instance, just this weekend, the following article appeared in the Sydney Morning Herald:

Here is a present depicted. The story begins with the words, "Children will be asked to draw pictures instead of spelling words as part of a new strategy to improve literacy test results in primary school". It goes on to note that "[t]he Department of Education is distributing a new teaching resource to schools, encouraging teachers to spend more time helping students develop their oral skills before learning how to spell specific words" (Patty, 2007, p11).

This is a 'present' for literacy teaching that contrasts greatly with the 'presents' I have witnessed in many of the classrooms visited in the course of my research. I have increasingly become concerned about the nature of some present-day literacy experience on offer to children in some classrooms during a study that evaluated the effects of bi-dialectal language use in classrooms with high numbers of Aboriginal children for the DET (Reid & Owens, 2005). In an interview with an eight-year-old, the following conversation took place:

I: What sort of story would you write? Do you go fishing, or what do you do?
L: I caught ... I'm a dropper. You've got to get on your boat and then tie this thing on a real big ... if there's a willow tree then tie it around it. And I wanted to put on the egg, and then the next morning on the dropper I got a six-, *seven*teen pound cod and then Onna, my dad's friend, went in and got it and put it in the boat.
I: Do you ever write stories like that in the classroom?
L: Yeah, we have sometimes.
I: When you write your stories in class, have a little think – what's the first thing you do when you write a story?
L: I can't do it.
I: Before you even start writing, do you think about things in your head first?
L: Yeah, what I'm going to write.
I: You think about things you're going to write? And what about the ARA; what about Nan, did she help you think about things?
L: Yes, she says, "Oh, we've got to put that in" or "You should have put this", and then she says it.
L: And what does she say things like?

I: Like ...
I: Say you were writing a story about catching a seventeen pound cod, what would she tell you to write?
L: That I should say ... write, "who caught the fish".

Here, eight-year-old Lyall, a Wiradjuri boy from the Murray-Darling Basin is showing a Wiradjuri researcher his writing, and talking about how he goes about writing in his classroom. There, spelling the words correctly is important, and the work he is talking about bears no relation to either his lived experience or the richness of the world he inhabits outside of it. My concern is that the text these two are discussing, the writing Lyall is asked to do now that he is in Year 3 and needs to be spelling, punctuating, making language choices appropriate to the text-type he is producing, is actually as follows:

> **BOO.**
>
> **My monster is a hairy, green, spotty, good monster. He is named BOO and he has lots of spiky fur. He scares big, ugly people. He is my best friend.**

Here, in Lyall's final copy, which is his fourth draft of this text, worked on for over a week, and carefully typed up on Friday, we see evidence of what I think might be pretty toxic literacy practices for Lyall. Is it significant that he hasn't 'bothered' to put his name on this text? What is this text doing? What is it *for*, except to practise adjectives, commas, and formal constructions of English grammar such as the passive formulation of 'is named'. This seems a very strange construction – and it places the relationship between Lyall and 'his' monster at some considerable distance, in fact removing Lyall from his sentence altogether. Lyall's writing, his literacy, has been made safe.

The will to safety in literacy teaching characterises our present, I am afraid. We have been convinced by the rhetorics of science, and the documents that tell us we must drill the children in phonics and text-types before they can tell their stories, and that some stories have more value than others, and some should not be told in the classroom at all. In the end, we have come to a present where many teachers are afraid to take risks, or take a chance, because we are not sure what will happen. Perhaps if we continue the Tarot we will find out.

Card 2: The immediate challenge

This step asks us to interpret and articulate (to 'lay on the table') what it is that we see to be the immediate challenge as we see it, and as we set out to take the action we want to take. This challenge might not be an issue directly related to the question, of course, it might be something that impacts on our ability to move quickly, or to do the things we want to do in our classroom. It may be the need to ask permission from the Principal to try something different, for instance, and to establish a different relationship with the AEA, or to address my own lack of skill in online media production – but this challenge will need to be addressed, as it will not go away. Knowing that it is there allows us to proceed with this knowledge in our consciousness, and to ensure we plan to address it as part of this process.

On the other hand, though, facing these challenges, small as they may seem when the size of a Tarot card, means stepping out of our safety zone – and of course this means that very often we put them off, leave them till later, once we have started our journey – and 'planning to address them' does not mean that they *are* addressed. It is easier not to challenge often, particularly when your colleagues, your school, the media you use over breakfast or in the car on the way to work, all indicate that you need evidence to show that what you are feeling you might want to do is sound and worthwhile literacy practice.

In her critical account of research which claims to prove that knowledge of sounds, or phonemic awareness, is the foundational building block of early literacy, and which is the 'evidence' upon which whole systems have based information for teachers, Denny Taylor writes:

> In positivistic research there is a total lack of recognition that literacy [...] is embedded in everyday activities, or that the use of complex symbolic systems is an everyday phenomenon constitutive of and grounded in the everyday lives of young children and their families (Taylor, 1998, p223).

Lyall does not get to embed his literacy in his life experience. He already knows how to select adjectives (and modify them, according to his social purpose of impressing his listener) very well in his oral language, in the story he tells about his fishing prowess. Allowing him to learn to write or communicate his enthusiasm and excitement in a range of modes may be more successful – may help his teacher achieve the goal of improving literacy outcomes for Lyall just as much as other children.

Changing the literacy program in Lyall's classroom will need us to talk to the Principal, and of course that will require us to explain WHY we want to make the changes we are suggesting. And that, of course, will require us to be able to argue a rationale for our case, one that is based on evidence and experience, from our own professional knowledge base as literacy teachers.

In Michael Singh's (1992) paper on the work of Sylvia Ashton-Warner, he makes the argument that her practice is more clearly 'professional' practice than that of teachers who simply follow the rules and syllabus set down by their employers without consideration of their situation of practice. He suggests that there are three "closely-related criteria [that] are normally employed to distinguish a professional from a non-professional occupation":

> First, the methods and procedures employed by members of a profession are based on research and a body of theoretical knowledge. Second, members of a profession have an overriding commitment to the well being of their clients. Third, to ensure that they can always act in the interests of their clients, a professional community reserves the right to make relatively autonomous judgements free from external, non-professional controls and constraints (Singh, 1992, p273).

It is to consideration of the basis on which we make our professional judgments that the Tarot takes us next.

Card 3: The distant past, the foundation or root of the subject matter of the question.

This is an important card, and those of you more familiar with psychology than Tarot may see the strategy implicit in asking us to speak and interpret our history in this way. Here, when we remember the question we are investigating as literacy educators, we are asked by the Tarot to remember *our* history, and call it into being as we think about our present and our possible futures.

Indeed, as Singh (1992, p273) notes: "There is a need for teachers to recover and reconstruct knowledge that allows them to more fully understand their own histories in order to be able to interrogate and analyse views of their professionalism". He goes on:

> If there is to be any chance for teachers to make changes which improve literacy education, it is important for them to have an understanding of the conflicts surrounding the genesis and evolution of ideas, practices and organisational modes presently taken for granted (Singh, 1992, p274).

Fifteen years ago, Viv Nicoll-Hatton wrote a PEN for PETA that focussed on the work of Don Holdaway, an international (New Zealand) literacy scholar, whose 1979 book *The Foundations of Literacy* highlighted the centrality of oral language for literacy learning in young children, and introduced the formal concept of 'shared book experience' into the practice repertoires of early literacy teachers. Nicoll-Hatton noted there something that I still find very telling in terms of teachers' awareness of our professional history: "Many teachers who successfully use the shared book approach in their classrooms may never have had cause to read Holdaway's *The Foundations of Literacy*, since his ideas have been incorporated into most state curriculum documents, teacher education courses, and inservice courses ..." (Nicoll-Hatton, 1992, p1). And for this reason, as she continued, many teachers:

> (for instance those who learned of the procedure 'second-hand' through teaching manuals) are not aware of the thinking and research that lie behind what appears to be a very simple classroom routine (Nicoll-Hatton, 1992, p1).

Later in this interview, Holdaway explained the rationale for the use of big books in the classroom, and in these reasons we find the traces of many of the challenges to formal, structured pedagogical approaches to literacy learning, the 'synthetic phonics' that Jackie Marsh referred to yesterday, that have continued ever since. Holdaway said:

> For one thing, we wanted a style of teaching which allowed all children to enjoy and cope with a challenging, ungraded, open literature at the centre of their instruction, [with] repetition producing 'favourite texts' suggested by the emergent literacy research.
>
> For another, we wanted print itself to be the focus of attention, and for this attention to be universal and under the control of the teacher. We wanted to teach phonics in context.
>
> We wanted a situation which was cooperative and supportive rather than competitive and corrective.
>
> We wanted to build a culture of trust and desire for written texts, a 'literacy club' from which no child was excluded.
>
> We wanted to use a literature so powerful that it would generate writing and every other form of real literate activity, including genuine publishing and book-making.
>
> We wanted every child to have an extensive inventory of text so familiar and loved that it would be a lifetime resource for all manner of literate preoccupations (Holdaway in Nicoll-Hatton, 1992, p2–3).

Now, while Holdaway's work is not actually the distant past for me, it is for my students – many of whom, perhaps like many of you, would never have read or would never make connections between the work of Holdaway, the work of James Gee in the United States, and that of leaders like Brian Cambourne, who worked with the idea of literacy acquisition in the Australian context. It may surprise you to know, too, that for many of the young teachers graduating and entering schools today, the really important and relatively recent writing of Alan Luke and Peter Freebody is similarly 'distant', and their notion of 'the Four Roles of the Reader' has become orthodox knowledge – and the principles behind it taken for granted – so that, unless we make use of heuristics like this to remind ourselves of them, they are rendered less important and less powerful as teaching methodologies.

I used this concern in a recent chapter for Robyn Ewing's new book the *Beyond the Reading Wars* (2006) where I described a particular reading method that was developed, quite brilliantly, by a creative teacher, George Jones, after his appointment to a little one-teacher school at 'Bundarra on the Gwydir' in north west NSW. Mr Jones quickly worked out that there was a huge range of literacy experience and capacity among the children in his classroom, and that he could not make best instructional use of the time they had in school if all the instruction needed to come through him. He worked out a system of phonics that would allow the children to remember the sounds that correspond to the symbols of print, and therefore to be able to self-correct using a form of kinaesthetic mnemonic ('auto feedback') as their body automatically moved to the position they had learned in correspondence with the sound.

As Holdaway (in Nicoll-Hatton, 1992) reminds us, the concept of learner self-correction is a key aspect of Marie Clay's historic contribution to our professional knowledge as literacy teachers. Her approach moves from the assumption that learning happens when we make mistakes, and then use our tentative strategies and insecure knowledge to take a risk and self correct – thus confirming and strengthening our knowledge of how print (and other semiotic forms) work.

The 'Jones method' for teaching reading, while employed successfully for over 20 years in Bundarra, and while it enjoyed nearly 10 years additional success in the classrooms of NSW teachers who were 'in-serviced' by Jones, started to lose its potency once he wrote and sold the manual, and it was placed on the reading list for teachers training colleges in NSW and Victoria – and once the teachers who took it up lost touch with the 'theory' and meaning – the situated professional knowledge, on which it was based.

Remembering our pasts, then, is crucial for successful change in literacy education. But we always teach in a closer relation to yesterday than last week, last year, or last century – and so it is no surprise that the Tarot asks us to think about this too. It is difficult work, and as Davies et al. (2007, p31) write, about their work with a group of teachers who were not interested in reading the material the researchers provided for them. They rejected accounts of an historical reality because, it seemed, "[t]here was [...] no way of understanding discourse at work, except through what was happening now". To understand this phenomenon, they have drawn on the idea of "[t]he neoliberal drive for what is new, as it is only the 'new' that can take us into the future" (Davies et al., 2007, p31). The Tarot reading considers this point as well.

Card 4: More recent past, including events taking place, not necessarily directly connected to the question.

Here we consider the constraints and circumstances that have had recent impact on our work – the policies and syllabi that are in place in our schools and systems; the political influences that require us to behave in certain ways: the rules or mores of our particular school or institution – timetables, staffing arrangements, and so on. We need to be clear about these issues – we have to stand somewhere in the present – we cannot pretend that the public media arguments and disputes over literacy and the best way to teach literacy are not our business. They are.

I used Denny Taylor's (1998) argument above to talk about the problems many teachers find with synthetic literacy programs and large number of required learning outcomes that are focussed on content delivery rather than the circumstances of delivery and the reception they may get. Even when teachers appreciate the regularity, security and safety of these scientifically-proven programs, they often report that the programs 'get in the way' of them knowing the children they are paid to teach.

In this regard, Taylor argues that when teachers are caught up in the rhetoric of the need to rely only on scientific 'evidence-based' research to guide their practice, the relationship between teachers and children is changed, so that the teacher's practice is no longer driven by the children in her classroom.

> Developing phonemic awareness in reading and writing classrooms in which teachers and children form literate communities has different social, cultural and intellectual significance than developing phonemic awareness in classrooms in which instruction takes the form of predetermined lesson plans that are given to children and used to control their learning (Taylor, 1998, p226).

But there are other influences that impact on our decisions as literacy teachers – as the discussion question posed at this stage of the Tarot Reading suggests, these do not necessarily have to be explicitly connected to the question. Here again, chance plays a hand. You might have just read a wonderful new book short-listed for the Children's Book Awards for instance; I am currently engrossed in an old, dog-eared copy Sylvia Ashton Warner's (1958) novel *Spinster;* a young teacher, Jemma Gascoyne, with whom I have worked on the River Literacies Project over the last couple of years (Comber, Nixon, Reid, 2007) found that her ability to remain committed to environmental action in her practice was assured when she discovered that her new colleague in the room next door was just as passionate about environmental issues as she was. These events will influence what we do, what direction we will take, and how we feel about what we are doing as teachers of literacy. They temper, sometimes, the ambitions that we may have – but at other times they extend and enrich them far beyond what we might originally have envisaged.

Card 5: The best that can be achieved. This is directly related to the question.

Here we are asked again to think about how fair, just and equitable access to literacy for all children can be achieved and what it will look like for the classrooms in which we work. In other words, and in the way that Boomer (1982) and Metcalfe and Game (2006) talk about the importance of 'imagining' what an action goal will look and feel like in its realisation, our planning is *creative* – it is a story we tell ourselves about what we and the other people who are implicated in our question will be doing, saying, producing and learning.

In a Tarot reading, of course there is an exciting element of beating chance, of risk, that knowing a potential future will give us an inside running as we make our way along the pathway towards a solution to the question we have put to ourselves (or to the cards). In a classroom there is just this same element of risk. The element of chance is always with us, and even when we plan something to the last detail there is always a large chance that something will 'happen' (an interesting word, by the way – which is related to 'happy', 'mishap' and 'happenstance', through the root word 'hap' which means 'chance', or 'good fortune' [Onions, 1966, p427]).

Sylvia Ashton Warner worked for years to achieve her educational dreams for the 'little ones' she taught in her New Zealand bush school. More than any other educational literature I have read, her account of her practice illustrates the importance of resilience and 'not giving up' until the best that can be achieved is achieved – even if not permanently. And in *Teacher*, Ashton-Warner (1963) shows poignantly how fleeting even the most hard-fought success can be. When she returns to the school where her methods were developed and honed over time, and where her 'little ones' grew up with a faith in education instilled through their earliest contact with the school system, she sees the way that her success has been cheapened and 'made safe' as it was adapted as orthodoxy in the school system. Her response, with those "sparkling five-year-old tears on an autumnal face" (Ashton-Warner, 1963, p224) – surely the most moving closing image of *any* body's book – is one that is shared by many who see their thinking mistaken, their work only half understood, and their achievements diminished.

Card 6: The Immediate Future. This indicates events in the next few days or week(s). This reading does not cover months.

At this point the Tarot provides an opportunity to interpret our sense of what *could* happen – remembering that we are not asked to consider this over the long term, but rather to think around and through the events we want to initiate in the next few days or weeks. This is the crunch of what we normally do as 'programming' – often without consideration of all the other factors that surround, underpin, and sometimes constrain our plans.

As teachers we are among the few professionals who see the mapping out of their immediate future as a key part (a required duty) of their practice. Garth Boomer, a key figure in the history of Australian curriculum studies, internationally known for his work on *Negotiating the Curriculum* (Boomer, 1982) argues there against an instrumental view of programming – and planning – that is not rooted strongly in the ongoing flow of classroom interactions, relationships and real events in the lives of children. In that book, Boomer outlines what he saw as a planning model that challenged me as a younger teacher to think differently about programming, simply because what he called "Justification of content" is included as a key concern for every program:

> This is where we justify the content chosen and make *hypotheses* about what things may be learnt.
>
> *Aim* – To decide what they already know and then to introduce new perspectives.
>
> *Key question* – This is where we outline the key questions that we think will be addressed. They may not be specifically 'treated' by the children, but they will be beneath all that is done.
>
> *Note* – The quality of the question will affect the quality of learning. The key question offers the teacher a philosophical framework which will give purpose, direction and shape to the learning activities. It will almost certainly imply a value stance (Boomer, 1982, p156–157).

For me, this requirement of us as teachers is a deeply professional requirement – to justify the things that go on in the time and space that we control. It is the only link I have found in the literature of school programming and planning in Australia, to the European notion of 'pedagogiek', which basically means 'upbringing', and which implies that all the work done by all the adults who interact in and on the life of a child, are implicated in a values-based project of induction and introduction of a new member of the social group. It requires us to make our values explicit, and if those values are actually centered around social justice, then they need to be foregrounded in our practice – and if they are centered around neoliberal individualism, then we need to be explicit about that too. For Boomer, there is no quality where we do not know what we are doing and why.

Card 7: The factors or inner feelings affecting the situation.

Here's something quite disconcerting for the non-mystic planner: the request to lay out for in(tro)spection our personal feelings as teachers about our working situation. The Principal's commitment to improving the BST scores among boys in the school, for instance, and your resentment that the 'boys' who are in focus here actually seem only to be some of them; my lifetime fear of singing out of tune in public (which began in the Year 4 Choir at South Girls and Infants State School, Toowoomba), which always seems to limit some of my larger creative plans; or the whole school's concern with addressing a growing problem with bullying, that needs to be dealt with on a number of levels.

Most of the time, as Sylvia Ashton-Warner (1958) says in the opening pages of her novel *Spinster*, "The thing about teaching is that while you are doing it no yesterday has a chance" (1958, p8). Once we are caught up in the passion and pleasure of the act and art of teaching little children, we often forget that we can't sing, or that the child who is reading the words and reading ahead as we all sing along together is the same child who failed again to sound out his reading correctly yesterday, as his fear of ridicule and teasing overcame all other feelings in that event. Paying attention to these inner feelings (both our own and those of our students) in this simple way is worthwhile in that while the Tarot asks us simply to note them, in so doing we acknowledge and respect them – and do not overlook or ignore them.

In reflecting on her work as a researcher of children at work in her classroom, Vivian Gussin Paley also bears strong witness to the importance of this sort of acknowledgement:

> The act of teaching became a daily search for the child's point of view accompanied by the sometimes unwelcome disclosure of my hidden attitudes. The search was what mattered – only later did someone tell me it was research – and it provided an open-ended script from which to observe, interpret, and integrate the living drama of the classroom.

> I began using the tape recorder to try to figure out why the children were lively and imaginative in certain discussions, yet fidgety and distracted in others […] wanting to return quickly to their interrupted play. As I transcribed the daily tapes, several phenomena emerged. Whenever the discussion touched on fantasy, fairness, or friendship ("the three Fs", I began to call them), participation zoomed upward (Gussin Paley, 2007, p154).

This work points us clearly (back) to the need to concern ourselves with children's lives outside of the classroom, argued by Ashton-Warner (1963) as a way to ensure that literacy is both meaningful and relevant in those lives.

Card 8: External influences. People, energies or events which will affect the outcome of the question and are beyond the Querent's control.

Here we are able to consider those things that will thwart or even possibly support us in our imagined changes – the time of the year and the school calendar come to mind immediately as factors that will impact on what it is that we plan and start to do. There may be other influences that emerge from the action as it unfolds, such as information about the skills or interests of a parent or grandparent, a travelling exhibition or a major news event. Some of these are things we cannot always work with if unpredictable, but by asking us to consider them in the planning process, the Tarot asks us to be open to opportunity and hence flexible – this is the meaning of this stage of the reading.

Card 9: Hopes or fears around the situation.

There are always great hopes for any statement of goal or quest. What would be the best that can befall us if we set out on a pathway to improve all children's literacy experiences in our classrooms? That they will all love me for having helped them earn the gift of reading? That their parents will write to the Principal about the wonderful things happening in my classroom? That I will catch Kane Edwards reading in the book corner instead of spitting into the giraffe's ears? That they will all achieve brilliant results on the tests and they will make a movie about them, starring Naomi Watts as me?

The instructions that are provided in the Tarot manual note here that we should "always bear in mind that hopes and fears are closely intertwined, therefore that which we hope for may also be that which we fear, and so may fail to happen" (Angel Paths Tarot). Indeed, as Cormack (2006, p130) says: "if history is any guide, we will experience a long period of experiment and change, with the old existing alongside the new, as teachers respond to the impact of changes in the materials they work with."

Card 10: Final outcome. This is a fairly self explanatory card.

We should remember the stoic advice of Antonio Gramsci to aim for what he described as an "optimism of the intellect, pessimism of the will", in relation to the final outcome of our planning and teaching for literacy – remembering, just as with the Tarot, the classroom plan is always subject to chance.

As Sylvia Ashton-Warner (1958) says: "The days happen along in their inadvertent way ..."

> I plan, but this is the surest way not to do a thing. Some other deeper mysterious plan takes over. I look for it sometimes, thinking I might submit my own will to it, thinking it would prove easier, if only I could put my finger on it beforehand. But I never can. [...]

> Yet I still plan in my wan way. I find some element of security in seeing ahead of me in a definite arrangement. It's a framework that amounts to a spacious shelter, and even though little eventuated that I have thought out first, I still do it. And as fast as my deliberations come to no fruition I make them again ... (Ashton-Warner, 1958, p31).

The Tarot provides its own advice here too: *However it is worth saying that if the card comes up somewhat ambiguous, once again it may be worth drawing three extra cards to clarify.*

Conclusion

In summary then, I have used the structure of one means of telling the future, the Tarot, to lay out a reading of our pasts, or some of them, and the sorts of considerations that I believe all of us need to reflect on, as teachers, as we plan the learning pathways for our own future directions in literacy teaching. A couple of years ago now, Bill Green (2003) asked a similar sort of Janus question in relation to English teaching – and as Jackie Marsh very usefully reminded us yesterday, our English teaching colleagues are in a very similar state of flux about the status of their subject:

> Where are we now? Where have we come from? Where are we going? These are questions arguably fundamental to English teaching, as a distinctive curriculum practice and a longstanding feature of schooling. They might seem removed from the immediate hurly-burly of English teachers' work [...] But such considerations are relevant and vital nonetheless, I suggest, and indeed central if we are truly to understand what English teachers do and what they are ... (Green, 2003, p135).

With eyes in the back of our heads, then, let us hope that we can move forwards into the future, treading strongly in our shared professional knowledge, and able to face the future knowing that we can support our 'little ones' to make mistakes, to learn from their errors, and to be supported in their efforts to communicate, enjoy and learn from the literate practices in which we allow them all to be fully engaged.

References

Angel Paths Tarot (retrieved 1 September 2007) Tarot Spread, www.angelpaths.com/spreads3.html.

Ashton-Warner S (1958). *Spinster*. London and Auckland: Heinemann.

Ashton-Warner S (1963). *Teacher*. London: Virago.

Boomer G (1982). Curriculum composing and Evaluating. In G Boomer [Ed], *Negotiating the Curriculum*, (pp150–163). Sydney: Ashton Scholastic.

Comber B, Nixon H, Reid J (Eds) (2007). *Literacies in place: Teaching environmental communication*. Newtown: Primary English Teaching Association.

Cormack P (2006). Reading in the primary English curriculum: An historical account. *Australian Journal of Language and Literacy*, 29(2): 115–131.

Davies B, Edwards J, Gannon S, Laws K (2007). Neo-liberal subjectivities and the limits of social change in University-Community Partnerships. *Asia-Pacific Journal of Teacher Education*, 35(1): 27–40.

Ewing R (2006). *Beyond the Reading Wars: A balanced approach to helping children learn to read*. Newtown: PETA.

Green B (2003). (Un)changing English: Past, present future?. In B Doecke, D Homer & H Nixon [Eds], *English teachers at work: Narratives, counter narratives and arguments*, (pp135–148). Kent Town, SA: Wakefield Press & AATE.

Green B, Reid J (2002). Constructing the teacher and schooling the nation. *History of Education Review*, 31(2): 30–44.

Gussin Paley V (2007). On listening to what the children say. *Harvard Educational Review*, 77(2): 152–163.

Metcalfe A, Game A (2006). *Teachers who change lives*. Melbourne: Melbourne University Press.

Nicoll-Hatton V (1992). Big books revisited: An interview with Don Holdaway, *PEN 86*. Newtown: Primary English Teaching Association of NSW

Onions C T [Ed, with G W S Friedrichsen & R W Burchfield] (1966). *The Oxford Dictionary of English Etymology*. New York and Oxford: Oxford University Press.

Patty A (2007). Every picture tells a story: So put those spelling books away. *Sydney Morning Herald*, 1 September 2007, p11.

Reid J (2006). Reading stories: Understanding our professional history as teachers. In R Ewing [Ed] *Beyond the Reading Wars: A balanced approach to helping children learn to read*, (pp16–25). Newtown: PETA.

Reid J, Green B (2003). A new teacher for a new nation? Teacher education, national identity and English in Australia (1901–1938). Paper presented at the British Educational Research Association Conference, Edinburgh.

Reid J, Owens K (2005) *The bidialectal approach to teaching standard Australian English*, evaluation report prepared for Aboriginal Programs Branch, Sydney: NSW Department of Education and Training.

Singh M G (1992). The literacy teacher as a professional: Insights from the work of Sylvia Ashton-Warner. *Australian Journal of Language and Literacy*, 15(4): 273–286.

Taylor D (1998). Beginning to read and the Spin Doctors of Science: An excerpt. *Language Arts*, 76(3): 217–231.

14
The significance of text in the teaching of reading in the early years

Kathleen Rushton
Faculty of Education and Social Work, University of Sydney

Abstract

This paper will explore some of the issues relating to the significance of text in the teaching of reading in the early years. The focus will be on the relationship of the learner's community to the teacher and the school. The sociocultural nature of the practice of reading, it will be argued, means that the context in which young children learn to read is of great importance. When texts are chosen for the purpose of teaching reading the individual student's engagement with the texts found in school and the student's oral language development must also be considered. The paper will begin to explore some criteria that teachers may need to include when choosing texts appropriate for all students in a classroom regardless of culture, ethnicity, economic or sociocultural background.

Introduction

In this paper I will attempt to define and clarify the significance of text in the teaching of reading and to focus on the relationship of the development of reading with the types of texts chosen to teach reading. In this paper 'text' in the context of teaching reading, will refer to the written texts used in a school. This definition also includes digital texts.

The role of the community in educational achievement is also highly significant. There is a strong correlation between the social and economic profile of particular communities and the educational success of the majority of students from those communities (Lokan, 2001). This cannot be accepted as either a natural or unchangeable correlation without considering the role of the school in the literacy development of individual students from a particular community.

In Australia there is a current debate around literacy education, which is particularly concerned with the achievements of Indigenous students. When these students were assessed by The Programme for International Student Assessment (PISA) in 2000 they were under-represented in the highest category of reading proficiency and while some achieved very high results, the group was over-represented in the lowest category (Lokan, 2001, pxi). This paper will examine the relevance of text in the teaching of reading especially in Australian Indigenous communities, in which under achievement in literacy has been recognised as a barrier to educational success. The relationship of the school to the learners' community will be explored as this is the context in which the teaching of reading takes place. Reference will be made to a case study, which aims to provide local communities with the ability to produce their own texts. Reading will be defined as a sociocultural practice and the development of criteria for choosing appropriate texts will be defined in reference to their level of difficulty and how this is mediated by both the development of oral language and engagement with the text.

The importance of the relationship of the school to the learners' community

Freire (1985) and Connell (1994) both address the alienation of disadvantaged students and show how poverty can result in what Freire calls "The culture of silence" (p73). These students are doubly disadvantaged as not only are they unable to access educational resources as easily as some other members of society but they also bear the personal responsibility for failing to do so. As Connell (1994) points out:

> Disadvantage is always produced through mechanisms that also produce advantage ... The beneficiaries of the current educational order are, broadly speaking, the groups with greater economic and institutional power, greater access to the means of persuasion, and the best representation in government and in professions (p15).

Freire (1985) reinforces the relationship of the dominated and the dominating cultures and how the poor are silenced by the oppressive social conditions under which they live. Connell and Freire, while not condemning teachers and their personal efforts to support disadvantaged students, do identify education systems as part of the apparatus of the state and therefore the dominant culture which supports systems which work to their own advantage (Connell, 1994).

Many students might find school a 'natural setting' in which to learn, and may therefore be acquiring knowledge at school because their understandings about language and education predispose them to learning in such an environment (Bernstein, 1971, 1990). Bernstein's theory of elaborated and restricted codes (Bernstein, 1990), supports the conclusions drawn by Connell and Freire and provides an example of how this disadvantage is realised in the personal literacy development of particular students. Students using restricted codes will often find it difficult to achieve the same level of success as students using elaborated codes. Older students may have mastered some aspects of reading, especially a basic ability to decode written text, but still struggle to read age appropriate educational texts (Freebody, 2005). However as Freebody has indicated in the four resources model of reading, (Freebody & Luke, 1991) decoding is only one aspect of the process. The understandings about language development, which inform most current syllabus documents, including the *English K–6 Syllabus* (Board of Studies NSW, 1998), describe reading as a complex process, which includes the development of critical analysis, grammatical knowledge and contextual understandings. In educational settings the learning process usually requires students to be able to independently read written texts to support their learning, especially in the later years. The understanding about the differences and complementarity of spoken and written language are therefore crucial in developing a pedagogy which could help students to read effectively. This in turn relies on understandings about the relationship of speech communities to school communities. This can be exemplified by a multi-site case study, which is being undertaken to further explore the significance of text in the teaching of reading.

A multi-site case study

The communities in this case study are spread across Australia but all have been identified as having a large number of Indigenous students achieving low levels of literacy. A specialist reading teacher, Margaret

Cossey, who recognised the need for reading materials which reflected the lives and language of contemporary Indigenous people has, over the last two decades developed Indij Readers. These books have been written and illustrated by Indigenous people and were produced collaboratively with consultation and advice from elders, community members and Indigenous organisations in each community. A Community Writers Kit is now being developed by Indij Readers as an extension of their original process of text development.

Many Indigenous students suffer the consequences of racial discrimination and marginalisation and the resulting inadequate health and education programs. This is coupled with a lack of cross cultural awareness and respect and has resulted in many Indigenous students performing below the benchmarks achieved by many other Australians. Many Indigenous students lack formal qualifications and fail to pursue higher or tertiary education and this can be directly related to their low literacy levels (Ewing & Rushton, 2007).

> Current literacy research (e.g. Cambourne, 2006; Louden et al., 2006) coupled with research about quality pedagogy (e.g. Education Qld, 2000; NSWDET, 2003; Lingard & Hayes, 2005) demonstrates that cultural relevance, links with prior background knowledge and engagement are vital factors if children are going to learn to read. Indigenous and non-Indigenous students alike need opportunities to read and engage with Indigenous stories. Literacy success correlates highly with self-efficacy and often leads to increased achievement at school and opportunities for higher education (p1).

The case study of the development of this Community Writers Kit is limited by its size, but it does include both urban and rural sites in three states. The data collected emphasise the importance of the relationship of Indigenous people to the land, the importance of local knowledge and understandings about communities and the development of literacy and its relationship to speech communities. Dr Robyn Ewing and Kathy Rushton (Ewing & Rushton, 2007) have prepared an Interim draft report for the project and quote one community author, who says:

It's not about Indigenous people getting language acquisition but it's about us using our language as a platform to say well we're going to make sure our kids read and write in terms of who we are as Indigenous people and our culture ... This is not the end it's only the beginning ... we look forward to what comes next! (p6)

Reading as a sociocultural practice

The model of reading outlined in many syllabus and support documents in Australia such as *English – a curriculum profile for Australian schools* (Curriculum Corporation, 1994), ESL Scales (Curriculum Corporation, 1994) and *English K–6 Syllabus* (Board of Studies NSW, 1998), acknowledge that reading is a sociocultural practice and that both the contexts of culture and situation (Halliday, 1994) define the meanings individual students will make when approaching a given text. The difficulty of any given text therefore varies for individual students, depending not only on their skills but their understandings about the cultural context and the situation in which they encounter the text. Every reader brings prior knowledge and understanding to a text and for teachers of students with low literacy levels, explicit literacy support must be based on a clear understanding of the reading process including how individual students approach a text. Meek (1988) demonstrates the importance of the text in the teaching of reading:

> The reading experts, for all their understanding about 'the reading process', treat all text as the neutral substance on which the process works, as if the reader did the same things with a poem, a timetable, a warning notice ... Not only that, these experts often fail to remind themselves that reading doesn't happen in a vacuum. The social conditions and surroundings are important too. For so long we have been inclined to think of reading as a silent solitary activity that we have neglected those things that are part of our reading together. ... The reading process has always to be described in terms of texts and contexts as well as in terms of what we think readers actually do (pp5&6).

Texts can be identified by the different audiences and purposes for which they are composed, and the structures and grammatical features which realise these choices. It is therefore of great importance to recognise that different types of texts make different demands on the reader and that these demands vary, especially in relation to the oral language development of the reader as well as their background knowledge of the subject matter of the text.

How children learn to read

Williams (2000), following Bernstein and Vygotsky, states that the explicit teaching of reading also requires the teacher to have both a clear understanding about the features of texts and the metalanguage to develop a discourse around the text. He suggests that developing a metalanguage is analogous to the learning of a foreign language:

> it might be argued: for children, the acquisition of a metalanguage differs from the acquisition of language precisely because it uses the semantics of the language as its foundation.
>
> This way of thinking suggests a different starting point for developing children's knowledge of grammar and, quite crucially, a different way of thinking about what grammatical knowledge might be for. Instead of conceiving of grammar in primary school as 'basic' descriptive work on parts of speech in isolated sentences, an alternative is to make exploring **how texts mean** ... Children's literature is a rich site for exploring these issues ... (p116)

A focus on social interaction in the classroom as the basis for learning is completely opposed to psychological behaviourist understandings about learning as identified in some approaches to the teaching of reading (e.g. Castles & Coltheart, 2004; Hempenstall, 1997 and Reynolds & Wheldall, 2007). Wells has defined a social constructivist approach in his definition of Vygotsky's notion of the Zone of Proximal Development (ZPD) as "not a context-independent attribute of an individual; rather it is constructed in the interaction between participants in the course of their joint engagement in a particular activity" (Wells, 1998, p333). He goes on to identify the ZPD as a site, which may engender unexpected understandings and may lead equally to change or stability. His understanding of the ZPD is that:

> the zone of proximal development is created in the interaction between the student and the co-participants in an activity, including the available tools and the selected practices, and depends on the nature and quality of that interaction as much as on the upper limit of the learner's capability (Wells, 1998, p318).

For teachers to support students effectively they need to take note of an individual's goals as well as the goals set by their communities and of the tools available to students including the texts they encounter in educational settings. This has implications for the classroom. Programs must be differentiated to meet the social, cultural and academic needs of the learners. It is also in contrast to a focus on the individual learner's reading ability being viewed, for instance, as a linear progression through a series of levelled texts designed by a publisher to 'test' or 'teach' reading 'skills'.

Developing criteria for choosing appropriate texts for teaching reading

Providing appropriately levelled texts for the teaching of reading

Marie M Clay (1991), who devised the Reading Recovery program, says: "that what is easy or difficult will vary from district to district, from school to school, and from child to child" (p201). The difficulty of any given text must therefore be seen to vary for individual students, depending not only on their skills but their understandings about the cultural context and the situation in which they encounter the text. Clay asserts that the difficulties in a text are always defined by the individual reader and that skilled teachers can develop an understanding of what constitutes an appropriate text for students learning to read.

Rose (Acevedo & Rose, 2007) in his work with Indigenous students states that students need support to read texts at the level of word, sentence and whole text because he recognises the need to teach students the patterns of language that they will encounter at each of these levels. He argues that the patterns of language found in texts will also differ according to their audience and purpose:

> For example, the language patterns of factual texts in science or society and environment are very different, from those in literary fiction, and both are different from the language patterns in arguments and text responses which evaluate issues or literary texts (p2).

Rose also acknowledges that students who are experiencing difficulty with literacy are not engaged with schooling, or reading, and are at risk of educational failure. He has recognised the importance of background knowledge when a reader is addressing a text however he does not focus on the possibility of particular texts being more or less engaging or supportive of the reading process.

Engagement

The importance of engagement in reading, however, is further underlined by the conclusions from recent research which show that students with the lowest levels of literacy make minimal progress during the middle years of schooling and this is compounded by a general decline in reading achievement for many students in the first two years of high school (DEST, 2005). This situation at least indicates that there is a lack of understanding about how to support lower achieving students in all grades. As Lokan has noted in the PISA report (2001) there is a correlation between engagement in reading and literacy achievement:

> The engagement with reading scale was significantly related to reading literacy achievement. With a measure of attitudes, it is usually not possible to disentangle whether positive attitudes lead to better performance, or the other way around, or a mixture of both. Efforts to raise students' appreciation of books and motivation to spend time reading should surely be of benefit, irrespective of which of them causes the other (pxi).

Some texts provide a bridge between the students' oral language and the written texts they will encounter within the education system. Within the classroom the engagement of young readers, from a range of backgrounds, can be achieved by skillful teachers if they choose the type of texts, which resonate with the particular young children in their own classes. These are texts which allow students the opportunity to participate with some understanding. These familiar texts will reflect the subject matter, wordings and grammatical features of the oral or written texts a child regularly encounters through participation in the discourse of their community. If this discourse is not congruent with the discourse of the school time must be given to building that familiarity with new the new discourse of the school (Smith, 1999).

The role of oral language in the teaching of reading

Thus the criteria for choosing texts must be based on a teacher's understanding of the oral language and literacy practices of the wider local community, and how they are reflected in the learning community within the classroom. An understanding of the relationship between the school community and the local community is crucial in the selection of appropriate texts, which will engage young readers. As Halliday notes: "spoken language favours the clause, where processes take place, whereas written language favours the nominal group. The locus of the constitution of things" (p99). It is clear that the patterns of language change from text to text depending on the audience and purpose; that particular audiences and purposes are privileged in our society; and that at the heart of learning to read is a familiarity with a range of patterns (Meek, 1988).

Halliday (1985) has also noted that teachers recognise that there is a role for oral language in the process of becoming literate (p96). He also differentiates between spoken and written texts, by identifying spoken texts as dynamic – presenting knowledge as a process – and written texts as synoptic – presenting knowledge as a thing that exists (p96). However Halliday argues that:

> In a literate culture, we tend not to take the spoken language seriously. This is not surprising, since not only has writing taken over many of the high prestige functions of language in our society, but also our highly valued texts are now all written ones. Written records have replaced oral memories as the repositories of collective wisdom and verbal art (p97).

This written way of knowing and sharing culture between generations has been challenged by many Indigenous peoples. As exemplified by Smith (1999) and Scollon (2001) there are other ways of knowing that are more highly valued by Indigenous peoples.

Halliday (1985) addresses one aspect of this difference when he explains that:

> Aboriginal languages are not, in fact, equipped to express the semiotics of Western societies – nor are European languages suited to the meaning styles of Aborigines. Each would have to adapt itself in order to meet such different demands (p92).

Smith (1999) would argue that this adaption has only been one way and it began to take place in Australia from the earliest times. It was not led by the dominant cultural group but by those who spoke the Aboriginal languages to which Halliday refers. As so aptly summarised by van Toorn (2006): "From these very early days, the history of Aboriginal literacy cannot be separated from the broader experience of Aboriginal oppression and dispossession" (p15). In reference to Rose, the patterns of Aboriginal English spoken by Indigenous people differ from the English of other Australians at the levels of word, clause and text. Halliday (1985) contends that:

> Learning is essentially a process of constructing meanings; and the cognitive component in learning is a process of constructing linguistic meanings – semantic systems and semantic structures. These systems of meaning, the ideational and interpersonal realities that we create in and through language, embody, as we have seen, two complementary perspectives: the synoptic and the dynamic (p98).

On the simplest level it is clear that the language of the written texts young students will encounter will be more familiar to some students than others and that this is an important consideration in the selection of texts.

Conclusion

In conclusion, choosing appropriate texts for teaching reading must be based on an understanding of the learner's needs as defined by the difficulty of the text for the young reader as well as the level of engagement the text produces. The difficulty of the text must not be reduced to a focus on the learner's skills as a decoder (Freebody, 2005) but must include the relationship of the young reader's community to the school, and what it means for the individual student learning to read (Bernstein, 1990; Connell, 1994; Freire, 1985). The choice of texts must above all engage young readers as poor and unmotivated readers spend less and less time reading and therefore compound the problem as they grow older (Lokan, 2001; Stanovich, 1986). If the teaching of reading is recognised as a sociocultural practice it is clear that the culture and social practices of the young student's community are important factors in the process of learning to read. Therefore, texts which reflect the social and linguistic resources of the local school community can provide important support to a young reader as it is this way of learning and knowing which will be most familiar to the young student.

References

Acevedo C, Rose D (2007). *Reading (and writing) to learn in the middle years of schooling*. Pen157 Marrickville: Primary English Teaching Association

Bernstein B (1990). Elaborated and restricted codes: overview and criticisms. In *Class, codes and control vol 4: The structuring of pedagogic discourse*, (pp94–130). London: Routledge.

Board of Studies NSW (1998). *English K–6 Syllabus*. Sydney: Board of Studies NSW.

Castle A, Coltheart M (2004). Is there a causal link from phonological awareness to success in learning to read? *Cognition*, 91(1): 77–111

Clay M (1991). *Becoming Literate: the construction of inner control*. New Zealand: Heinemann Education

Connell R W (1994). Poverty and Education. *Harvard Educational Review* 64 (2): 125–149.

Curriculum Corporation (1994). *English – a curriculum profile for Australian schools*. Victoria

Curriculum Corporation (1994). *ESL Scales*. Victoria.

(DEST) Department of Education, SaT (2005). *Teaching Reading Report and Recommendations*. Canberra: Australian Government.

Dufficy P (2000). Through the lens of scaffolding: Genre pedagogy and talk in multilingual classrooms. *TESOL in Context*, 10(1): 4–10.

Ewing R, Rushton K (2007). *Interim report: Researching the development of a community writer's kit and series 3 literacy resources*. Unpublished manuscript, University of Sydney.

Freebody P (2005). Hindsight and foresight: Putting the four roles model of reading to work in the daily business of teaching. In Healy A, & Honan E (Eds), *Text next: New resources for literacy learning*. (pp3–17) Sydney: Primary English Teaching Association.

Freebody P, Wyatt-Smith C (2004). The assessment of literacy: working the zone between 'system' and 'site' validity. *Journal of Educational Enquiry*, 5(2): 30–49.

Freire P (1985). *The politics of education: culture power and liberation*. New York: Bergin & Garvey

Halliday M A K (1994). *An introduction to functional grammar*, 2nd Edn. London: Edward Arnold.

Halliday, M A K (1985) *Spoken and written language*. Victoria: Deakin University Press

Hammond J, Gibbons P (2001). What is scaffolding? In J Hammond (Ed), *Scaffolding teaching and learning in language and literacy education*, (pp1–14). Newtown: Primary English Teaching Association.

Hasan R (1996). Literacy, everyday talk and society. In R Hasan & G Williams (Ed), *Literacy in Society*, (pp377–424). Harlow: Addison Wesley Longman Limited.

Hempenstall K (1997). The Whole Language-Phonics controversy: An historical perspective. *Educational Psychology: An international journal of experimental educational psychology*, 17(4): 399–418.

Lokan J (2001). *15-up and counting, reading, writing, reasoning: how literate are Australian students?: the PISA 2000 survey of students' reading, mathematical and *scientific literacy skills*. Melbourne: Australian Council for Educational Research Ltd.

Mahn H, John-Steiner V (2002). The Gift of Confidence: A Vygotskian View of Emotions. In G C Wells & G Claxton (Eds), *Learning for life in the 21st century: Sociocultural perspectives on the Future of Education*, (pp46–58). Oxford, UK: Blackwell Publishers.

Meek M (1988). *How texts teach what readers learn*. Stroud: The Thimble Press.

Reynolds M, Wheldall K (2007). Reading Recovery 20 Years down the Track: Looking Forward, Looking Back. *International Journal of Disability, Development and Education*, 54(2): 199–223

Scollon R (2001). *Mediated Discourse: the nexus of practice*. London: Routledge

Smith F (1999). Why Systematic Phonics and Phonemic Awareness Instruction Constitute an Educational Hazard. *Language Arts*, 77(2): 150–155.

Smith L Tuhiwai (1999). *Decolonizing Methodologies: Research and indigenous peoples*. Dunedin: University of Otago Press.

Stanovich K E (1986). Matthew effects in reading: some consequences of individual differences in the acquisition of literacy. *Reading Research Quarterly*, 21(4): 360–407

van Lier L (2004). *The Ecology and Semiotics of Language Learning: A Sociocultural Perspective*. Norwell: Kluwer Academic Publishers.

Van Toorn P (2006). *Writing never arrives naked: Early Aboriginal cultures of writing in Australia*. Canberra: Aboriginal Studies Press

Vygotsky L (1986). *Thought and Language*. Cambridge: The Massachusetts Institute of Technology.

Wells G (1998). Some Questions about Direct Instruction: Why? To Whom? How? And When? *Language Arts*, 76(1): 27–35.

Williams G (2000). Children's literature, children and uses of language description. In L Unsworth (Ed), *Researching language in schools and communities: Functional linguistic perspectives*, (pp111–129). London: Cassell

15
Debating and public speaking as oral literacy: promoting democratic education

Dr Ben Spies-Butcher
Macquarie University

This paper is a reflection on the NSW Department of Education debating and public speaking programs and efforts to make these programs more inclusive and democratic.

This paper is largely a reflection on my experience as a teacher/trainer and adjudicator in debating and public speaking for the Performing Arts Unit in the NSW Department of Education and Training. My experience is over roughly a decade, from the late 1990s, and is concentrated in working with primary school students, both at a state level and in regional and school specific programs, primarily in south-western Sydney.

The skills of oral literacy clearly go beyond those learned in debating and public speaking. Oral literacy is about a broader notion of communication. Nonetheless, these skills are an important component of our ability to communicate, and particularly our ability to gain recognition and respect for our ideas and opinions. These skills are particularly important because they are central to much of the way in which our society publicly deliberates, and because these skills are often used as an informal mechanism for stratification and establishing (or more likely reinforcing) social hierarchies.

The history of public speaking and debating in NSW offers an insight into a process of democratisation that has been taking place in the state's schools. Skills that were once confined to a social elite are increasingly becoming part of the mainstream education curriculum. In the process the definitions of public speaking and of debating, the skills and the judgement of what constitutes 'good speech' have also begun to change.

This is not to argue that these skills have lost their hierarchical characteristics altogether. Public speaking and debating remain a very particular form of communication – even within the public realm where people come to discuss politics, social organisation and how we collectively live together.

As a reflection, this paper is also informed, although perhaps less explicitly, by other experiences. I have also worked in the non-government sector, with social movements, particularly around issues of Indigenous rights and issues of peace and conflict. I have also been an active member of the Greens, a party that operates via consensus, a very different discursive principle to the implicit logic of debating.

In this paper I want to argue that the developments within public speaking and debating in NSW are to be welcomed. I argue these developments represent two separate but connected processes. Firstly, public speaking and debating have been opened up to more students. New competitions have emerged, skills have been incorporated into other aspects of the curriculum and schools previously excluded have been included. Secondly, the nature of debating and public speaking has itself begun to change. Aspects of affectation most closely associated with status and class have been diluted, there has been a shift away from formalism and there has been greater attention paid to the skills of listening and engaging with the ideas of others.

These changes make for a more democratic public sphere. They do so for different reasons that reflect the nature of the different changes. Not only do these developments promise a more inclusive public debate in the sense that more students, from more diverse backgrounds, participate, but the nature of that debate may also be more inclusive because of the values it embodies. This is far from an ideal picture. But it appears a step in the right direction.

The changing face of debating and public speaking

Many aspects of public speaking and debating have the characteristics of what Pierre Bourdieu (1984) termed 'cultural capital'. Cultural capital refers to the cultural resources that allow privilege to be transferred between generations. Bourdieu argued that elements of the education system were largely dedicated to this process. Educational systems, he argued, set in place structures where those from wealthy and middle class backgrounds prospered at the expense of working class children. By doing this, the education system obscured the processes of class reproduction – making the success of the better off appear to be the result of skill and hard work, rather than the privileges of birth.

Something of this process certainly appears to be in place in the realms of debating and public speaking. For some time these activities were dominated by a relatively small number from relatively elite schools. There is a very strong tradition of debating, for example, amongst the elite Greater Public Schools (GPS) in NSW. Within the public system the strongest debating traditions are in inner city selective schools, such as Sydney Boys and Sydney Girls, North Sydney Boys and North Sydney Girls and Fort Street.

A shift to a more inclusive approach has begun. Here I focus on the public system, primarily because this forms the great bulk of my experience, but also because it is in the public system that we would expect to find the best test on inclusion. The number of schools, students and competitions have all increased rapidly over the past 10–15 years. Prior to 1990 the Department of Education ran three debating competitions, for Years 9 and 10, Year 11 and Year 12. The Department also ran a public speaking competition for senior high school students sponsored by the *Sydney Morning Herald*, although this began about 25 years after the debating competitions.

The number of competitions began to expand in the 1990s. A junior high school public speaking competition, sponsored by Legacy, began in 1995 and a primary school competition for students in Years 3–6 began in 1996. A primary school debating competition, for Years 5 and 6 began in 1995 and a similar competition for Years 7 and 8 began in 1998. The nature of these competitions has also changed in some respects, although this is discussed later in the paper.

The number of students involved, and of schools, has also increased. In 2006 over 1300 teams entered the debating competitions. Teams typically comprise four students, although many schools rotate members throughout the competition allowing greater participation. Over 2000 primary school students entered the primary public speaking competition – the Multicultural Perspectives Public Speaking Competition – in 2007.

These are still relatively small numbers. However, this represents the tip of a much larger iceberg. In many schools, those involved in formal competitions are only a small proportion of those that engage with debating or public speaking. Many schools have internal competitions, or mini-regional competitions with neighbouring schools, to allow greater participation. Those that excel are then entered into the more formal statewide competitions. Likewise, debating and public speaking skills are increasingly being integrated into assessments for core subjects, such as English and History. It is becoming increasingly difficult to complete a school education without having to get up in front of your class and make a case.

From my experience some of the most important changes were taking place at the edges of the formal competitions. The Department also runs a series of skills workshops and training days for students and teachers. These 'flying squads' travel around the state, from the Riverina to the North Coast, from eastern Sydney to the far west of the state. A typical event will include students from a number of neighbouring schools, usually a significant proportion (sometimes all) of a particular year. A typical day might have anything up to a couple of hundred students in total.

The workshops usually run all day and involve a number of experienced debaters and public speakers giving an overview of the skills involved, followed by students practising those skills in small groups. The trainers are generally drawn from the pool of adjudicators, who are made up of the more successful high school debaters once they have left school. The training is focused on broad skills development, and so involves a number of theatre-type games that focus on getting students comfortable with being in front of an audience and thinking on their feet. The days also include brainstorming activities designed to teach students how to think creatively about arguments and how to structure their case.

These one-off interventions are generally supported by a longer term commitment from key teachers in different regions of the state. These teachers usually run the local competition and coordinate with neighbouring schools, as well as promoting debating and public speaking in their own school. There have been a number of key teachers around the state who have championed the cause, and this has been a key factor in the expansion of debating, particularly beyond the traditional heartland of the inner-city, northern Sydney and the selective schools.

Perhaps the most salient indicator of the success of these teachers, supported by the Arts Unit within the Department, has been the success of individual schools from outside the core zones of traditional success. Colo High School has twice won the Year 9 and 10 competition. Oxley High School in Tamworth won the inaugural Year 7 and 8 competition and Dubbo Public School has won the Year 5 and 6 competition. These are not the only examples, but they highlight the point.

More broadly there is a pattern of broad participation from around the state. In 2007 there were a total of over 1400 teams involved in debating competitions. The largest single group came from south-west Sydney (212). There are reasonable numbers from all regions of the state, the lowest being 71 teams from the Northern Tablelands region.

It is important not to overstate the trend. The high school representative teams remain dominated by a handful of selective schools, although this partly represents broader dynamics in the education system. There also remains a strong tradition of private schools paying for private coaches to assist their teams – a luxury very few public schools can afford.

Nonetheless, the trend appears positive. One of the concerns in recent years has been that funding to the flying squads has declined. It is an expensive line item – involving staff travelling and staying around the state, as well as leave for teachers to take students. But it is also demonstrably valuable to the process of democratising these skills.

Beyond the programs supported directly through the Arts Unit of the Department, which runs both the competitions and the flying squads, there have been other initiatives that have directly targeted schools outside the normal core of debating and public speaking.

I have been involved in a number of targeted coaching programs within the public system that in some ways mimic the private coaching offered within private schools. The main differences have been both that the students involved have fair less experience, and that the programs are generally targeted at a broader audience than those engaged in competition debating or public speaking.

The most notable of these experiences was in south-west Sydney. The district office, led by Kathy Rushton, began a speaking and listening program for students in a number of primary schools, supported by funding for disadvantaged students. The program ran for a number of weeks after school, and received strong support from a number of principals. Many of the students were from non-English speaking backgrounds, particularly from Arabic cultures, although none had significant problems with understanding English.

The program helped to establish internal debating competitions in and between a number of schools in the region, driven particularly by Auburn North Public and the district office. This is a region that had no prior formal debating or public speaking tradition, and is now one of the most economically and politically marginalised parts of Sydney. Now it is one of the regions with the highest participation in debating. The feedback from parents about the program has been extremely positive. Parents clearly place a high value on seeing their children speak in public, particularly where they are engaging with big ideas and advancing an intellectual case.

The response of parents highlighted for me the cultural significance of speaking skills. Being able to make a case publically, and engaging in argument, is highly valued. I think part of the reason for this is the cultural capital that comes with public speaking – it is associated with power and authority. But it also reflects that power and authority directly. Public speaking and debating are important tools in a democracy. They enable views to be put and people to be persuaded. It is particularly important for those groups who are marginalised from mainstream public discourse, and whose experiences are likely to be different from the experiences of those that dominate public debate.

Building a culture of debating and public speaking, normalising these skills, throughout our schools is an important step towards building a more inclusive and a more democratic society. The efforts of principals, teachers and those working in the Department have all contributed to a significant expansion in the reach of public speaking and debating. Of course, there remain limitations, but these efforts have had real results.

Changing the nature of debating and public speaking

Not only has debating and public speaking expanded in terms of the numbers and backgrounds of those involved, it has also changed in terms of the nature of the skills themselves. The way in which the main competitions are judged has been changing over time. These changes have been driven from within the public system and the leadership role that has increasingly been played by the Arts Unit, and its director, Lloyd Cameron, as the number of competitions and the number of participants has expanded.

The changes have been similar in both debating and public speaking. However, the issues are perhaps most pronounced in debating. Here, adjudication has traditionally focused on three broad areas. These areas are known as the 'three Ms' – manner, matter and method.

Manner is generally related to the way in which material is presented. It includes things like speaking clearly, modulating your voice and dressing appropriately. Matter relates to the substance of what is presented and

Method relates to the structure of the material – from simple things like ensuring you have an introduction, to more complex concepts such as ensuring your definition is consistent with your material and that you structure your case to allow the other side to engage appropriately.

The three Ms provide a definition of 'good speech'. And until relatively recently this understanding was codified through a marking formula. Each speaker would receive a mark out of 100 – consisting of a mark out of 40 for each of manner and matter and a mark out of 20 for method. The totals for each speaker would then be added and the team with the highest score would be judged the winner.

This obviously defines good speech in a particular way. It gives significant weight to the way ideas are presented, because of the high mark for manner. More particularly, the definition of 'good' manner becomes very important. Including aspects of presentation like dress has a particular impact, but so too does 'speaking clearly'. For many people, having an accent makes someone's speech less clear. It can also tend to encourage more theatrical performances.

Both the construction of manner and the weighting of manner within the marking system tended to reinforce existing preconceptions about what classified good speech. Just as importantly, focusing on manner tended to encourage participants to learn material by rote, and to regurgitate, rather than to engage.

Debates happen fairly quickly. Speakers will talk for 4–10 minutes, depending on the level. There may be a minute or so between speeches while an adjudicator notes things down and to allow the next speaker to gather their thoughts. That does not leave much time to listen to what has been said, absorb it and then develop a response. Those who do attempt to engage will almost always make mistakes. They will stumble, they may repeat themselves, they may have to stop and think for a moment.

The construction of manner and the weight it is given militate against genuine engagement. Students who engage tend not to do as well at manner as those who just reiterate what they were always going to say –

sometimes in a form that attempts to anticipate what their opponents might have said and therefore feign engagement.

It is perhaps obvious why I might have a problem with such a marking system. It encourages a form of speech that I regard as less democratic, and it discourages speech that is far more democratic. The idea of debate, at least in the public realm of civil society and politics, is surely to contribute to what John Stuart Mill would call the 'market place of ideas' – to do the sort of job we imagine of science; to put forward propositions and to test them by looking for evidence and challenging their logic.

To focus on the way things are said, rather than on what is said, is to encourage a form of debate that lacks substance. Moreover, it is to define authoritative speech in ways that are almost entirely cultural, rather than ways that are based on more substantive and objective criteria. I am not arguing that debate necessarily leads to truth, but I believe there are clear benefits to defining good speech in ways that minimise attributes that are part of a person's cultural inheritance and maximise those attributes that are part of a broadly scientific approach to knowledge.

Fortunately, this desire is exactly what has informed the changes in adjudication and the definition of good speech in recent years. Adjudicators, particularly at senior levels, increasingly mark according to a different system. Rather than awarding marks for each speaker and then calculating totals, debating is generally adjudicated accord to a principle of seizing the initiative – reflected in the manual for high school debating 'Taking the Initiative'.

This is a less well defined measure, but it attempts to capture the way one might ideally wish people to participate in the public sphere. It rewards genuine engagement with other people's ideas. It also encourages teams to structure their case to allow a real debate, rather than trying to define the other side out of the game or use clever logical tricks to prevent the other side having a fair chance. Of course it still takes account of the substance of what is said, it just encourages each speaker to try and engage with where the debate is up to and add their new substance in this light, while also challenging what their opponents have said before them.

This style of adjudication specifically rewards those students who attempt to rebut their opponents. Adjudicators are even told, as are teams, that the odd umm or ahh is to be encouraged if it means that people are genuinely trying to engage with ideas. As a result, the traditional aspects of manner, while not irrelevant, are now far less significant than they once were.

Likewise the way matter is judged has changed. Where once quoting great historical events was considered the pinnacle of good substance, now debaters are encouraged to use material that is topical and current, drawing from popular culture, news and current affairs.

In public speaking competitions this has gone one step further. The main primary schools competition is explicitly focused on multiculturalism. The competition thus makes the lived experience of students a legitimate source of material, particularly for those from minority cultures. It encourages people to reflect on their experience and the experiences of others, and to engage in contemporary debates about identity and living together.

Together these changes have meant not only an expansion in who participates in speaking, but a transformation in how the parameters of speech are defined. The result, I suggest, is both a more inclusive and a more democratic practice. One that teaches students to listen to each other, think about what others are saying and genuinely attempt to engage with those ideas.

This is not to say that Bourdieu's fears have been fully allayed. No doubt debating and public speaking, like most of the education system, play a role in reproducing, rather than removing, inequality. But these have been important steps in the right direction. Encouraging even greater participation, and continuing to encourage a reflexive and critical appraisal of the way competitions are set up and judged and how students are taught, must continue. Given the importance of these oral literacy skills to both the prospects of individual students and to our democracy, we need to pay attention to how these aspects of education continue to evolve.

References
Bourdieu P (1984). *Distinction: A social critique of the judgement of taste.* London: Routledge.

16
Research based criteria for the design and selection of literacy and thinking tools

David W Whitehead
School of Education, University of Waikato
Hamilton, New Zealand

Abstract

This paper describes criteria for the design and selection of literacy and thinking tools. The criteria are that tools should be: (i) teaching focused (ii) learner focused, (iii) thought linked (iv) neurologically consistent, (v) subject specific, (vi) text linked, (vii) developmentally appropriate, (viii) culturally responsive, and (ix) assessment linked.

Introduction

The importance of establishing criteria for the design and selection of literacy and thinking tools (Whitehead, 2001; 2004a) lies in the need for teachers to justify what they do. The reason for using literacy and thinking tools might be very general, for example 'the need for literate, future-focused thinkers who can create new knowledge and ensure the survival of society', or 'the need for a populace that understand how views are socially constructed and not always based on evidence'. Alternatively, the reason might be very specific, for example, 'the need to meet the evidence based reading comprehension needs of students'. Whatever reason we adopt, embedding a selection of literacy and thinking tools into an already over-crowded, over-specified, subject focused curriculum is problematic. It is made even harder in some institutions, notably secondary schools and universities, characterised by unproductive, hermetically-sealed silos of subject specific discourses that too long ago created intellectual no-fly zones, and that too long ago closed down the kinds of interdisciplinary dialogues crucial to the development of a literate and thoughtful population. But the question: "Which tools should we use in our classrooms?" inevitably leads us to consider criteria against which we might design and select those tools, and ultimately, justify what we do.

I use the 'tool' metaphor, rather than the more common term 'strategy', to emphasise the instrumental nature of these pedagogical aids, and I describe the tools illustrated in this paper in terms of both 'literacy' and 'thinking' because, as Guthrie and Wigfield (2001) note, the processes of inquiry learning [in science] are similar to text comprehension strategies recommended by the US National Reading Panel (National Institute of Child Health and Human Development, 2000) and the types of thinking outlined by the [Australian] Curriculum Council (1998).

A bird is ...	A bird can ...
Before	**Before**
1. An animal that can fly	1. Fly
During	**During**
2. Linked to dinosaurs	2. Crush seed in its beak
After	**After**
3. An avian	3. Migrate
Examples of birds are ...	**Birds have ...**
Before	**Before**
1. Crow	1. Feathers
During	**During**
2. Parakeet	2. Bills and beaks
After	**After**
3. Humming bird	3. Webbing and talons

Figure 16.1. A simple *Concept Frame* tool about birds.

Literacy and thinking tools are construction tools for the mind. Just as carpenters use tools to construct houses, literate thinkers use tools to construct and use knowledge. Just as hammers are built to drive in nails, some literacy and thinking tools are purpose-built to evoke specific types of thinking and for use with specific subjects and text types. Like the range of tools used by carpenters, literacy and thinking tools can be, procedurally and cognitively, more or less sophisticated. For example, the simple *Concept Frame* tool (see Figure 16.1) assists students to record and use their conceptual understandings. More specifically, this tool, discussed in greater depth later in this paper, engages students in recording words evoked by four generic headings (A xxx is ..., A xxx can ..., xxx have, Examples of xxx are ...). The recorded information can then be used to write or critique a report or description text.

Identifying design and selection criteria

The focus of this paper is not to describe tools for use in the classroom but rather to provide examples of tools that are consistent with criteria that allow us to justify what we do. The method used to identify nine criteria that allow us to justify the design and select literacy and thinking tools, involved the use of meta-analyses and literature reviews. These describe the characteristics of effective research-based pedagogy (Hattie, 1992, 2003; Hipkins, 2002; National Institute of Child Health and Human Development, 2000), and the application of recent understandings about learning from educational and cognitive psychologists (Ashcraft, 2007; Brophy, 2001; Sadoski & Paivio, 2001), and neuroscientists (Shaywitz & Shaywitz, 2007; Willis, 2007a, 2007b; Wolfe, 2001).

In part, the criteria emerged from a 2002 New Zealand Ministry of Education (MOE) literature review of significant New Zealand and international research published as the *Curriculum, Learning and Effective Pedagogy: A Literature Review in Science Education* (Hipkins et al., 2002). The selection of studies for inclusion in the 2002 MOE review was based on five characteristics, including whether the studies indicated (i) quantitative evidence of increases in student understanding and performance on authentic tasks, and (ii) qualitative evidence of improved student understanding, and attitudes in the classroom. The researchers who compiled this review defined 'effective pedagogy' in relation to student achievement.

Broadly, this literature review recommends that students might experience more success where pedagogy and curriculum are characterised by:

- learning experiences that are couched in meaningful contexts

- learning experiences that include sharing the purposes for learning with students
- student conversations with teachers that include explicit modelling of the type of discourse needed to achieve learning intentions
- the use of literacy strategies (or tools) that help students cope with the text features.

Findings from this review, together with those from other researchers referenced above, are used to identify criteria that might be used to justify each of the literacy and thinking tools described in this paper.

Criteria for the design and selection of literacy and thinking tools

The literacy and thinking tools described in this paper are consistent with nine research-based criteria. The criteria, derived from and supported by the literature reviewed in association with each tool, are that tools should be:

1. teaching focused
2. learner focused
3. thought linked
4. neurologically consistent
5. subject specific
6. text linked
7. developmentally appropriate
8. culturally responsive
9. assessment linked.

The use of each of the tools described in this paper can be justified in terms of more than one criterion. From a research paradigm perspective, justification for the inclusion of the teaching and learner focused, developmentally appropriate, thought linked and assessment linked criteria stem, primarily, from the research of cognitive, educational and developmental psychologists (Block & Pressely, 2001; Brophy, 2001; Neisser, 1976). The research paradigms of functional systemic linguists (Halliday, 1985; Martin, 1985), evolutionary psychologists (Pinker, 2002) and the epistemological studies of philosophers (Russell, 1912) provide justification for the text linked and subject specific criteria. Justification for the inclusion of the neurologically consistent criterion reflects recent research from neuropsychologists (Gazzaniga, Irvy & Mangun, 2002; Willis, 2007a; Wolfe, 2001).

1. Justification for a teaching focused criterion

The difference between tools consistent with the teaching focused criterion and tools consistent with the learner focused criterion is like the Chinese proverb: Give a family a fish and they will eat for a day; give them a fishing line and they will eat for a lifetime. Tools consistent with the teaching focused criterion are like fish. Tools consistent with the learner focused criterion are like the fishing line.

A justification for the inclusion of a teaching focused criterion lies in the claim that literacy and thinking tools should align with what excellent teachers do. Excellent teaching is associated with student achievement. In this respect, a meta-analysis of research describing the behaviours of excellent teachers conducted by Hattie (1992; 2003) noted that teachers account for about 30 per cent of the variance in student achievement. What teachers know, do, and care about is crucial to student achievement. More specifically, Hattie reports that teachers' feedback (effect size 1.13), instructional quality (effect size 1.00) and direct instruction (effect size .82) are key 'quality of teaching' variables.

A characteristic of excellent teachers identified by Alton-Lee (2003) that relates to Hattie's 'instructional quality' variable is 'teacher responsive to student learning processes'. This responsiveness is expressed when teachers scaffold learning, provide feedback on students' task engagement, encourage reflective thinking and engage students in goal oriented assessment.

Additional characteristics of excellent teachers identified by Hipkins et al. (2002) are again that they (i) scaffold conversations and investigative skills with explicit modelling of the type of text appropriate to the type of learning to be achieved, (ii) engage students in the co-construction of meaning that acknowledges their existing ideas (Ruddell, 2002), (iii) model different types of questions associated with inquiry and (iv) engage students in types of rich instructional dialogue that support critical and logical thinking (Alvermann & Hayes, 1989; Brooks, 1993; Goldenberg, 1993; Martin, Sexton, Wagner & Gerlovich, 1997).

Together these research findings point to excellent teachers as having a significant influence on student achievement. To be consistent with the teaching focused criterion, literacy and thinking tools must be shown to facilitate these characteristics of excellent teaching.

Teaching focused tool

The *concept cartoon* (see Figure 16.2) is designed to assist teachers who use co-construction pedagogy to restructure students' existing conceptual knowledge. It facilitates scaffolding through dialogue that models how we reason. *Concept cartoons* enable teachers to model different types of questions associated with inquiry learning and, through these questions, involve students in types of subject specific argumentation that, combined with responsive feedback, serve to modify the known and link to the new (Naylor, Keogh, & Downing, 2001).

The visual format and minimal written text of the *concept cartoon* tool together with their potential to help students express diverse and complex viewpoints make them effective teaching focused literacy and thinking tools. Best of all, the user-friendly cartoon format removes any potential embarrassment that might occur when students justify their own views to their peers.

As illustrated in Figure 16.2, *concept cartoons* take the form of cartoon styled drawings that illustrate students' subject specific conceptions (or misconceptions) and allow for the presentation of alternative ideas as a means of evoking ideas that don't fit comfortably with students' existing beliefs (cognitive dissonance).

Through discussion around a teachers' initial observation, ("Some birds have beaks curved at the end") and then through dialogue that evokes critical and reflective thinking, this teaching focused tool enables students to make intellectual leaps to a 'Big Scientific Idea'. The ideas beginning with 'BUT ...' recorded in *concept cartoon* callouts take the form of pseudo-questions, and can come from either the teacher, who understands some common misconceptions students might have about the topic, or from students, with teachers taking a 'back seat'.

Figure 16.2. A completed *concept cartoon* tool.

This tool enables teachers to help students learn effectively by talking themselves to meaning and is consistent with many of the teaching focused criteria associated with excellent teaching.

The intermediate *acrostics* tool (see Figure 16.3) is consistent with both the teaching and learner focused criteria. A key word from a current topic is written down the left of the acrostic and words beginning with each letter recorded mid-way (top word) and at the end of a series of lessons on that topic. Students then select the best word associated with each letter and construct a sentence that uses that word. The *acrostics* tool is consistent with both the teaching and learner focused criteria because it can be used by the teacher, as scribe, with a class or used independently by students as a revision tool. It can also be used as an assessment tool, for example by students recording words beginning with each letter of a few key words associated with a topic selected by the teacher.

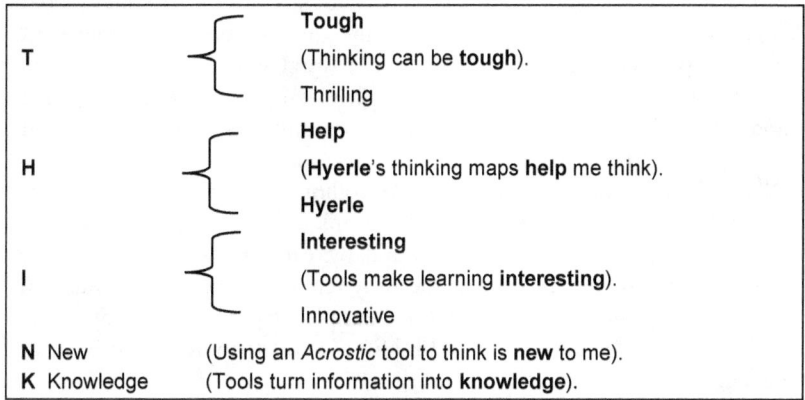

Figure 16.3 An intermediate *acrostic* tool.

2. Justification for a learner focused criterion

Learning tools are like fishing lines because they equip students with a means of becoming lifelong, literate thinkers. Two broad reasons for the use of tools consistent with a learner focused criterion are that (i) democratic societies need literate thinkers who can use a range of literacy and thinking tools independently and (ii) tools that align with this criterion are consistent with our understanding of learning as an active and complex process. More specifically, research by cognitive psychologists (Ashcraft, 2007) and neuropsychologists (Willis, 2006) suggests that students learn when they (i) maintain attention on a task,

(ii) are motivated to learn, (iii) encounter vivid and interesting experiences and (iv) are able to repeat the same experience and apply their understanding. This research also explains how we represent and modify concepts. Tools consistent with the learner focused criterion should reflect these findings and, in consequence, assist students to learn.

A learner focused tool

The *concept frame* (see Figure 16.1) is designed to help students achieve deliberate and purposeful outcomes with texts, independently. It is consistent with the learner focused criterion to the extent that it reflects the way psychologists think concepts are represented in memory. For instance, research by evolutionary psychologist Steven Pinker (2002) supports the claim for an innate ability among humans to represent direct experiences of the physical and natural world as concepts. He notes that in every human society, people classify, (conceptualise) plants and animals into species-like groups. Cognitive psychologists suggest concepts are represented in memory as connected 'meaning nodes' (Blaut, Stea, Spencer & Blades, 2003; Collins & Loftus, 1975; Farah & McClelland, 1991). These include 'example', 'dynamic', 'classification' and two types of 'attribute' nodes. Similarly, each sector of a *concept frame* (see Figure 16.1) aligns with the way concepts are represented in memory by providing learners with 'example' (types of bird), 'dynamic' (A bird can ...), 'classification' (A bird 'is ...) and 'attribute' (Birds have ...) headings.

This tool is also consistent with the principles of formative assessment. The 'Before', 'During' and 'After' (a series of lessons) headings invite students to record their developing understandings and allow teachers to assess student progress.

3. Justification for a thought linked criterion

Tools that align with the teaching and learning criteria construct learning as an active cognitive process. They are consistent with a definition of literacy as language in use – use implying thought. The thought linked criterion justifies the design and selection of tools on the basis of the types of thinking they evoke. In part, support for a thought linked criterion stems from research that describes the role of *generic* and *thematic* types of thinking in learning (McComas, 1998). For example, the [Australian] Curriculum Council (1998) notes that when students plan science investigations, (although clearly this applies to other subjects), they engage in at least three distinctive *generic* types of thinking. These include (i) critical thinking ('exploring ideas and materials, reviewing background information, identifying variables'), (ii) creative thinking ('thinking laterally, making predictions, inventing strategies for investigation'), and (iii) metacognitive thinking ('clarifying purposes, reflecting on their knowledge and experiences') (Curriculum Council, 1998, p222). Other researchers highlight the role of caring (and ethical) thinking (Lipman, 1977; Millett, 2003; Pohl, 2000).

There are overlaps among these types of *generic* thinking. For example, critical thinking requires principled reasoning, a critical spirit, and a rational and ethical passion (Eisner, 1985) – qualities also associated with epistemologically subversive students who are creative thinkers and who show creative curiosity, reflectivity and fascination in a subject. Metacognitive thinking is integral to all these types of thinking and significantly associated with student achievement (Scott, Asoko, & Driver, 1992). Literacy and thinking tools that evoke metacognitive thinking have, arguably, the largest impact on student achievement of any teaching practice (Donovan, Bransford, Pelligrino, 1999; Georghiades, 2000). However, it should be acknowledged that students' ability to engage in metacognitive thinking is not exclusively dependent on the use of tools designed to evoke this type of thinking. As Georghiades (2000) notes, short 'metacognitive instances' that involve brief discussions, thinking and writing tasks, and group activities can assist students to reflect on their own thinking using their own language.
In addition to these four *generic* types of thinking, justification for the inclusion of a thought linked criterion is provided by three common 'scientific themes' outlined by the American Association for the Advancement of Science (1996. These themes represent different types of *thematic* thinking, including (i) systemic, (ii) temporal-causal, and (iii) model thinking, all of which transcend disciplinary boundaries. First, systemic thinking allows learners to think about the 'whole' (for example the theme of a story) in terms of its parts (for example a narrative episode). System thinking also allows us to think about parts in terms of

how they relate to one another and the whole, for example how the relationships among episodes provides texture to the whole story.

Second, there are two components of temporal-causal thinking, which are (i) change and (ii) scale. For example, in respect to change, much of our comprehension of characterisation in narrative is concerned with comprehending how a character's psychological state changes, and the scale of that change. Change might be subtly signalled by a raised eyebrow, or dramatically signalled by a pique of rage. We also comprehend the rate at which things change, for example, the gradual development of abiding love and the instant onset of jealousy.

Third, model thinking allows us to represent ideas, objects and events (Gilbert & Boulter, 2000) as metaphor, analogies and visual mental images. I believe that model thinking should be made an explicit focus of learning because, as Coll (2005) argues, mental models, such as visual images, are central to our understandings of physical and psychological phenomena that may be unavailable to direct experience. In the form of analogies, metaphors or visual mental images, model thinking allows students engaged with the content of any subject to reflect on, discuss and critique both their understandings of concepts and those held by others (Taylor, 2000).

Evidence supporting the inclusion of a thought linked criterion acknowledges the need for tools that assist students to engage in generic and thematic types of thinking.

Thought linked tools

Literacy and thinking tools consistent with the thought linked criterion can, variously, evoke *generic* and *thematic* types of thinking. For example, *generic* creative thinking and *thematic* modelling can be evoked by the use of visual imagery tools such as *RISE* (Read, Image, Share and Evaluate) (Whitehead, 2001; 2004a). This involves teachers reading to or with students, then asking students to construct visual images representing objects, events, settings or people described in the text. Next, students are asked to share their images and then evaluate their images against the author's description as the text is re-read, or the illustrations as they are revealed. Consistent with the learner focused criterion this tool can be used by students independently.

A range of tools can be used to evoke critical thinking, including the *concept frame* when used to critic the content of text. Ethical issues can be addressed using *y-chart* tools that evoke caring thinking (Whitehead, 2001). There are also tools described by Fogarty (1994) that assist us to think metacognitively. These include the use of questions that prompt students to ask, "Which tool should I use to think about that idea?" Systemic and temporal-causal types of *thematic* thinking can be evoked through the use of *flow diagram* tools (see Figure 16.5).

Just as it would be unwise to define generic types of thinking as mutually exclusive, so too it is unwise to assume a single, clear and certain link between tools and types of thinking. Tools may simultaneously evoke more or less challenging types of creative and critical thinking. Consequently, the multiple types of thinking evoked by any single tool render popular classification such as 'creative thinking tool' as unspecific and problematic. But the fact that tools might evoke multiple types of thinking should not deter teachers from their professional responsibility to understand the types of thinking associated with their practice. Nor should this be used to dismiss the thought linked criterion as a means of justifying the design and selection of literacy and thinking tools.

4. Justification for a neurologically consistent criterion

The types of thinking described in relation to the thought linked criterion have their genesis and residence in the brain. It is unsurprising, therefore, that a neurologically consistent criterion should emerge from a review of recent literature from neuropsychologists. This criterion emerges from research by cognitive neuroscientists (Gazzaniga, Irvy & Mangun, 2002; Willis, 2007a, 2007b; Wolfe, 2001) and stipulates that literacy and thinking tools should be brain-friendly, that they should align with the way the brain learns naturally. Visual (mental) images associated with model thinking are neurologically consistent and have a long tradition in thought experiments and education (Dagher, 1995; Gilbert, 2005; Gilbert & Boulter, 2000). Visual (mental) images can be used to understand objects, events and ideas that are unfamiliar to students (like starvation) or abstract, like time, or unavailable to direct inspection (sometimes because objects and events are hidden, like mental illness, sometimes because they are too small to see, and sometimes because they would take more than a lifetime to observe, such as fossilisation). Like any mental model, visual images are likely to be (i) wrong in some key respect, (ii) simple or complex, (iii) more or less understood as imaginary rather than real, and (iv) more or less representative of students' understandings of the things they are meant to illustrate (Dyche, McClurg, Stephans, & Veath, 1993). It should be also noted that some people cannot image (Treagust, 1993; Whitehead, 1995).

Justification for the inclusion of this criterion is, naturally, based on an understanding of the literate brain. At a general level the brain processes verbal language (words, mathematical and scientific symbols and formula), and non-verbal language (illustrations and mental visual images) in two separate but connected systems (Sadoski & Paivio, 2001) – reading and writing are not exclusively verbal. These systems provide at least two ways of knowing. The verbal system provides one way of knowing about a person, for example, stating in a sentence: "Stanley Yelnats was persistent." The non-verbal system provides another way of knowing about Lord Rutherford, for example, by forming a visual mental image of him walking across a dried up lake bed eating onions.

At a specific level, neurological justification for the use of visual imagery tools comes from findings which show that functionally specific areas of the cerebral cortex permit the generation and manipulation of images (see Figure 16.4). Areas at the back of the brain in the occipital lobe which are crucial for sight (visual perception), are also crucial to the representation of mental models as images (Kosslyn, Ganis, & Thompson, 2001). These areas work in concert with areas on the left side of the brain that associate images with words, and areas on the right side of the brain that allow us to think about the spatial extent of images. The motor cortex area on the left side of the brain is implicated in the rotation of image (Tomasino, Borroni, Isaja, Rumiati, & Farah, 2005) and all these areas work under the direction of the prefrontal cortex that acts like an executive decision maker, allowing us to consciously image and engage in imagery thinking. Justification for the neurologically consistent criterion lies in understanding the parts of the neural network that facilitate modelling and other types of thinking.

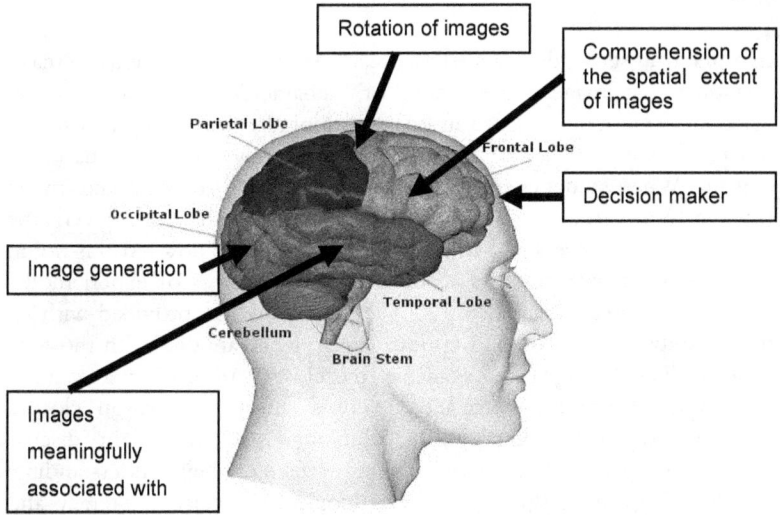

Figure 16.4 Areas of the brain involved in visual mental imagery

A neurologically consistent tool

Tools consistent with this criterion align with the way the brain learns. When teachers use tools and texts to engage students in different types of thinking, they operate on the brain as assuredly as neurosurgeons. The neural fabric of the brain is restructured or pruned every time a literacy and thinking tool is used. In this sense, the very structure of our brain – the relative size of different regions, the strength of connections between them, even their functions – reflects the pedagogy we use. Like sand on a beach, the brain bears the footprints of the decisions we have made, the tools we have used and the conversations we have conducted.

Visual imagery tools prompt students to generate and manipulate different types of visual mental images. For example, the use of a visual image to think about changes in a character's psychological state requires the generation of transformational images that represents those changes of state. Zooming in on that representation, or changing one's imaginary position in respect to that character can offer 'insight' into that character's psychological state and provide viable re-view and retrieval cues.

In a practical sense, during a lesson, teachers might ask students to make a static visual image, for example, of a character that is not moving. Then students might engage in imagery thinking by making their image move, allowing them to 'see' the character involved in a narrative episode. When students are asked to share the things they imaged (move from a non-verbal to a verbal representation) they are given the opportunity to express and further clarify what they know. At this point, and consistent with findings of behavioural indicators of expert model use (Coll, France, and Taylor, 2005), they should be provided with an opportunity to compare and critique their mental models with those of experts. These might be available by closely re-reading a text or examining illustrations that accompany a text. As a lesson closure designed to foster metacognitive thinking, students might discuss whether images and imagery thinking affected their understanding; whether the use of this type of neurologically consistent literacy and thinking tool helped them learn.

Tools consistent with the thought linked criterion serve as an interdisciplinary adhesive, as a super-set that connects disciplines. These tools have a unifying effect across the curriculum and allow teachers to redefine knowledge as a way of knowing. Visual imagery tools are whole brain tools, but justification for their design and selection lies in understanding the parts of the neural networks that facilitate the generation and use of the images. Like visual imagery tools, all literacy and thinking tools should be neurologically consistent because teaching and learning should align with how the brain learns naturally.

5. Justification for a subject specific criterion

While some literacy and thinking tools, like *thinking maps* (Hyerle, 1996) and cooperative learning tools such as *think-pair-share* (McTighe & Lyman, 1998) suit most subjects, other tools are more suited to specific subjects because they align with their language and epistemological characteristics (the types of thinking that underpin how those subjects construct knowledge). For example, scientists probably have more use for *flow diagram* tools than most other subject specialists because the reading and writing of explanations, and the cause and effect thinking inherent in their work and those literate tasks, are central to the traditional way scientists construct knowledge. However, note that creative thinking is a crucial antidote to the tyranny of empiricism.

A subject specific tool

The simple *flow diagram* illustrated in Figure 16.5 is well suited to science because it helps students explain changes in, for example, the states of matter. This tool also helps them acquire the verbal and visual language associated with these changes. Specifically, this tool assists students use 'causal link' words and visual text features associated with the academic language of scientific explanations ('because', 'so', 'when', etc). It is also formative, supporting conceptual development over time by requiring students to draw a series of sketches that represent and stretch their understandings, and to draft and re-draft their understandings as captions.

1. Sketches drawn over a series of lessons, explaining the process of water evaporating from the ocean.	2. Sketches drawn over a series of lessons, explaining the process of water vapour condensing into rain drops.
Final draft caption explaining events in the pictures using 'because'. Water evaporates from the ocean <u>because</u> warm air heats the water and molecules escape as water vapour.	*Final draft caption explaining events in the pictures using 'so'.* <u>So</u>, the warm humid air rises into the sky and begins to cool and turn into rain drops.
4. Sketches drawn over a series of lessons, explaining the process of snow melting into water.	3. Sketches drawn over a series of lessons, explaining the process of water freezing.
Final draft caption explaining events in the pictures using 'when'. <u>When</u> snow or ice heats up (or loses cold), it becomes a liquid again, and when it heats up even more, it becomes a gas or water vapour again.	*Final draft caption explaining events in the pictures using 'when'.* <u>When</u> water gets cold enough, it becomes a solid called snow, or a solid called ice like in hailstones.

Figure 16.5 A simple captioned *flow diagram* tool describing changing states of matter.

The three *flow diagram* sketches and caption in Figure 16.6 illustrate a student's developing understanding of evaporation, the subject specific language used to explain this process, and their ability to use the visual language of science. The student understands that the space between molecules of water vapour make it less dense than water, that scientists use schematic diagrams and that water vapour is better suited to an explanation of evaporation than steam.

Figure 16.6 Sketches drawn over a series of lessons, exploring the process of water evaporation

6. Justification for a text linked criterion

Support for a text linked criterion is linked to the claim that specific subjects preferentially evoke certain types of thinking, and the additional claim for links between types of thinking and text types. Indeed, Pontecorvo (1993) goes so far as to suggest that "forms of discourse become forms of thinking" (p191). Implicit in this claim is that different types of thinking can be evoked through specific discourse practices (including reading and writing specific text forms). Additionally, the thinking associated with, for example, writing a factual report, is both a response to epistemology of the subject of the report, (that is, to subject specific ways of knowing) and to the type of thinking evoked by the type of text commonly used by that subject. These claims seem to underpin a key recommendation by Hipkins et al. (2002) that "students need to be coached in communication styles" (p179). Indeed, Lemke (1990) notes that a hallmark of engaging in learning is the opportunity to acquire subject specific discourse, a position consistent with that of functional systemic linguists (Halliday, 1985; Martin, 1985) who make links between the social construction of knowledge and text forms.

Further evidence justifying the inclusion of a text linked criterion comes from research that suggests comprehension is enhanced if readers make use of (i) text features associated with 'conventional' genre, and (ii) top level text structures including cause-effect, compare-contrast, and problem-solution structures typical of paragraph (Duke & Pearson, 2002; Goldman, 1997).

A text linked tool

Literacy and thinking tools that evoke types of thinking similar to that evoked by a text students are required to read, write or talk are probably best used when students read, write or talk those texts. This is because of the synergies generated between subject specific, thought linked and text linked criteria. These synergies are illustrated by the links between the *concept frame* tool (see Figure 16.1) and the report text about birds (see Figure 16.7). The tool is consistent with the text linked criterion because it is designed to help students comprehend or construct report texts and engage in the type of thinking associated with those tasks.

Specifically, the *concept frame* tool evokes, in part, attribute thinking – students are prompted to list (see 1–3 in the 'Can' and 'Have' sectors of the *concept frame*) the attributes of an object, event or idea. In turn, report texts represent the outcome of attribute thinking – they too record the attributes of objects, events and ideas. Given that both the *Concept Frame* tool and report texts evoke similar types of thinking they should, consistent with the text linked criterion, be used together.

From a linguistic perspective the *concept frame* tool is also consistent with the text linked criterion. Different parts of a *concept frame* reflect some of the 'conventional' structural features of report genre. One structural feature of a report, usually found toward the beginning, classifies the topic ("Birds are ... animals that fly"). Students can use information from the unshaded sector of the *concept frame* (see Figure 16.1) to help them write this part of a report. Information from the shaded sectors of the *concept frame* can be used to write the body of a report (identified in the shaded area of Figure 16.7). This information might be written as in simple sentences ("Birds can chirp"), or as more complex sentences and paragraphs that reflect deeper understandings.

Title: Birds of a Feather

Engagement
  Our <u>parakeet</u>, Wally, squawks and his cage sometimes smells. Wally is a bird and has a curved beak and beautiful feathers.

Classification
  Most birds are <u>animals that fly</u>. But there are some birds, like emus and kiwis that don't fly. All birds have <u>feathers</u>. Some birds like parakeets have colourful feathers, and some like the bald eagle are mostly dark in colour. All birds are <u>avian</u>.

Body
Anatomy
  All birds have <u>feathers</u>. Some feathers are long like the tail feathers of a peacock. Some feathers are colourful and others black like those of a crow. Feathers are hollow inside which makes them light.
  All birds have <u>beaks</u>. Some are curved, others are long and thin, others are short and strong, and others are flat and wide. The type of beak a bird has and what it eats are related.
  All birds have <u>wings</u>, but not all birds can fly. Some sea birds have wings up to two yards long. The emu has stumpy wings and can not fly.

Behaviour
  Most birds can fly. Some birds like the humming bird fly very fast. Other birds like the <u>eagle</u> soar and glide and don't flap their wings as fast as a <u>humming bird</u>.
  You might think that all birds can <u>chirp</u>, but the <u>parakeet</u> we have at home makes a loud screeching noise that doesn't sound like a chirp. Many small birds chirp, especially the ones with short strong beaks for <u>eating grain</u>.
  But not all birds eat grain. Birds with different shaped beaks eat different things. For example, humming birds eat nectar from flowers and eagles eat meat and fish.

Figure 16.7 A short annotated report text about birds linked to a simple *concept frame*. Note: Underlined words are from the simple *concept frame* tool about birds (see Figure 16.1)

7. Justification for a developmentally appropriate criterion

The progression from the use of tools by teachers and later learners is consistent with the teaching focus and learner focus criterion signals that tools need to be developmentally appropriate. The justification for this criterion lies along at least three dimensions. The first is that the design and use of tools should scaffold students from a dependence on the teacher to an independence from the teacher. The second is that tools should provide a challenge to learners. This dimension is consistent with research by Locke & Latham (1992) that suggests achievement is enhanced to the degree that students and teachers set challenging goals, and that the greater the challenge the higher the probability of students seeking, receiving, and assimilating feedback information. The availability of developmentally appropriate tools at three levels of challenge reflects this research.

Third, and consistent with calls from educational psychologists for developmentally appropriate teaching and differentiated instruction (Brophy, 2001), tools consistent with this criterion need to be designed for use with students at different levels of social, academic and cognitive maturity. Thus the developmentally appropriate criterion reflects beliefs about variations in students' attention spans, and in the types of text-related intellectual tasks they encounter in classrooms. Consistent with these three dimensions, the tools used to illustrate criteria described in this paper have been designed at three developmental appropriate levels; simple, intermediate and complex. For example, the simple *concept frame* (see Figure 16.1) provides students with just four headings that assist them to gather and record information. In terms of Bloom's (1956) taxonomy this evokes little more than recall and understanding. In contrast, intermediate and complex *concept frames* (see Figures 16.8 and 16.9) require students to work with five headings and to further process information in each sector of each frame. In terms of Bloom's (1956) taxonomy this requires students to analyse and synthesise information.

What these three developmentally appropriate levels do not assume is that students' age should determine which tools they use. If eight-year-old students are capable of using intermediate rather than simple tools, they should be encouraged to use them. Many students in the early years of schooling are capable of abstract thinking even when presumed to be operating at a concrete operational stage. However, the more abstract thinking evoked by some complex tools might signal the need to scaffold their use, that is, to use them in ways consistent with the teaching focus criterion rather than the learner focus criterion. Teachers can plan to use tools at an appropriate level, but bear in mind that levels should never deny students opportunities to think.

A developmentally appropriate tool

The developmental appropriate levels of the three *concept frames* illustrated in Figures 16.1, 16.8 and 16.9 are designed to provide students with challenges appropriate to their intellectual development and experience. The simple level tool probably best suits 5–8-year-old students, or students using literacy and thinking tools for the first time. The intermediate level tool is designed to challenge the thinking of 8–12-year-olds and should suit students who can already use simple tools confidently and independently. The complex level tool is designed for use in secondary schools or with gifted and talented students, who will probably begin to use a range of tools in combination.

Is … / is a …		BIRDS	Are …	
Order	Belongs to a group		Order	Things about them
3.	Animals that fly		2.	Pets
2.	An avian		1.	Expensive to keep
1.	Animal with feathers		X	Colourful
X.	A noisy thing		3.	Meat eaters
Can …		Has … /has a … /have …		Examples	
Order	Actions	Order	Things they have	Order	Examples
4.	Chirp	1.	Feathers	2.	Eagle
2	Fly	2.	Claws	1.	Crow
1.	Eat grain	3.	Wings	3.	Sparrow
5.	Spread disease	4.	Curved beaks	4.	Chaffinch
3.	Dirty windows	5.	Stubby beaks	5.	Kiwi

Figure 16.8 An intermediate *concept frame* tool about birds.

For example, when used as a teaching tool, a simple *concept frame* (see Figure 16.1) can be used as a text-linked, pre-writing tool. This tool enables teachers to assess and record before, during and after a series of lessons, and to collaborate with students as they use each sector of their completed frames to write simple pattern sentences, for example, 'A bird can ...', A bird has ..., A bird is ..., An example of a bird is ..., or a more complete report text.

In contrast, students may find the intermediate and complex *concept frame* tools more challenging. At the intermediate level students are asked to further attend to what they know by ordering information in each sector of the *concept frame*. This order will be reflected in the structure of their written report texts. They might also decide that some information doesn't align with what they want to write in their report, and signal this with an 'X' beside the word (see Figure 16.8).

A complex level *concept frame* requires students to generate additional ideas by using the 'Examples' words (see right hand bottom sector in Figure 16.9) to construct and answer questions. To achieve this students would begin with a name of a bird listed in the 'Examples' sector, for instance 'Eagle', and add a sector header word ('is', 'are', 'can', or 'has') to 'Eagle' to construct their question. For example, 'An eagle is ...?', or 'Eagles can ...?' or 'An eagle has ...?' Students then conduct further research and record answers to those questions in the appropriate sector of the *concept frame*. For example, 'Eagles can ... catch rabbits' so 'catch rabbits' would be recorded under the 'can' sector heading of the *concept frame* (see point 6. '*Catch rabbits*' under 'Can' in Figure 16.9). In addition, the complex *concept frame* requires students to group information. Figure 16.9 illustrates how groups have been made for 'damaging' things birds can do, and for examples of birds that are 'meat eaters' and 'grain eaters'.

The developmentally appropriate criterion reminds us that literacy and thinking tools should be designed at three levels of 'challenge' that align with students' social and cognitive strengths.

Is ... / is a ...		Are ...	
	BIRDS		
Order	Belongs to a group	Order	Things about them
3.	Animals that fly	2.	Pets
2.	An avian	1.	Expensive to keep
1.	Animal with feathers	X	Colourful
X.	A noisy thing	3.	Meat eaters
		4.	Threatened

Can	Has ... /has a ... /have ...	Examples
Order Actions Groups	Order Things they have	Order Groups
4. Chirp	1. Feathers	2. Eagle ⎤ Meat eaters
2 Fly — Damaging	2. Claws	1. Crow ⎦
1. Eat grain ⎤	3. Wings	
5. Spread disease ⎬	4. Curved beaks	3. Sparrow ⎤ Grain eaters
3. Dirty windows ⎦	5. Stubby beaks	4. Chaffinch ⎦
6. Catch rabbits		

Figure 16.9. A complex *concept frame* tool about birds.

8. Justification for a culturally responsive criterion

A further criterion that can be applied to justify the design and selection of literacy and thinking tools is cultural responsiveness. This criterion is aligned to the belief that students should think about their own and others' thinking, and more specifically, should reflect on the ways in which indigenous cultures construct knowledge.

A culturally responsive tool

The *universal perspective* tool (Whitehead, 2004b) is culturally responsive because it enables students to engage in a type of worldview thinking that has its genesis in indigenous cultures. The tool enables students to appreciate the perspective of people who see themselves as one within a connected universe (connected to nature, society and supernatural realms). First, this tool requires students to identify whether an author has constructed identities that were universally connected to, or separated from a culturally specific zeitgeist. It then requires them to appreciate the effect on meaning of a non-universal perspective, and finally to think critically about an author's text by asking why they adopted (or didn't adopt) a universal perspective. Literacy and thinking tools consistent with the culturally responsive criterion can assist us to communicate interculturally and appreciate the perspectives of others.

9. Justification for an assessment linked criterion

The forms of assessment teachers use have a powerful influence on the kinds of instruction students encounter, and the kind of learning they can accomplish. Underpinning the assessment linked criterion is the belief that there is nothing inherently wrong with assessing the content and processes we teach, as long as we concurrently and regularly assess in ways that reflect how that content and those processes were taught. The assessment linked criterion is, therefore, consistent with the use of literacy and thinking tools that engage students in formative assessment (Black & Wiliam, 1998).

The use of tools as concurrent and formative learning and assessment measures is consistent with Neisser's (1976) claim that assessment items should be constructed in such a way that students recognise and treat them as familiar and representative of the actual learning experience – that is, that they should be *ecologically valid* items. Thus, tools that align with the assessment linked criterion as assessment items, simultaneously assess both subject content and students' ability to use the tools employed to teach and learn that content. This criterion goes to the heart of how we teach and our understandings of how we learn.

The use of literacy and thinking tools as assessment items may require some teachers to change their pedagogical metaphors of 'knowledge-as-object', 'mind-as-container'. This pair of metaphors fails to reflect that knowledge, and especially the procedural knowledge associated with the use of literacy and thinking tools, which is something that does things, or makes things happen (Castells, 2000). If we accept that knowledge has what Lyotard (1984) calls *performativity*, it follows that the assessment of literacy and thinking should be consistent with Claxton's (2004) 'school as gymnasia', 'fit mind', and 'mental exercise' metaphors. When we work out at the gymnasium we don't look at the equipment, we use it, just as we use literacy and thinking tools to manipulate what we know and construct new meanings. Tools consistent with the assessment linked criterion should tell us how well a student can use what they know.

An assessment linked tool

The assessment item illustrated in Figure 16.10 can be used as a planned, formative, pre-test item to gauge students' prior knowledge of a topic, and as an ecologically valid summative post-test item (assuming the tool was used concurrently to learn the content). Assessment linked tools provides teachers with opportunities to test as they teach; to assess not only what is taught (about rocks), but also how it is taught.

A rock is ... 1 2 3	A rock can ... 1 2 3
Examples of rock are ... 1 2 3	A rock has ... 1 2 3

Figure 16.10 A simple *concept frame* tool used as a pre- and post-test item

Instruction: Define the meaning of a rock as accurately as you can by completing the simple *concept frame*.

Conclusion

The use of literacy and thinking tools consistent with these nine design and selection criteria impact on how we plan and conduct our lessons, assess learning and view the role of education in society. For example, learning intentions and success criteria will identify tools linked to texts and types of thinking. Lessons will align more with co-construction than transmission models of teaching, and assessment will become more formative. The use of knowledge by a population of literate thinkers will be valued by society. Changes will occur to curriculum and teacher education programs, to the extent that tools for gathering, processing and reflecting are valued as part of our schools' culture along with content.

The use of literacy and thinking tools, justified against these nine research based criteria, provides a way of addressing a tendency among some teachers to rely on their pedagogy, a bit like a drunk uses a lamp-post – to support the way they teach rather than to shed light on alternative and justifiable pedagogies. Moreover, some teachers only use their lamp-post. Too often we seize on what we know and on historic precedent to support the way we teach without the justification of research based criteria. We resist looking for future directions because we have adopted comfortable labels. I believe the use of tools that align with these nine criteria should be an integral component of our programs, and should be prized, not only because their application leads to attractive learning opportunities, but also because the journey toward those destinations is extremely satisfying and motivating for both teachers and learners alike.

References

Alton-Lee A (2003). *Quality teaching for diverse students in schooling: Best evidence synthesis.* Wellington: Ministry of Education.

Alvermann D, Hayes D A (1989). Classroom discussion of content areas reading assignments: An intervention study. *Reading Research Quarterly*, 24: 305–335.

American Association for the Advancement of Science (1996). *Benchmarks for science literacy.* New York: Oxford University Press.

Ashcraft M (2007). *Cognition.* New York: Pearson.

Black P J, Wiliam D (1998). Assessment and classroom learning. *Assessment in classroom learning: Principles, policy and practice*, 5(1): 7–74.

Blaut J M, Stea D, Spencer C, Blades M (2003). Mapping as a cultural and cognitive universal. *Annals of the Association of American Geographers*, 93(1): 165–185.

Block C C, Pressely M (Eds), (2001). *Comprehension instruction: Research-based best practices*. New York: Guilford.

Bloom B (1956). *Taxonomy of educational objectives*. New York: Longman, Green and Co.

Brooks J G, Brooks M G (1993). *In search of understanding: The case for constructivist classrooms*. Alexandria, VA: Association for Supervision and Curriculum Development.

Brophy J (Ed), (2001). Subject-specific instructional methods and activities. *Advances in Research on Teaching, Vol. 8*. New York: Elsevier.

Castells M (2000). *The rise of the network society, 2nd Edn*. Oxford: Blackwell.

Claxton G (2004). Mathematics and the mind gym: How subject teaching develops a learning mentality. *For the learning of mathematics*, 24(2): 27–32.

Coll R K (2005). The role of models, mental models and analogies in chemistry teaching. In P Aubusson & A G Harrison (Eds), *Metaphor and analogy in science education*. Dordrecht: Kluwer.

Coll R K, France B, Taylor I (2005). The role of models/and analogies in science education: implications from research. *International Journal of Science Education*, 27: 183–198.

Collins A, Loftus E (1975). A spreading activation theory of semantic processing. *Psychological Review*, 82: 407–428.

Curriculum Council (1998). *Curriculum framework for kindergarten to year 12 education in Western Australia*. Osborne Park, WA: Author.

Dagher Z R (1995). Analysis of analogies used by science teachers. *Journal of Research in Science Teaching*, 32(3): 259–270.

Donovan M S, Bransford J D, Pellegrino J W (Eds), (1999). *How people learn: Bridging research and practice*. Washington: National Academy Press.

Duke N, Pearson P D (2002). Effective practices for developing reading comprehension. In A E Farstrup & S J Samuels (Eds), *What research has to say about reading instruction, 3rd Edn*, (pp205–242). Newark, DE: International Reading Association.

Dyche S, McClurg P, Stephans J, Veath M L (1993). Questions and conjectures concerning models, misconceptions and spatial ability. *School Science and Mathematics*, 93(4): 191–197.

Eisner, Elliot W (1985). *The art of educational evaluation: a personal view*. London: Falmer Press.

Farah M J, McClelland J L (1991). A computational model of semantic memory impairment: Modality specificity and emergent category specificity. *Journal of Experimental Psychology: General*, 120: 339–357.

Fogarty R (1994). *How to teach for metacognitive reflection*. Arlington Heights, IL: Skylight.

Gazzaniga M S, Irvy R B, Mangun G R (2002). *Cognitive neuroscience, 2nd Edn*. New York: Norton.

Georghiades P (2000). Beyond conceptual change learning in science education: Focusing on durability, transfer and metacognition. *Educational Research*, 42: 119–139.

Gilbert J (2005). *Visualization in science education*. Dordrecht: Springer.

Gilbert J, Boulter C (2000). *Developing models in science education*. Dordrecht: Kluwer.

Goldenberg C (1993). Instructional conversations: Promoting comprehension through discussion. *Reading Teacher*, 46(4): 316–326.

Goldman S R (1997). Learning from text: Reflections on the past and suggestions for new directions of inquiry. *Discourse Processes*, 23(3): 357–398.

Guthrie J T, Wigfield A (2001). *Engaging in reading through science: Motivating strategies across the disciplines*. Paper presented at the Crossing Borders: Connecting Science and Literacy conference, Baltimore, MD.

Hattie J A (1992). Towards a model of schooling: A synthesis of meta-analyses. *Australian Journal of Education*, 36: 5–13.

Hattie J (2003). *Teachers Make a Difference: What is the research evidence?* Paper presented to the Australian Council for Educational Research, October 2003.

Halliday M A K (1985). *An introduction to functional grammar*. London: Edward Arnold.

Hipkins R, Bolstad R, Baker R, Jones A, Barker M, Bell B, Coll R, Cooper B, Forret M, Harlow A, Talyor I, France B, Haigh M (2002). *Curriculum Learning and Effective pedagogy: A literature review in science education*. Report to the Ministry of Education.

Hyerle D (1996). *Visual tools for constructing knowledge*. Association for Supervision and Curriculum Development: Alexandria, Va.

Kosslyn S M, Ganis G, Thompson W L (2001). Neural foundations of imagery. *Neuroscience*, 2: 635–642.

Lemke J L (1990). *Talking science: Language, learning and values*. Norwood, NJ: Ablex.

Lipman M (1977). *Philosophy in the classroom*. Montclair State College, Upper Montclair, NJ: Institute for the Advancement of Philosophy for Children.

Locke E A, Latham G P (1992). Comments on McLeod, Liker & Lobel, *Journal of Applied Behavioral Science*, 28: 42–45.

Lyotard J F (1984). *The postmodern condition: A report on knowledge*. Manchester: Manchester University Press.

Martin J (1985). *Factual writing: Exploring and challenging social reality*. Geelong: Deakin University Press.

Martin R, Sexton C, Wagner K, Gerlovich J (1997). *Teaching science for all children*, 2nd Edn. Boston: Allyn & Bacon.

McComas W F (1998). *The nature of science in science education*. Dordrecht: Kluwer.

McTighe J, Lyman F (1988). Cueing thinking in the classroom: The promise of theory-embedded tools. *Educational Leadership*, 45(7): 18–24.

Millett S (2003). Thinking tools for teaching ethics across the curriculum. *Critical and Creative Thinking*, March, 2–13.

Ministry of Education (2006). *Effective literacy practices in Years 5–8*. Learning Media: Wellington.

National Institute of Child Health and Human Development (2000). *Report of the National Reading Panel. Teaching children to read: An evidence-based assessment of the scientific research literature on reading and its implications for reading instruction*. Washington: Author.

Naylor S, Keogh B, Downing B (2001). *Dennis likes a good argument: Concept cartoon, argumentation and science education*. Paper presented at the annual conference of the Australasian Science Education Research Association, 11–14 July.

Neisser U (1976). *Cognitive psychology*. New York: Appleton-Century-Crofts.

Pohl M (2000). *Learning to think, thinking to learn: Models and strategies to develop a classroom culture of thinking*. Highett, Vic: Hawker Brownlow Education.

Pontecorvo C (1993). Forms of discourse and shared thinking. *Cognition and Instruction*, 11(3&4): 189–196.

Pinker S (2002). *The blank slate*. New York: Penguin.

Ruddell M (2002). *Teaching content reading and writing, 3rd Edn*. New York: Wiley.

Russell B (1912). *The problems of philosophy*. Oxford: Oxford University Press.

Sadoski M, Paivio A (2001). *Imagery and text*. Mahwah, NJ: Lawrence Erlbaum.

Scott P, Asoko H, Driver R (1992). Teaching for conceptual change: A review of strategies. In R Duit, F Goldberg & H Niederer (Eds), *Research in physics learning: Theoretical issues and empirical studies* (pp310–329). Kiel: Institute for Science Education at University of Kiel.

Shaywitz S E, Shaywitz B A (2007). What neuroscience really tells us about reading instruction. *Educational Leadership*, 64(5): 74–76.

Taylor I J (2000). *Promoting mental model-building in astronomy education*. Unpublished PhD Thesis, University of Waikato, Hamilton.

Tomasino B, Borroni P, Isaja A, Rumiati R, Farah M (2005). The role of the primary motor cortex in mental rotation: a TMS study. *Cognitive Neuropsychology*, 22(3&4): 348–363.

Treagust D F (1993). The evolution of an approach for using analogies for teaching and learning science. *Research in Science Education*, 23: 293–301.

Whitehead D (1995). *The design and validation of a visual imagery ability questionnaire*. Unpublished PhD Thesis, University of Waikato, Hamilton.

Whitehead D (2001). *Top tools for literacy and learning*. Auckland: Pearson Education.

Whitehead D (2004a). *Top tools for teaching thinking*. Auckland: Pearson Education.

Whitehead D (2004b). *World-view perspectives*. Paper presented at the Language, Education and Diversity conference, University of Waikato, November, March 2004.

Willis J (2006). *Researched based strategies to ignite student learning*. Alexandria, Virginia: Association for Supervision and Curriculum Development.

Willis J (2007a). The gully in the 'brain glitch' theory. *Educational Leadership*, 64(5): 68–73.

Willis J (2007b). Toward a neuro-logical reading instruction. *Educational Leadership*, 64(6): 80–82.

Wolfe P (2001). *Brain Matters: Translating the Research to Classroom Practice*. Alexandria, VA: Association for Supervision and Curriculum Development.

www.ingramcontent.com/pod-product-compliance
Lightning Source LLC
Chambersburg PA
CBHW071735150426
43191CB00010B/1587